REINSURING HEALTH

REINSURING HEALTH

Why More Middle-Class People Are
Uninsured and What Government Can Do

Katherine Swartz

Russell Sage Foundation • New York

The Russell Sage Foundation

The Russell Sage Foundation, one of the oldest of America's general purpose foundations, was established in 1907 by Mrs. Margaret Olivia Sage for "the improvement of social and living conditions in the United States." The Foundation seeks to fulfill this mandate by fostering the development and dissemination of knowledge about the country's political, social, and economic problems. While the Foundation endeavors to assure the accuracy and objectivity of each book it publishes, the conclusions and interpretations in Russell Sage Foundation publications are those of the authors and not of the Foundation, its Trustees, or its staff. Publication by Russell Sage, therefore, does not imply Foundation endorsement.

Library of Congress Cataloging-in-Publication Data
Swartz, Katherine.
    Reinsuring health : why more middle-class people are uninsured and what government can do / Katherine Swartz.
        p. cm.
    Includes bibliographical references and index.
    ISBN (cloth) 978-0-87154-787-3   ISBN (paper) 978-0-87154-788-0
        1. Insurance, Health—Government policy—United States.   2. Medically uninsured persons—Government policy—United States.   I. Title.
HG9396.S93   2006
368.38′200973—dc22   2006040505

Text design by Suzanne Nichols.

RUSSELL SAGE FOUNDATION
112 East 64th Street, New York, New York 10021
10 9 8 7 6 5 4 3 2 1

For Frank

Contents

About the Author

KATHERINE SWARTZ is an economist and professor of health policy and economics at the Harvard School of Public Health.

Preface

Since the mid-1970s, the federal government has conducted nationally representative surveys of the U.S. population to learn more about those who do not have health insurance. Twenty-five years ago two-thirds of the uninsured lived in poverty or had incomes just above the poverty level, and two-fifths were children. For policymakers determined to reduce the number of uninsured, the message was clear: expand Medicaid and create programs aimed at children. The country made progress in both of these directions—but to the consternation of many, the number of uninsured continued to rise. As of January 2006, the U.S. had 45.5 million uninsured people. Among these are almost 14 million middle-class people; being uninsured is an increasingly common problem for middle-class adults.

The growth in the number of middle-class people among the uninsured requires us to take a new look at the reasons why people are uninsured. It also requires that, in addition to programs targeted at the poor and near-poor, we develop new policies to provide incentives for insurers to make health insurance more widely available. These are the subjects of this book.

Acknowledgments

As my family and friends know all too well, *Reinsuring Health* has been a long time coming. I wrote this book with the hope that it would contribute to the public's understanding of why so many Americans are uninsured and what might be done to remedy the situation. I would dearly like to see this great country develop a policy that would guarantee health insurance for all Americans.

The first version of the book was almost completed while I was on leave and in residence at the Russell Sage Foundation during the 2000–2001 academic year as a visiting scholar. I am most appreciative of that opportunity and for the generous support of the people at the foundation. Eric Wanner deserves special thanks for his support of the project. The Robert Wood Johnson Foundation also provided generous financial support, including funding for the initial project that ultimately led to this book. I am grateful to David Colby for his many expressions of encouragement for the writing of the book. The Harvard School of Public Health also provided financial support during the last year when I substantially revised the book. Thanks also go to Arnie Epstein, chair of my department, for encouraging my efforts to address a wider audience than my academic colleagues. While I was writing the first draft of the book, I was fortunate to spend a month at the Rockefeller Foundation Conference and Study Center in Bellagio, Italy, when my husband was a fellow in residence there. I wrote more in that one month than I have ever been able to write anywhere else, and I thank the people there for that.

I owe enormous debts to the many people who read all or parts of the working drafts of the book. They were generous in giving their time, and their constructive comments, questions, and suggestions greatly improved the book. Joe Newhouse read both of the working drafts and provided insightful comments and suggestions. I appreciated his constant reminders to be precise, even when trying to simplify explanations. My father, Clifford Swartz, also read both working drafts. He also asked good questions that made me rework explanations. I am not sure whether both are gluttons for punishment, but I am enormously grateful to them for the detailed comments and suggestions they made.

Linda Blumberg, Judy Feder, Deborah Garnick, Alan Monheit, and Steve Zuckerman all provided extremely thoughtful and detailed comments on the first working draft. I hope they will see where their attention to details and suggestions for reorganizing the book's themes reshaped the book. Each deserves special thanks. I also am grateful to Bruce Abbe of Communicating for Agriculture for his many comments and suggestions relating to chapter 5 and state high-risk pools. His comments made me rethink and rework my discussion of these pools. Ed Pasterick of the Federal Emergency Management Agency also provided details and comments that greatly improved my understanding of the federal government's role in flood insurance (see the appendix). Janet Rosenbaum, a student in the Harvard Ph.D. program in health policy, gave me very useful feedback on four of the chapters of the first working draft. Particularly helpful were my discussions with Karen Pollitz about the differences between the uninsured people I interviewed and those she has written about who lack health coverage. Finally, two anonymous reviewers provided very useful comments and suggestions for ways to improve the book, and I am grateful to them. Despite their extensive input, all these people may not agree with everything I say, and they certainly are not to blame for errors that may remain.

I do not want to name the uninsured people I spoke with, but I am very grateful for their willingness to spend time talking candidly about their circumstances and experiences. I only hope that this book helps get them health insurance soon. Other people talked with me about reinsurance and those industries and parts of the economy where there has been a marked increase in the use of nonpermanent employees. I am grateful especially to Ari Wolfe, Meghan McGuire, Lee Koromvokis, Steve Gunther, Steve Barley, Michael Hartman, Harry Shuford, Barbara Helfgott Hyett, Elise Peterson, Susan Houseman, Paul Osterman, Thomas Kochan, Oscar Reyes, Frank Ellero, Franklin Shaffer, Peter Buerhaus, Susan Garfield, Tamara Swartz, Beth Cooper Lawrence, Nanci Healy, Susan Walker, Cathy Perron, Nick Lemann, Jaci Coleman, Andrew Cooper, Nancy Hallberg, Deborah Jackson Weiss, and Judith Moldover.

I am indebted to a number of friends and colleagues who provided me with information or explanations that were otherwise hard to find; Laurie Pascal, Julian Pettingil, Patricia Swolak, Randy Ellis, Michelle Mello, and David Autor were particularly generous in this regard. Jim Mayhew of the Centers for Medicare and Medicaid Services and Jim Rice of the Bureau of Labor Statistics' Quarterly Census of Employment and Wages were more than generous in helping me find data I could not find myself in libraries or on the Web, in some cases because it is now considered "old."

I could not have described the uninsured and the changes in their characteristics over the last twenty-five years without the help of three outstanding graduate students in economics at MIT: Cynthia Perry, Elizabeth Oltman Ananat, and Jessica Cohen. At various stages, they analyzed different years of Current Population Survey data with cheerfulness and care. I am particularly indebted to Elizabeth Ananat for analyzing the March 2005 CPS in October and November 2005, while she was finishing her own dissertation.

Many of my Harvard School of Public Health students and students in the Ph.D. in Health Policy Program at Harvard heard me talk about issues that are in the book and provided good comments, questions, and suggestions that I hope are reflected in the arguments presented here. I also received helpful comments from seminar participants at Western Michigan University (the Department of Economics Werner Sichel Lecture-Seminar Series, cosponsored by the W. E. Upjohn Institute); the Sloan School of Management Industrial Relations Group; Columbia Medical School Department of Medicine; Rutgers University Center for State Health Policy; and several seminars at Harvard University.

I would be remiss if I did not thank the librarians at the Boston Public Library, Harvard University, and Massachusetts Institute of Technology. Their ability to find government documents in the archives and their helpful attitudes are warmly appreciated. Internet Web searches are wonderful, but they cannot replace the efforts of humans who know history.

I am especially grateful to my editor, Nancy Kirk. Her editorial suggestions and probing questions about what I meant to say greatly improved the clarity of the text. Nancy also found and put me in touch with people who either are uninsured or could provide context for what has been happening in a variety of industries where people are being shifted to nonpermanent employee status and so have lost health insurance. Nancy's encouragement also helped me get past writer's block at one crucial point, for which I am very appreciative.

Suzanne Nichols, director of publications at the Russell Sage Foundation, never seemed to waver in her belief that I could write this book. Her generosity in providing encouragement every step of the way helped enormously, and I thank her for that—and for her humor.

Many friends have heard me talk about this book for quite some time, and I appreciate their patience. I particularly want to thank Linda Dorman, Ronnie and Bob Hartman, Laurie and Ross Pascal, Linda Silberman and Vic Goldberg, Chuck and Barbara Herz, Dick and Mary Jo Murnane, Ronny Frishman, Marilyn Ellwood, Jim Hester, and Charlie Clotfelter for their support and interest.

My parents, Barbara and Clifford Swartz, and my mother-in-law, Florence Levy, have been constant in their support of my efforts in writing this book. My mother-in-law has a great ability to ask just the right questions, and I appreciate the interest all three have shown in the project. My children, David and Marin Levy, were wonderful in asking about the book and engaging in conversations about its content. David also helped me locate several people who work on contract and have had problems getting health insurance. I could not ask for more from either of them.

This book is for my husband, Frank Levy. Without his support, encouragement, and willingness to discuss my ideas and read too many drafts, I never would have finished.

Chapter 1

A Health Insurance System in Crisis?

S usan Mitchell* does not have health insurance. She is a freelance editor and writer who until three years ago was an employee of a medium-sized company in Washington, D.C. Health insurance had been part of her compensation. Susan writes public relations announcements and edits documents that are sent to the firm's clients. When the company felt pressure to reduce its labor costs, it eliminated Susan's job but asked whether she would work on a freelance basis, doing the same work she had been doing as an employee.

By changing the terms of Susan's employment, the company reduced its fringe benefit costs—Susan is no longer eligible for the company's health insurance and pension benefits. She had the option to continue her health insurance coverage under a government provision known as COBRA (Consolidated Omnibus Budget Reconciliation Act of 1985). COBRA enables people who have been laid off or who leave a job to continue in the group insurance policy for up to eighteen months as long as they pay 102 percent of the total premium themselves.[1]

For several months, Susan kept up the payments for the company's health insurance. Then trouble began. Because the company offered a relatively generous policy, the total premium was $1,137 a month for coverage for two adults. Susan's husband, Ed, works on commission as a wholesaler for small boat and marine products in the northern Virginia and Maryland area. The company Ed works for treats its salespeople as independent contractors and does not offer them a health insurance plan. Between them, the Mitchells earn about $70,000 a year, and they were confident that they could find good coverage for less than $1,137 per month. They discovered, however, that at fifty-four and fifty-three years

---

*Susan's name has been changed to protect her identity, as have the names of all the uninsured people I describe in the book. None of the people described is a composite.

of age, they were viewed as suspect applicants. They applied to several insurance companies for individual health insurance but could only find policies that would cost them even more than they were already paying. Now they are uninsured, and Susan is looking for a job that offers a decent health insurance benefit. With each passing month, however, it is clear that Susan's profession is changing: as it moves into the freelance realm, opportunities for editing and writing jobs are scarce with firms that offer permanence and benefits.

THE UNINSURED ARE NO LONGER ONLY THE POOR

In 2004, 45.5 million Americans under age sixty-five did not have any type of health insurance. Among them, 36.5 million were adults, and two-thirds of these adults were employed. Another 7 percent of the adults were actively looking for work, so only one-quarter of these uninsured adults were out of the labor force. Many working adults are in situations similar to that of the Mitchells: they are in jobs or employment circumstances that do not include employer-sponsored health insurance.

Most Americans think of the uninsured as low-income people who work for small employers that do not offer health insurance or are temporarily unemployed. That image is partially correct. Among all people under age sixty-five without health insurance, the majority (70 percent) are poor or low-income. But as the number of uninsured has grown over the past twenty-five years, the likelihood that a middle-class person will be uninsured has increased too. Today one in ten working-age adults (twenty-three to sixty-four years old) with an annual income above the median household income ($44,430 in 2004)—putting them in the middle class—are uninsured; in 1979 only 6 percent fit this description.[2] Over the past twenty-five years, more and more middle-class people like the Mitchells have found themselves uninsured or scrambling to pay for health insurance. Health insurance is now out of reach not only for low-income people but also for a growing share of middle-class Americans.

Until recently, if the economy was doing well, the proportion of the population with private health insurance increased. Because this was accepted wisdom, most of the incremental efforts to increase insurance coverage were targeted at the poor and near-poor. But the number of uninsured did not decline markedly during the late 1990s in spite of a tight labor market and low unemployment rates.

What has changed over the last three decades to cause more middle-class people to be without health insurance? Why are more workers of all incomes uninsured? What do these changes imply for efforts to increase private health insurance coverage? There are two key parts to the answer.

Significant Shifts in Employment

During the last twenty-five years, there have been three important shifts in employment. The first is the continued decline in manufacturing employment and the related decline of unionized, blue-collar jobs.[3] As late as the early 1980s, manufacturing employed almost 22 percent of all workers; even at 22 percent, benefits practices in manufacturing played a standard-setting role for the rest of the labor market.[4] The example these jobs could set for the rest of the economy had been significantly reduced by 2004, when only 11 percent of all workers were in manufacturing. The changes since 1979 in employment by industry are eye-opening. Two of the service industries, known as "business and professional services" and "education and health services," now employ the largest shares of the labor force (12.4 percent and 12.7 percent, respectively). Between 1979 and 2004, the number of people working in each of these industries more than doubled. Employment in "leisure and hospitality services" and "financial-activities services" also grew more quickly than the labor force as a whole. The service-providing industries as a group not only absorbed people who lost manufacturing jobs but also absorbed the 46 percent growth in the size of the labor force between 1979 and 2004.

The decline of manufacturing jobs had important implications for health insurance provision. During the years from the 1940s to the 1970s, health insurance coverage grew as a fringe benefit that was strongly associated with union manufacturing jobs. These jobs—especially those connected to the manufacture of automobiles and airplanes, basic materials such as steel and aluminum, and items for the booming housing market such as durable appliances and crafted windows—also paid salaries that enabled people with just a high school education to be solidly in the middle class. David Autor estimates that between 1979 and 1999 the fraction of workers who were in blue-collar occupations slipped from 32 percent to less than 25 percent.[5]

The decline in manufacturing's share of all jobs also gave rise to the second employment shift: a rising share of workers employed in small firms, which are far less likely than large companies to offer health insurance. Approximately 52 percent of firms with three to nine employees offered health benefits in 2004, while 99 percent of firms with more than two hundred employees offered coverage.[6] If nothing else had changed in the economy except the shift from manufacturing to services, the proportion of workers without health insurance would have increased simply because the services sector has many small firms.

A third shift in employment has been the change in employer-employee relationships, which has caused a growing number of people (like Susan Mitchell) to be self-employed or to work as temporary or contract workers. The number of self-employed workers has grown at almost the same rate as the size of the labor force.[7] In 1979, 9.8 percent of the workforce reported that they were self-employed; by 1996 that fraction had risen to 10.5 percent. This increase does not include the growing number of people who work as independent contractors. People who are independent contractors often have long-term relationships with firms and work on projects that last as long as a year, sometimes followed by other projects and new contracts offered by the same company. In surveys of workers, independent contractors may respond that they are regular employees. Anecdotal evidence and ethnographic studies of occupations suggest, however, that the number of nonpermanent employees—independent contractors and temporary workers with assignments of a month or more—has increased in the last ten years. Firms that sponsor health insurance for employees typically do not offer it to nonpermanent workers in order to save on insurance costs per worker, as was the case with Susan Mitchell's employer.

The Rising Costs of Medical Care

The second part of the answer to the question of why more middle-class people are uninsured today is that medical costs (after adjusting for inflation) are far higher than they were twenty-five years ago. In 1980 total health care expenditures per person in the United States were $2,535 (in 2004 dollars); in 2004 they were $6,280.[8] The explosive growth in options for treating diseases, conditions, and traumas cannot be overstated. Diagnostic tests and imaging equipment now available were unheard of before the 1980s. MRI (magnetic resonance imaging) machines were not invented until 1983, and they have already progressed through several generations of improvements. Laparoscopic surgery has reduced many complicated and dangerous surgeries to outpatient procedures, with the patient returning home in the evening and being ready to resume normal activities within twenty-four to forty-eight hours.[9] Prior to 1980, many conditions, including arthritic knees and hips, torn rotator cuffs, or hernias, would have been much more difficult to treat. Many went untreated because of concern that the treatment was too dangerous.

The 1970s mark the beginning of our ability to treat health care problems that we now label "chronic." Before then, physicians had few choices to offer people with cancer, cardiovascular disease, or arthritis. Today

4

medical providers don't tell patients whose knees ache, "Take some aspirin; such pains are part of growing old." There are now better pain relievers for arthritis and the option of joint replacement surgery. The surgical techniques available for treating orthopedic or joint problems were only gleams in surgeons' eyes fifteen years ago. Similarly, treatment options for cancer and cardiac conditions are strikingly improved. People who would have died of cancer within months now have ten-year survival rates accompanied by longer "disease-free" time. The change from being doomed by a diagnosis to being a cancer survivor is due to advances in surgical techniques and the development of new chemotherapies and new drugs that permit more aggressive use of chemotherapies. The creation of drugs that break up stroke-causing blood clots and drugs that lower blood pressure and cholesterol levels has significantly altered how cardiovascular diseases are treated. All these pharmaceuticals were developed over the past twenty-five to thirty-five years and have become recommended treatment options during the past decade. Although the costs of these drugs per person are often low (less than $1,000 a year for some of the prescriptions for cardiac conditions), the number of people in the population who have these conditions can be in the many millions. This is one reason why total health expenditures have grown so much.

Other advances related to a wide variety of acute medical problems have occurred in the last twenty-five years. We are now able to save many more babies born prematurely, and we can even perform life-saving surgery on babies in the womb. Surgeons routinely do organ transplants for many more types of organs and tissue and have created techniques that save people who have suffered traumatic injuries that only a decade ago they would not have survived. New drugs have dramatically improved treatments for mental illnesses and for infectious diseases that were unheard of in the 1970s—for example, HIV/AIDS and SARS.

These medical advances, however, have greatly increased our average expenditures for health care. True, they have brought enormous benefits and improved the quality of life for millions of people. At the same time, the new options create considerable variation in the costs for treating a particular problem. How an oncologist decides to treat a cancer patient depends enormously on the stage of the cancer, the underlying health of the patient, and the patient's ability to tolerate chemo and radiation treatments. Even having a baby can vary in costs by $10,000 or more depending on whether the delivery is vaginal or caesarean and on the types of complications that may arise. The increased variation in costs of care and the growth in average costs of medical care mean that insurers are less able to predict costs for individuals and small groups of people. The risks for insurers are greater than they were twenty-five years ago.

Since health insurance premiums closely track expenditures for medical care, they also have more than doubled (after adjusting for inflation) since 1979. The rapid rate of growth in health insurance costs has been an eye-popping contributor to the cost of labor for companies facing increased competitive pressures. The decline in U.S. manufacturing jobs in the 1980s was a response to lower labor costs abroad. In the 1990s employers responded to rising labor costs by shedding employees who were not part of their "core business competencies" and outsourcing jobs to business service firms that often were small and did not offer health coverage. Within the last five to eight years, companies have become more aggressive about hiring more people as nonpermanent employees as another way to restrain labor costs.

As a result of these employer responses to the increased cost of health insurance, it is no longer just the poor and low-income who cannot afford health insurance. The growth in the number of middle-class people who are uninsured has been faster than the growth of people with middle-class incomes; thus, the chance that a middle-class, working-age adult will be uninsured has risen to one in ten. Many of these people are self-employed or working in small firms that do not offer insurance. Their only option for obtaining coverage is the individual insurance market, where premiums are higher than they are in large companies.

These middle-class workers fall into two groups. In one group are young and healthy people who have never spent—nor can they imagine spending—more than a couple of hundred dollars a year for medical care. They have limited knowledge of potential health problems and associated medical costs. Moreover, they often misunderstand the concept of insurance—that by paying a premium they are paying to avoid the risk of having to pay for expensive care themselves. Thus, when the annual premium is greater than $3,000 or $4,000 for an individual or $8,000 for a family policy, they balk at paying. Most people, even those with employer-sponsored health insurance, tend to resist paying more than 5 percent of their income for health coverage.

The other group of middle-class people who are uninsured are over forty-five years of age or have had some health problems. They are far more likely to face much higher premiums or to have trouble obtaining insurance. They often have their applications turned down or are offered policies with severe restrictions on the services covered. Depending on their age, they frequently cannot find a decent insurance policy for less than $700 a month for single coverage, $1,000 a month for coverage for two adults, or more for a family policy. If they are denied coverage, there is not much they can do to obtain coverage; if they earn only a little more than the $44,400 threshold for being middle-class and are offered policies at these premiums, they may not be able to afford them.

INSURER AVOIDANCE OF PEOPLE LIKELY TO
HAVE HIGH EXPENSES

Sixty-three percent of Americans under age sixty-five had health insurance through an employer or union (employment-based coverage) in 2004.[10] They constitute the vast majority of people with private health insurance. Another 7 percent purchase individual (nongroup) private insurance. Everyone else in the United States is either uninsured or has some type of public insurance. As we saw with Ed Mitchell when he was insured, many of the 63 percent with employment-based coverage have their insurance through a spouse or parent whose employer or union sponsors it. If the worker loses that coverage, the loss affects the spouse and children too.

People with employment-based insurance are beneficiaries of two significant advantages that greatly reduce their out-of-pocket costs for health insurance. One is the fraction of the premium paid by the employer.[11] In the case of an individual policy for just the employee, employers generally pay between 70 and 95 percent of the premium; on average they pay 84 percent.[12] Employers pay, on average, 74 percent of family policy premiums, although the percentage varies considerably.

The second advantage of employment-based coverage is that it is significantly less expensive per person to sell insurance through employer groups than to individuals. Insurance sold through groups carries a lower risk for an insurer because almost everyone in the employer group enrolls in the group policy. The insurer does not worry that the people who want health insurance are those who believe they will need expensive medical care in the coming year. In the case of small groups (especially those with fewer than twenty-five employees) and individuals, insurers face a greater risk of high medical costs per person. Without many people over whom the risk of very high costs can be shared, the premiums are higher than in large groups. The higher premiums often are high enough to discourage healthy people from enrolling, so it is likely that the applicants are those who suspect they will have high medical expenses. Premiums per person also are lower in large groups because insurers save on costs related to administering the policy and collecting premium payments. Employers often take on many of the tasks of those two functions. It is also less expensive for insurers to market a policy to one large group than to hundreds or thousands of separate individuals.

Thus, the 63 percent of non-elderly Americans with employment-based health insurance have a relatively good deal: the premiums are lower, and the employer typically pays a large fraction of it. In 2005 the average total premium per month for employer-sponsored health plans was $335 for single coverage and $907 for family coverage. Workers in large companies were paying average out-of-pocket costs of about $55 per month for single coverage and about $200 per month for family coverage.[13]

People who do not have access to employment-based coverage lack these advantages. The only other source of private health insurance is the individual (nongroup) market. It can be difficult to find a suitable policy, and part of the search may involve consulting with an insurance agent, whose main interest is selling a product. Even if a person succeeds in identifying a desirable policy, the most significant factor that affects the premium is insurers' concern that the policy has attracted "adverse selection." Adverse selection occurs when a disproportionate share of people who apply for health insurance suspect that they have medical problems that will require expensive medical care in the near future.

The potential threat of adverse selection in the small-group and individual insurance markets is real. Because we have a voluntary system of health insurance purchases, young and healthy people are less likely to apply for and buy coverage. The result is a catch-22: insurers charge higher premiums for small-group and individual coverage because the risk of people with high costs is greater than it is in the large employer groups. In response to the higher premiums, young and healthy people decide that, because their own expected medical costs plus whatever they are willing to pay for the value of insurance are less than the premium, they will not buy coverage.

Insurers have responded to the increased threat of adverse selection in the small-group and individual insurance markets by becoming more sophisticated in their use of mechanisms to avoid it. They spend a great deal of effort and money trying to select the most desirable applicants—those who they expect will be low-cost—and protecting themselves from others who they predict will be high-cost. They deny coverage to some people based on their age and prior medical history; they offer restricted coverage; and in states where they are required to insure anyone who applies, they charge unaffordably high premiums of $1,500 or more per month. The end result is that young and healthy people can obtain individual insurance at relatively low premiums, especially in states where insurers are permitted to use a wide variety of selection mechanisms. But those older than forty and those who have had health problems are frequently unable to obtain coverage at all.[14] In states where the premiums must be the same for everyone regardless of age or health status (known as community-rated premiums), middle-aged and less healthy people can obtain coverage, but the premiums are generally high. Young and healthy people resist paying these premiums and are more likely to be uninsured.

THE IMPLICATIONS OF BEING UNINSURED

Being without health insurance is a risky business, although it may not seem so at first glance.[15] People who are young and healthy generally do not become sick, so it is reasonable to assume that their yearly medical expenses will be close to zero. Indeed, half of all those under age sixty-five spent less than $500 (in 2005 dollars) on medical care in 1996.[16] We do not have the expenditure data for 2005 yet, but because these people are healthy, the $500 amount is likely to be only slightly higher in 2005. (The increase will reflect changes in the practice of medicine since 1996 that are not accounted for with adjustments for inflation between 1996 and 2005.) But these people face risks—they might get hurt in a car accident or become ill with a condition that requires long-term medical attention. The risks of a period without health insurance can extend beyond the time without coverage. As insurers have become more selective about whom they cover with small-group or individual policies, any type of prior medical problem can cause a person to be denied coverage or charged significantly higher rates than a similar healthy person.[17] Even an indication of a future problem, such as above-normal blood test levels, can result in denial of coverage. In addition, individual and small-group insurance policies generally do not cover services for at least a year for preexisting medical conditions. Thus, even for healthy people the risks of being without insurance include the risk of difficulty in getting health insurance in the future.

For people who are older or for those who have had medical problems, the risks of being uninsured are more apparent. If such a person has a chronic condition or is diagnosed with a cancer or other life-threatening illness, the risk is that he or she will not get the same quality of care that an insured person would receive.[18] This risk then expands to becoming sicker or dying earlier than an insured person with the same disease. These risks are genuinely frightening to people as they age.

Society also runs risks by having a significant number of uninsured people. Typically, they do not seek medical care when they first notice symptoms, and they do not visit physicians for regular checkups or for preventive care, such as screenings for cancer. When they do seek medical care, their problems often cost more to treat because they were neglected at an early stage. Medical care provided to uninsured people is not free—we all pay for it in the form of higher taxes and the higher prices charged by medical providers.

THE PLAN OF THIS BOOK

This book is about people who do not have health insurance and what might be done to help them. The book is divided into three parts. The first part describes why people are uninsured, while the second part examines government policies that might make private health insurance more affordable and available to these people. The third part is about the need for a new health insurance structure that would enable more people to have health insurance.

In chapter 2, we begin by analyzing who is uninsured and the changes over the past twenty-five years in the types of people who are uninsured. Specifically, we explore why being uninsured is now a problem confronting the middle class and people twenty-five to forty-four years of age. Changes in the economy, employer-employee relationships, demographic patterns, and new public programs to cover poor and low-income children have affected the population of the uninsured. In discussing how the uninsured have changed since 1979, I rely on a nationally representative dataset—the Current Population Survey (CPS), conducted by the U.S. Census Bureau—and on information obtained from interviews with more than forty people who are uninsured or who run small businesses and struggle with offering coverage to their employees. I use the experiences of six middle-class uninsured workers and three small-business owners to illustrate the reasons why being without health coverage now threatens millions of Americans. Unlike the CPS, the sample of people I spoke with is not a scientific sample, but these interviewees do represent a wide variety of occupations and experiences in the labor force.

The focus in chapter 3 is on why some people have problems obtaining health insurance as part of the compensation they receive for work. We examine job options for different types of people and the impacts of changes in the U.S. labor market over the past twenty-five years on employer-sponsored health insurance coverage. We also investigate the relationship between premiums and employer-group size and its effect on workers' chances of having employer-sponsored coverage.

How insurers compete with each other and why some people cannot buy insurance is the subject of chapter 4. Insurers are very concerned about adverse selection, and they compete by using selection mechanisms to reduce their risk of covering very high-cost people. As a result, people who might incur high medical costs have difficulty obtaining health insurance; either they are denied coverage or they are charged very high premiums. If the risk of extremely high-cost people were lowered, insurers would reduce both premiums and their use of selection mechanisms that prevent people from buying coverage.

If we want to maintain private insurance, proposals to expand health coverage must address insurers' risk of extremely high-cost people. The second part of the book investigates three proposals that might address this risk and thereby make private insurance affordable and accessible to more people. In chapter 5, we examine two potential mechanisms for reducing insurers' fear of adverse selection: high-risk pools and an assessment mechanism that might be used to relieve carriers of the financial burden of high-risk enrollees. Both of these mechanisms rely on predicting who in a group of people is likely to have high medical costs.

Chapter 6 focuses on a third mechanism for addressing the risk of adverse selection: the federal government reinsuring the small-group and individual insurance markets. Reinsurance is insurance for insurers, protecting them from extreme risks. If the federal government were to provide a reinsurance program that took responsibility for people who have the top 1 percent of all medical expenses among everyone covered by small-group or individual insurance, it could reduce premiums for such coverage by 20 to 40 percent. How much premiums might decline would depend on how the reinsurance is structured. In addition, because a government-sponsored reinsurance program would reduce insurers' incentives to select against people they suspect will be high-cost, more people would find that insurance is available to them when they apply. The reductions in premiums together with the increased availability of coverage might induce as many as one-third of the uninsured to become insured. The total costs of such a program would depend on the structure of the reinsurance. A rough estimate is that it would cost between $6 billion and $20 billion a year to help at least 15 million uninsured persons purchase coverage in the individual and small-group insurance markets. This is about the same amount of money being discussed to help clean up after Hurricanes Katrina, Rita, and Wilma just in 2005. By comparison, the annual federal tax subsidy for employer-sponsored health insurance is now estimated to be more than $140 billion.[19]

There are precedents for government taking the worst risks in other situations, enabling markets to operate more efficiently. Today the catastrophe reinsurance markets and secondary mortgage markets would not exist without the federal government's assumption of responsibility for the worst risks in these markets. Three health-related government programs also make the government responsible for large shares of the costs of the highest-risk cases. Medicare has provided additional payments to hospitals for very expensive cases (known as outliers) since 1983. Medicare pays a hospital for 80 percent of its costs above the threshold that defines an outlier case. The Medicare prescription drug benefit (Medicare Part D) established risk corridors such that if an insurer has an individual with expenses in excess of a complicated formula of costs, the Centers for Medicare and Medicaid Services provides a reinsurance payment. Among the state programs for the uninsured, Healthy New York stands out as the first with an explicit reinsurance component that reimburses insurers with enrollees who have annual expenses above a threshold defined on a per-person basis. Healthy New York reimburses insurers

11

for 90 percent of a person's annual costs between $5,000 and $75,000. In 2004 the program paid out less than $35 million for such expenses, less than what had been budgeted for the reinsurance pool.[20] These precedents are described more fully in the appendix.

The third part of the book is about how we could move from the current situation of rising numbers of uninsured to a situation where health insurance would be affordable and accessible for more people. Why the United States needs a new structure for its system of health insurance and how it might be configured are the focus of chapter 7. The appendix, as noted, describes precedents for government taking responsibility for the worst risks.

A FINAL NOTE

Although the lack of health insurance now extends well into the middle class, the majority of the uninsured are poor or low-income. The primary way to help poor and low-income uninsured has been obvious for some time. We need to expand government assistance—we cannot continue to believe that they will be able to buy private coverage on their own. The economic boom of the late 1990s provided ample evidence that a strong economy and tight labor markets do not cause health insurance to trickle down to large numbers of the working poor. But because many others have proposed and written about policies that would help the poor and low-income uninsured, the problems they face in obtaining health insurance are not the focus of this book.[21]

Instead, this book focuses on what is different about the uninsured today and on policies that could allow us to maintain a system of health insurance based on private insurance. The uninsured are different from those of twenty-five years ago in three significant ways. They account for a larger share of our under-sixty-five-year-old population: one in six are now uninsured. More middle-class people now face the prospect of being uninsured: one in ten working-age, middle-class adults are without insurance. An increasing number of people are in skilled occupations that ensure middle-class incomes but do not always come with employer-sponsored health insurance. And perhaps most sobering, a significant number of adults twenty-five to forty-four years of age are uninsured—so many that between 20 and 25 percent of all adults in this twenty-year age cohort are uninsured. This is not good for them, and it's not good for the country's ability to maintain private insurance.

We are on the edge of a crisis. Health insurance is out of reach for an ever-expanding number of people. Unless we do something quickly to help younger adults and middle-class people buy health insurance, our system of private insurance will collapse.

PART I

Why People Lack Health Insurance

Chapter 2

The Growing Ranks of the Insured: Who Lacks Health Insurance?

If you want to have a career in broadcasting, journalism, advertising, graphic design, filmmaking, or interior design, prepare to live without health insurance. Even many high-tech computer-related occupations, such as software programming, hold out the same prospect. None of this was true twenty-five years ago—but when it comes to health insurance, we are in a new economy.

Sam (not his real name) is a thirty-four-year-old sports broadcaster who does play-by-play announcing. He has a master's degree in journalism from one of the top three broadcast journalism schools in the country and is in his seventh year of television sports broadcasting. Sam has moved twice already to climb the ladder of television sports broadcasting and now works in a medium-sized city with many sports teams. He hopes his next career jump will be to a large city. Although Sam's career progression is quite successful, he has not been an employee of any of the stations for which he has worked. As a result, he has not been eligible for group health insurance through any of the radio and cable television companies for whom he broadcasts. Technically a freelancer, he has to string together contracts to earn a steady income. Among his gigs is announcing arena football games—the city's team plays seventeen games between January and June—for one of the city's cable stations. (Arena football, played indoors, is generally a much faster and higher-scoring game than regular football, so play-by-play announcing is more like that for basketball or ice hockey.) Sam has worked two seasons as a sideline reporter for NFL games for one of the major networks, and he has done play-by-play announcing for NFL-Europe games. With his various contracts, he earns more than $45,000 a year. But out of that he must pay income taxes and the full 15.3 percent payroll tax for Social Security and Medicare, living expenses, and payments on loans he took out to get his master's degree. Not much is left over for health insurance, which he keeps meaning to look into.

Behind the camera that brings us Sam and other announcers are highly skilled camera men and women. They too have experienced a shift in fortunes over the last decade. Brian is one of them. In his late forties, Brian is sought after to film interviews for segments that are shown on news broadcasts on the major television networks and public broadcasting stations. Two decades ago, cameramen and sound technicians were employees of these networks. But with the push to reduce production costs and the advent of lightweight, relatively inexpensive cameras making it possible for many less experienced people to come into the video business, midcareer cameramen like Brian have been forced to become freelancers. This is particularly problematic because they often have experienced shoulder injuries from lugging around the heavier camera equipment that was the norm until just recently. Brian still earns a middle-class income, but after accounting for inflation, he earns less now than he did a dozen years ago. Moreover, pursuing filming assignments, which increasingly are given as one-day rather than multiple-day jobs, has added to the stress in his life. Although producers who are his age or older are familiar with his reputation as a creative and skilled cameraman, many of them have left the business in response to the budget cuts imposed by networks and broadcast companies. Brian finds that he has to cultivate younger producers so that they will call him for assignments. If he worked in Los Angeles, he most likely would be a member of a union of production people. But he doesn't, and with his forced shift in employment status to freelance, he lost access to group health insurance. Brian and his wife divorced several years ago, so he cannot obtain health insurance through her employer. Brian worries a lot about not having health insurance, but he feels that he cannot afford the $500 monthly premiums he has been quoted.

Most of us would assume that getting a college degree in computer science and engineering would be a sure ticket to a secure job that pays a good salary. But over the last decade, computer programmers, software engineers, and hardware engineers have increasingly found themselves forced to work as independent contractors or employees of contract houses.[1] What happened to Paul is common. Paul graduated five years ago with a master's degree in computer science from a top Midwest university. He found a job in Texas working for a large computer software firm that provides technical support to large U.S. companies. But within a year of starting work, he was told that he could either continue as an independent contractor or work for a contract house. (Contract houses act as agents or middlemen in obtaining short-term and long-term contracts for skilled workers. They are the employer of record for tax purposes—they obtain the contracts from the places where they send workers and then they pay the workers.) Either way, Paul would continue doing the same job he had been hired for, but he would no longer be an employee of the company and he would have to find his own health insurance. After working as an independent contractor for half a year, he moved back to his home state in the Midwest to join a start-up that was being financed primarily by a large computer company. But here too he has found himself not an employee: the seventy-plus workers at the start-up are all employees of a contract house, and health insurance is not part of the compensation. He still does not have health insurance, largely because, with college loans and the costs of moving to and from Texas to pay off, he thinks it is too expensive.

WHAT IS OBSCURED BY THE NUMBERS ON THE UNINSURED

Of the 45.5 million uninsured Americans under age sixty-five, 13.75 million (three out of ten) have incomes that are above the median household income level of $44,400 in 2004—that is, they are in the middle class. If that is surprising, it is just as surprising to apply a similar yardstick to the uninsured in 1979 and discover that three out of every ten were middle-class in that year as well.[2] This similarity is deceiving, however, because the uninsured today are very different from the uninsured of twenty-five years ago. To start with, in 1979 almost 40 percent of the uninsured were children under the age of nineteen. Today, only 20 percent of the uninsured are children, and the number of uninsured children is actually smaller today than it was in 1979 (see table 2.1). While

Table 2.1   Ages of Non-Elderly Uninsured, 1979 and 2004

	1979		2004	
Age Cohort	Number Uninsured (Millions)	Percentage of Uninsured	Number Uninsured (Millions)	Percentage of Uninsured
Younger than 19	10.784	39.3%	9.034	19.9%
19 to 24	4.974	18.1	8.001	17.6
25 to 34	4.112	15.0	10.174	22.4
35 to 44	2.438	8.9	8.108	17.8
45 to 54	2.349	8.5	6.257	13.7
55 to 64	2.818	10.3	3.934	8.6
Total	27.470	100.1	45.508	100

Source: March 1980 and March 2005 Current Population Surveys.

the number of uninsured children shrank, the number of uninsured adults grew. If the number of uninsured adults had stayed the same while the number of uninsured children declined, the proportion of all uninsured who are adults would be higher today compared to 1979 simply because the number of uninsured children declined. But instead, we have both an increase in the proportion of uninsured who are adults and a large increase in the number of uninsured adults—adults like Sam, Brian, and Paul. In fact, the number of uninsured adults increased so much that the uninsured now represent 17.8 percent of all people under the age of sixty-five, whereas in 1979 the uninsured were 14.7 percent of the non-elderly.

The changing nature of the uninsured is a result of four major factors:

- The changing economy

- Changing employer-employee relationships that result in more people not being permanent employees

- Falling birthrates and changing marital patterns

- Expanded programs to insure poor and lower-income children and poor adults

THE CHANGING ECONOMY

The U.S. economy has undergone significant changes in the last quarter-century. A healthy, vibrant economy constantly responds to shifts in consumer tastes and to potential changes in production costs. New products and new firms emerge, less costly ways of producing older products are invented, and, inevitably, older products or older production methods are replaced. Few of us, for example, would want to go back to using typewriters instead of computers. Although we may be nostalgic for products no longer manufactured or for old ways of making some things, unless people value old-fashioned goods and production methods enough to pay for them, they disappear. In the normal course of change in an economy, workers are forced to change jobs. The U.S. economy's dynamics can be seen in the monthly statistics on hires and separations from jobs. In the winter of 2005, about 140 million people were working, and in February 2005, 4.6 million people were hired and 4.2 million people voluntarily or involuntarily left their jobs.[3] Thus, about 3 percent of the workforce changes jobs every month, reflecting a significant amount of dynamic change.

Workers can generally find new jobs with salaries comparable to those in their previous jobs when demand is high for their skills. But if a worker's skills become outdated by new production methods, or if demand drops for the product the worker helped to make, he or she may have trouble finding a similar job or any job with a comparable salary. The Industrial Revolution marks the best-known rapid change in employment opportunities. The rate at which many occupations were eliminated in the nineteenth century owing to the mechanization of work was unprecedented. At the same time, new job opportunities and occupations were created by the new machinery. The twentieth century also witnessed distinct shifts in employment opportunities and employee-employer relationships. Some of the shifts in manufacturing opportunities caused large migrations of people within the United States. Detroit, Chicago, Los Angeles, and other cities grew because people left farms and rural areas between the 1920s and the 1960s to take jobs making cars, washing machines and other household appliances, air conditioners, pharmaceuticals, telephones, and airplanes—products that were just being developed at the beginning of the century.

The Shift Away from Manufacturing to Service-Producing Industries

By the 1980s, the employment shifts were becoming more rapid as manufacturers in other countries began to offer serious competition not only for durable goods such as cars and appliances but also for electronics and textiles. Cheaper labor abroad as well as changes in transportation made it possible for foreign-made goods to be competitive with American goods. The number of people employed in manufacturing in the United States fell by 1.5 million between 1979 and 1984, and even after the country recovered from the 1981 to 1983 recession, manufacturing employment never returned to its pre-recession level of 19.4 million. In 1989 manufacturing employment was just under 18 million, and it continued to fall steadily thereafter. By 2004 manufacturing employment was about 14.3 million. But because the total workforce grew by 41.6 million people between 1979 and 2004, the proportion employed in manufacturing fell from 21.6 percent to 10.9 percent (see figure 2.1). This is a stunning change in just twenty-five years.

The people who were hurt most by the shift from goods-producing to service-producing industries were the people who had not gone to college. Manufacturing jobs, especially those in durable goods production such as steel, cement, automobiles, and household items like refrigerators, were relatively well paid. Because they also were often unionized, health insurance was typically part of their compensation. From the 1950s through the late 1970s, high school graduates could work in these jobs and expect to live a comfortable, middle-class life. But with the sud-

Figure 2.1   Percentage of Employment in U.S. Manufacturing and Services Sectors, 1979 to 2004

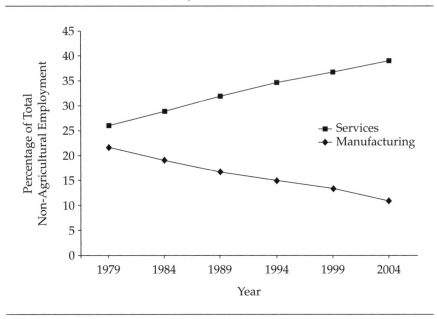

Source: U.S. Department of Labor, Bureau of Labor Statistics, *Employment and Earnings,* in Council of Economic Advisers, *2005 Economic Report of the President* (Washington: U.S. Government Printing Office), table B-46.

den decline in such jobs, many less-skilled and less-educated workers found themselves forced to take pay cuts, lose health insurance, and slide away from their middle-class lives.

Some of the people who are now between poverty and middle-class and do not have health insurance are people who a decade or more ago earned as much as two times what they are now earning—and had health insurance. They now show up as having incomes below the middle-class threshold. The significantly higher probabilities of being uninsured for people with incomes between two and four times the poverty level (see table 2.2) reflect the shifts in the economy that have caused changes in people's incomes as well as in health insurance. (The poverty level is adjusted each year to account for inflation. Also, because it differs by family size, it provides a way of comparing people's incomes across family size. In 1979 the poverty level was $7,412 for a family of four (in 1979 dollars); in 2004 it was $19,307.)

Table 2.2 Family Income Relative to the Poverty Level for the Non-Elderly Uninsured, 1979 and 2004

Family Income Relative to Poverty	1979			2004		
	Number Uninsured (Millions)	Percentage of Uninsured	Simple Probability of Being Uninsured	Number Uninsured (Millions)	Percentage of Uninsured	Simple Probability of Being Uninsured
Below poverty level	7.651	27.9%	35.0%	11.476	25.2%	33.7%
1 to 1.49 times poverty level	4.291	15.6	27.9	6.443	14.2	30.8
1.5 to 1.99 times poverty level	3.785	13.8	21.2	6.444	14.2	28.0
2 to 2.99 times poverty level	5.124	18.7	12.8	8.692	19.1	20.4
3 to 3.99 times poverty level	2.863	10.4	8.6	4.808	10.6	12.9
4 times poverty level or higher	3.757	13.7	6.5	7.646	16.8	7.8
Total	27.470	100.1	14.7	45.508	100	17.8

Source: March 1980 and March 2005 Current Population Surveys.

The Rise in Small-Firm Employment

Luckily for most of the people who lost their manufacturing jobs, or who lost the expectation of taking a job in a steel mill or automobile plant after graduating from high school, the service-producing part of the economy grew tremendously in the late 1980s and early 1990s.[4] Between 1984 and 1994, the service-providing industries of business services, health and education services, and leisure and hospitality increased employment by about 11 million, and between 1994 and 2004 their employment grew again by 10.8 million.[5] Employment in all the industries in the service-producing part of the economy grew by 44.7 million between 1979 and 2004. Figure 2.2 shows the percentage changes in employment in the major industries over this period.

A significant consequence of the shift in employment from manufacturing to services and the subsequent rapid growth in the service-producing industries is an increase in the fraction of workers employed by small firms. Unlike the goods-producing part of the economy, the service-producing sector is dominated by small firms. In 1979, 37 percent of all private-sector workers (that is, not including government workers) were em-

Figure 2.2   Percentage Change in Employment in Major Industries, 1979 to 2004

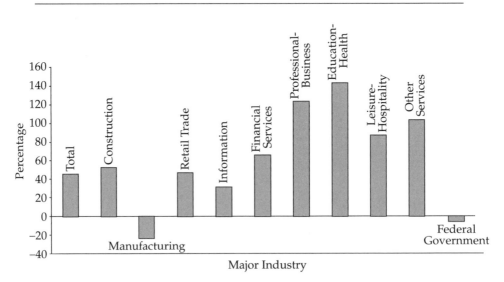

Source: U.S. Department of Labor, Bureau of Labor Statistics, *Employment and Earnings,* Council of Economic Advisers, *2005 Economic Report of the President*, table B-46.

ployed in establishments with fewer than fifty workers; 28 percent of all
workers were employed in establishments with five hundred or more
workers.[6] Preliminary data from the first quarter of 2005 show that 43.7
percent of private-sector workers worked in establishments with fewer
than fifty workers.[7] The fraction of private-sector workers employed by
establishments with five hundred or more workers had fallen to 17.2
percent.

As discussed in more detail in chapter 3, large firms are far more likely
to offer health insurance to their employees than are small firms, in large
part because the premiums per person are much lower for large firms.
Thus, simply because goods-producing jobs as a proportion of all jobs in
the economy fell from 28 percent in 1979 to less than 17 percent in 2003,
there was a substantial decline in the number of workers employed in
large firms where health insurance was a standard part of compensation.
Even if nothing else had changed in the economy over the last twenty-
five years, the shift in employment to service-producing industries and
smaller firms would have increased the number of uninsured.

CHANGES IN EMPLOYER-EMPLOYEE
RELATIONSHIPS: MORE
NONPERMANENT EMPLOYEES

Just as competitive cost pressures have caused shifts in the economy,
cost pressures are altering employer-employee relationships. What happened to Susan Mitchell, Sam, Brian, and Paul has happened to millions
of other people who had good jobs and incomes. Since the mid-1990s,
many companies have laid off employees and then hired people (sometimes even their old employees) on a contract or temporary basis to do
much of the same work. Occasionally the temporary freelance people are
there for so long that they call themselves "permalancers."

Employers have restructured their employment practices primarily to
save on labor costs.[8] When a person is an employee, an employer has to
pay the employer share of taxes for Social Security and Medicare (currently 7.65 percent), as well as taxes for unemployment insurance.[9] Employers also are required to collect and transmit the employee's income
taxes to the federal and state governments. If, in addition, an employer
provides fringe benefits, such as a pension plan or health insurance, it
pays a portion of the costs of these benefits too. Thus, changing a job to
one that is done by a temporary employee, consultant, or independent
contractor saves an employer a lot of money. The restructuring of work
from employee relationships to contract or temporary work has enabled
whole industries and firms to reduce their labor costs.[10] It is only now

becoming apparent that this restructuring has created a significant shift affecting the labor force.

Sam's and Brian's situations illustrate this shift. The stations that broadcast the games that Sam covers keep their production costs low by contracting with freelance broadcasters. Similarly, the relatively recent cost pressures on cable and television news divisions cause producers of feature segments to hire cameramen like Brian on a daily basis when they decide to film an extended interview or a special event. In previous decades, they simply would have used production workers who were on staff. Now they consider the benefits and costs of shooting and editing new video versus having a person provide the essence of the story in a studio or perhaps using archival video footage. This is now the norm in broadcast journalism. With the exception of the best-known reporters and anchors on national news shows on the major broadcast networks, most workers in the broadcast industry are freelancers or independent contractors. In medium and small city markets, and at the local cable companies in large cities, most people in broadcasting work as independent contractors and do not get health insurance or other benefits. The situation is identical at most magazines: only a very few executives and senior editors are employees. The rest, including some of the best-known authors in print journalism, work on a contract basis and do not receive health insurance or other fringe benefits. Many of them have joined the ranks of the uninsured because they cannot afford the coverage they are offered when they apply for individual health insurance or because they have been offered policies with strict limitations on coverage for their medical conditions.

Within the last decade, other industries have been similarly restructuring their workforces. Many software programmers lost jobs that were outsourced to India. The sharply lower costs of digital cameras and software to edit video have enabled a new generation of young people to compete with Brian for work in advertising. As companies downsized over the past few years, many laid off communications people like Susan Mitchell. Running through all these examples is the fact that there are more people available now to do various types of previously specialized jobs. As a result, many workers have to settle for the work terms that companies are setting. They are not in a position to demand permanent employment, much less health insurance.

The restructuring of work has two other benefits for companies trying to respond to changes in demand and to please Wall Street. By relying more on temporary workers and people who do contract work, firms can ramp up production during periods when they are not sure that increased demand for their goods or services will last. It is then easy and relatively cheap to cut back production if the increased demand recedes.

In addition, over the past five years Wall Street analysts have noted when companies appear to have larger numbers of employees than their competitors. Temporary employees and contract workers often are not counted in such comparisons. The relative efficiency calculations of output per worker can appear favorable if more of the work is done by temporary and contract workers.

Increased Numbers of Self-Employed and Contingent Workers

The shift in employment relationships and the restructuring of work are reflected in the increasing numbers of people who are freelancers and independent contractors, like Sam, Brian, Paul, and Susan Mitchell. Such people are described as contingent workers or self-employed.[11] Contingent workers are people who work in situations that are structured to be short-term or temporary. They may work as temporary employees who almost always obtain work through temporary service agencies. Another group of contingent workers are those who accept consulting contracts to do a specific job over a specified time period. There is some overlap between self-employed people and contingent workers. Some self-employed people are independent contractors: they take on work assignments within one or perhaps a few companies over the course of a year. But most provide business services for which they have many customers or clients. Certified public accountants, lawyers who practice on their own, construction contractors, and interior decorators are examples of self-employed people with many clients.

It is difficult to obtain national data that have tracked the numbers of self-employed and contingent workers for many years. The survey that the Bureau of Labor Statistics uses to estimate the self-employed changed most recently in 1994, so the data before and after are not directly comparable.[12] Since 1967, the BLS has distinguished between incorporated and unincorporated self-employed people; it is the unincorporated who are typically referred to as self-employed in their publications. In the late 1970s about 6.8 million non-agricultural workers were self-employed. The number grew throughout the 1980s and early 1990s, reaching almost 9 million in 1993.[13] After the survey changed in 1994, the number of non-agricultural, self-employed workers hovered around 9 million until the economic boom of 1999, when it fell to 8.8 million. In 2003 the number was 9.3 million. Another 4.8 million people were incorporated non-agricultural, self-employed workers.[14] Among all self-employed workers, about one-fourth were uninsured.[15]

National data on contingent workers were collected only between 1995 and 2001. Steven Hipple of the BLS estimated that the percentage of Americans who worked on a contingent basis between 1995 and 1999 was 4.3 percent of the workforce.[16] These contingent workers are concentrated in particular occupations. Hipple estimates that 29 percent of college and university instructors were contingent workers in 1999.[17] Almost one-quarter of all library clerks worked on a contingency basis. Other occupations with high rates of contingent workers include physicians, biological and life scientists (perhaps working in diagnostic laboratories), photographers, interviewers, general office clerks, and receptionists and typists.[18]

There is some concern that the contingent worker survey questions did not fully capture the magnitude of contingent work. For example, people who work for contract houses and have an employer of record may not have answered the questions in such a way that their contractor status would have been noted. As a result, the BLS estimates of the numbers of self-employed and contingent workers are likely to be too low. We have to rely on case studies of what has been happening in various industries where shifts to temporary workers and contract work have been documented to get a more complete picture of the extent to which various occupations now have nonpermanent employees. Stephen Barley and Gideon Kunda estimate that in the late 1990s between 15 and 30 percent of the technical workforce in Silicon Valley were independent contractors.[19] By one estimate, about 5 percent of all nurses today work as "travel" nurses: they are placed by agencies that supply registered nurses, practical nurses, physical therapists, and other medical personnel.[20] The nurses accept thirteen-week (three-month) assignments that are primarily at hospitals but also include summer camps, college-abroad programs, and cruise ships. Another study estimates that nearly 43 percent of all teaching faculty in colleges and universities were part-time or adjunct faculty in 1998.[21] Since almost half of all universities and colleges do not offer health insurance to part-time faculty, and part-time faculty are paid substantially less than tenure-track faculty, colleges and universities save a lot of money by hiring people as adjunct faculty. People in all of these occupations have had to shift their expectations not only about job and income security but about their health insurance and pension savings as well. Many of the people are recent additions to the ranks of the uninsured.

Entrepreneurs and 1099 Employees

Contributing to the increase in the number of people working as independent contractors or temporary employees has been a change in how entrepreneurs and inventors transform their inventions into businesses. Unlike household names like Michael Dell and Bill Gates, inventors of new products today are more likely to set up small companies and arrange for much of the manufacturing of their product to be done overseas. In the services sector, there has been a virtual explosion of entrepreneurs who have come up with ideas for specialized services to sell to other companies. One of these is thirty-three-year-old James, an uninsured computer software engineer. He graduated from a nationally known small college and worked for Viacom for several years. During his first two years at Viacom, he was a permalancer and did not have access to health insurance benefits. Then James became a regular employee with health insurance. After he left Viacom to join a start-up company, he maintained his Viacom-sponsored health insurance for eighteen months under the COBRA regulations, but since it expired he has been uninsured. James has been involved with a number of start-up companies offering Internet Web design and hosting services; he helped start several of these, and he owns one that now has fifty clients. As he said, however, start-ups are usually hard-pressed for cash and often fail; health insurance is just one of those items on the "back burner" that he will buy if he ever gets enough clients to earn "real" money. When James does hire other people, they work as independent contractors.

Another relatively new entrepreneur is forty-nine-year-old David, who worked for twenty years for a large consulting company before starting his own company six years ago. David graduated from a prestigious university with a bachelor's degree in economics; he also knows a lot about computer software processes. He started his own company when he realized from his consulting work that there are a lot of businesses that want to track particular companies' earnings and other financial information. He developed a program that does that and sold the service to a number of companies. His "employees" are not technically employees; they all work as independent contractors.[22] They include six or seven women who want to work at home and have flexible hours. Their work involves taking information from various sources and putting the data into David's predeveloped program, and then creating reports that are sent to the business clients. David expressed some frustration that he cannot provide them with health insurance, but he says that he cannot afford it.

Although the surge in the inventiveness of business services has increased jobs, many of the business-services entrepreneurs are like David and James: they do not technically have employees. Instead, the people who work for them are "1099 workers" who theoretically are independent consultants. They receive a 1099 statement of "miscellaneous" income instead of a W-2 income statement, which employees get for income earned the previous year. Although James tends to hire highly skilled computer software people, many other business-services entrepreneurs are like David and hire people without specific skills. Those 1099 workers without specific skills who work from home typically earn anywhere from the minimum wage to $10 or $12 per hour.[23] Skilled or not, 1099 workers are part of the growing number of uninsured in the United States.

The Rise in Temporary Government Employment

Cost pressures to reduce labor costs by reducing employees and hiring people on a temporary basis also are affecting all levels of government. In earlier decades, government employees often had lower salaries than their private-sector counterparts but were rewarded with job stability and generous benefits. In some places, that is still true, but it is quite common today to find new government hires working in temporary positions that do not come with health insurance or other benefits. The federal government has shrunk its workforce since 1989, when 3.1 million people were federal employees. By 2004 the number had fallen to 2.71 million.[24] While the number of federal employees has declined, the number of state and local government employees has grown steadily since 1985. In 2004 about 17 million people worked for state and local governments; almost 8 percent of these workers were uninsured.

FALLING BIRTHRATES, CHANGING MARITAL PATTERNS, AND INCREASED FEMALE LABOR FORCE PARTICIPATION

So far, we have focused on the economic factors that significantly changed the composition of the uninsured between 1979 and today. But during the same period significant demographic changes that particularly affect children and younger adults were occurring too. These demographic changes also have affected changes in who is uninsured. As noted earlier, one of the most striking differences between the uninsured in 1979 and 2004 is the decline in the number of uninsured children and the halving of the proportion of the uninsured who are children. Today only 20 percent of the uninsured are children (as we saw in table 2.1). The decline in the fraction of the uninsured who are children is a product of two independent factors: declines in birthrates and changing marital patterns, and expansions in government programs to insure poor and low-income children. While policymakers' attention was focused on expanding programs for children, the demographic changes affecting the types of families in which children were being raised were occurring with little notice.

The first of these demographic changes is the slow but steady decline in the birthrate among women fifteen to forty-four years of age. As can be seen in figure 2.3, the birthrate was 15.9 per 1,000 such women in 1980; by 2003 the birthrate had fallen to 14.1 births per 1,000.[25] (For comparison, during the baby boom years the birthrate was between 24.1 and 26.6 per 1,000 women.) The decline in the birthrate is echoed by an 18.5 percent decline in the number of children under age eighteen per household between 1979 and 2004.[26] During this period, families with children went from being a slight majority of all families (52.5 percent) to less than half of all families (47.2 percent).[27]

The decline in the birthrate occurred among both whites and blacks, and birthrates have been declining among teenage women and holding steady for unmarried women fifteen to forty-four years of age since 1995.[28] The birthrate for teenagers is now 33 percent below its most recent peak, in 1991.[29] Since 1991, the birthrates for non-Hispanic white and non-Hispanic black teenagers have fallen the most: 38 percent for the white teens and 45 percent for the black teens. The birthrate for Hispanic teenagers has declined by 21 percent since 1991.

As a result of the drop in birthrates, there are fewer children per

Figure 2.3   **Birthrates for All Women Age Fifteen to Forty-Four and for White and Black Women, 1980 to 2003**

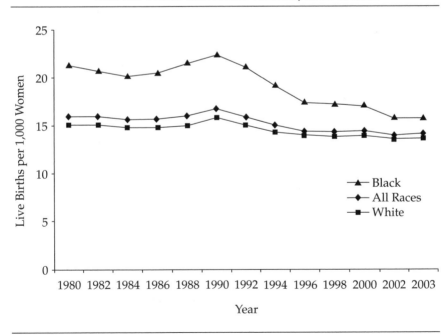

Year

Source: National Vital Statistics Reports 54, no. 2 (September 2005).

adults in the population today than in 1979. The decline in the number of children per adults probably would have caused the share of children among the uninsured to decline, even if public health insurance programs for poor and near-poor children had not been significantly expanded after the mid-1980s. Or to put it another way, the shift in the uninsured population so that younger adults are a larger share than they were in 1979 is partly a result of the decline in the number of children per adults.

The second significant demographic change since 1979 is the steady rise in the median age of first marriage for men and women.[30] As figure 2.4 shows, in 1979 the median age at first marriage for men was 24.4 years, and for women it was 22.1 years.[31] By 2004 the median ages were 27.4 years for men and 25.8 years for women. These increases are extraordinary. We have to go back to 1890 to find a median age of first marriage for men (26.1 years) that approaches the current number. The year 1890 also saw the highest median age of first marriage for women

Figure 2.4   Median Age of First Marriage for Men and Women, 1969 to 2004

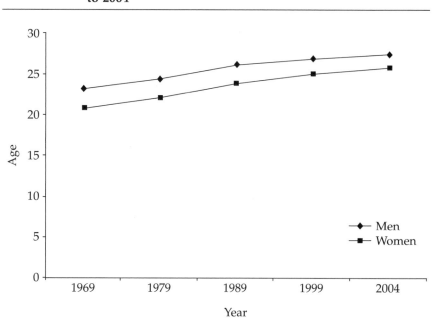

Source: U.S. Department of Commerce, U.S. Census Bureau (see chapter 2, n. 31, this volume).

(22.0 years) until 1979. These sharp increases have had significant effects on household and family structures, as well as on the proportion of families headed by married couples in which children live. Today a higher fraction of all men fifteen years of age and older have never been married compared with men in earlier years.[32] As can be seen in figure 2.5, in 1980, 29.6 percent of all men had never married; by 2004 this proportion was 32.6 percent.[33] The trend is similar for women fifteen years of age and older: in 1980, 22.5 percent had never been married, and by 2004, 25.6 percent had never married. Divorce rates have also increased over the last twenty-five years. By 2004, 8.2 percent of all men fifteen years of age and older were divorced, and 10.9 percent of all women were divorced.[34]

The changes in median age of first marriage and higher divorce rates have had a significant impact on household and family structures. More

Figure 2.5   **Percentages of Persons, Age Fifteen and Older, Who Are Never-Married or Divorced, 1970 to 2004**

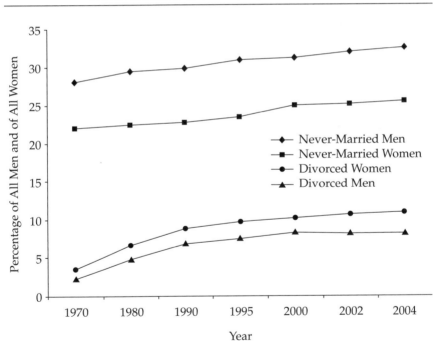

Source: U.S. Department of Commerce, U.S. Census Bureau (see chapter 2, n. 33, this volume).

single men and women have their own households. But if we look just at families (which consist of related people: married adults with or without children, or adults with children), the proportion of all families with children under eighteen years of age went from being the majority (52.5 percent) of all families in 1979 to less than half (47.2 percent) in 2004.[35] If we examine just families with children, the proportion headed by a married couple fell from 81 percent in 1979 to 72 percent in 2004; the proportion headed by a mother only increased from 17.4 percent to 22.9 percent in the same period.

Another way of looking at how changes in adults' marital status affected children can be seen in figure 2.6. In 1979 a little more than three-fourths of all children under the age of eighteen lived with two parents.[36] By 2004 the proportion of all children living with two parents had dropped to two-thirds. By the same token, in 1979, 17 percent of all children lived with just their mother, but by 2004 the percentage had risen to almost one-quarter.

Figure 2.6   Living Arrangements of Children Less Than Eighteen Years Old, 1979 to 2004

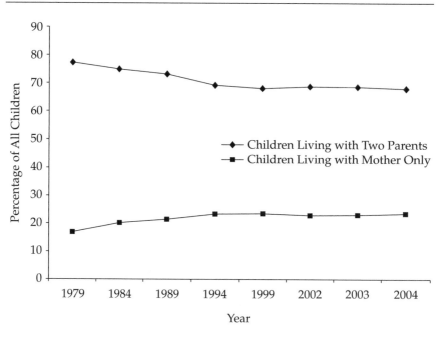

Source: U.S. Department of Commerce, U.S. Census Bureau (see chapter 2, n. 36, this volume).

Both the rise in median age of first marriage and the growth in the number of single men and women living in their own households are consistent with the increase in the share of younger adults who are among the uninsured today compared to 1979. It is not clear whether the absence of responsibility for dependents causes young people to be uninsured or whether it's the other way around. But either way, having more young adults without health insurance is a concern. As an emergency department physician said to me when commenting about the young-adult car accident victims he sees, "You may not need health insurance 99 percent of the time, but when you do, the costs of its absence go right up."

A third factor affecting household structure has been the rising labor force participation rate of women, especially married women and women with children under the age of six. In 1980 just over half (51.5 percent) of all women sixteen years of age and older were in the labor force; by 2003 the percentage was almost 60 percent.[37] As can be seen in figure 2.7, the increase in women's labor force participation rates is even more striking for women with children younger than eighteen: by 2003, 73 percent of all single mothers and 69 percent of all married mothers were in the labor force. Among women with children under the age of six, the participation rates also jumped, to 70 percent and 60 percent for single and married mothers, respectively. Thus, many more families today have incomes coming from women, and many more children, especially those under the age of six, have mothers working for pay.

This rapid change in women's participation in the labor force had a dramatic impact on family incomes in the 1980s and 1990s, particularly in families where the husband did not have a college education.[38] The earnings (after accounting for inflation) of these men fell or did not grow during the 1980s and 1990s.[39] The sharp decline in manufacturing jobs and the subsequent increase in service-sector jobs described earlier particularly affected men with only a high school education. But because their wives entered the labor force, these men and their families were able to maintain middle-class incomes.

Equally important, the increase in women's labor force participation has meant that many families have access to health insurance that they might not have if the husband's employer does not provide health insurance. The ability of families to get health insurance from a second earner has cushioned the effect of the employment restructuring of the past decade. Among the independent contractors, consultants, and small-business owners I interviewed, those with health insurance said over and over again that without the health insurance provided by their spouses' jobs, they would not be able to have the careers they do. If women had not returned to the labor force in the numbers they have, the

Figure 2.7   Labor Force Participation Rates of Women, 1970 to 2003

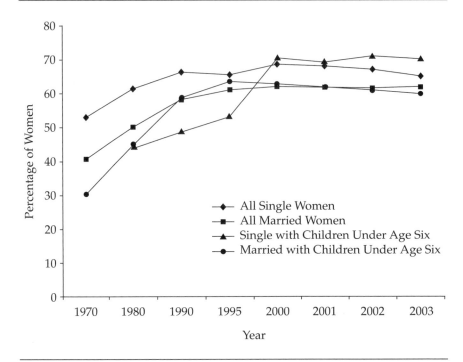

Source: U.S. Department of Labor, Bureau of Labor Statistics (see chapter 2, n. 37, this volume).

employment restructuring of the last decade would have dramatically increased the number of uninsured. Another effect of the presence of a second earner is that many families are deciding who will stay home with young children on the basis of which adult is more likely to have continued access to employer-based health insurance.[40]

All of these changes in demographics, marital status, and labor force participation rates have changed the types of family and financial circumstances in which children are growing up. Surprisingly, in spite of all the changes, the proportion of children living in families with incomes below the middle-class threshold of the median household income did not change over this period, remaining around 45 percent. But among children in families below the middle-class threshold, the proportion who were uninsured fell from 28 percent to 18 percent. The reason for this relates to the fourth factor that has affected changes in the uninsured population since 1979.

THE EXPANSION OF PUBLIC PROGRAMS FOR
POOR AND LOW-INCOME CHILDREN AND
POOR ADULTS

Since the 1960s, efforts to help the uninsured have focused on very low-income people. The general expectation in the post–World War II era was that larger firms were more efficient at producing goods and services and that people would gravitate to larger firms for employment. Since large firms were more likely to offer health insurance, the assumption was that health insurance would become more widespread as more less-skilled workers found employment in the larger firms. To the extent that policymakers tried to help working people obtain health insurance, the effort was implicit in job training programs rather than through any explicit policy. Initiatives to help the uninsured focused on raising Medicaid's income eligibility caps and on state programs to help the uninsured poor. The targets of these initiatives were children and single mothers or people with health problems that prevented them from working—people who did not have financial means to purchase health insurance. They were viewed as being first on a priority list of "deserving" uninsured people in need of assistance.

The initiatives to cover more of the uninsured poor have been modestly successful during the last two decades and have primarily affected children. In the late 1980s the income eligibility limits for Medicaid were raised across the country so that all children under the age of six with family incomes below 133 percent of the poverty level were eligible for Medicaid. In addition, Medicaid eligibility was phased in for children age six to nineteen who had family incomes below the poverty level. Since 2002, all poor children under age nineteen are eligible for Medicaid. In 1998 the State Children's Health Insurance Programs (SCHIPs) were launched.[41] The SCHIPs provide medical coverage to children with family incomes above their state's income cap for Medicaid eligibility. In 2003, thirty-eight states and the District of Columbia had SCHIP income eligibility caps of 200 percent of the poverty level or higher. Together, Medicaid and the SCHIPs covered almost 30 million children in 2003—almost 40 percent of all American children.[42]

WHO IS NOW UNINSURED?

With many poor and near-poor children now covered by Medicaid and the SCHIPs, there are now fewer uninsured children than there were twenty-five years ago (see tables 2.1 and 2.3). The fraction of all children who are uninsured has fallen from 17 percent to just under 12 percent. The uninsured age groups that have grown particularly are twenty-five-to thirty-four-year-olds and thirty-five- to forty-four-year-olds. Two out of every five uninsured people today are between the ages of twenty-five and forty-four; in 1979 people in this age range accounted for just under one-quarter of the uninsured.

More shocking is the fact that the chances of being uninsured for people in these age groups have doubled since 1979, as table 2.3 shows. Today someone twenty-five to thirty-four years old has a better than one-in-four chance of being uninsured, and someone thirty-five to forty-four years old has almost a one-in-five chance. Those are very bad odds. The high number of uninsured adults in these age groups has implications for other family members too. People twenty-five to forty-four years of age are often heads of families and need health insurance to cover children and pregnant women.

For young adults who are in very good health, the possibility of a serious medical problem must seem remotely small. Interviews indicate that most view health insurance premiums as high relative to their expected medical expenses. It was striking that those under age forty spoke about health insurance as if it were prepaid medical care. They seemed to ignore the fact that insurance would enable them to shift the risk of high costs to insurers in exchange for a known monthly cost. Yet most knew that they did not have enough money to pay for serious medical care. Indeed, among the uninsured in general, many are in debt for the cost of medical care for what are covered services for people with insurance.[43] Monthly payments for medical debts are another expense that reduces an uninsured person's ability to pay for health insurance.

The shifts in the economy and employer-employee relationships and their effects on the insurance status of adults can be seen clearly in the higher educational attainment of today's uninsured adults. In 2004, 37 percent of uninsured adults had a four-year college degree or had completed some college courses (including a two-year associate's degree); in 1979, 28.6 percent of uninsured adults had this level of education (see table 2.4). But more sobering are the increases since 1979 in the simple chances of being uninsured for adults with all levels of education except postgraduate degrees. The chances doubled for adults who did not complete high school or who did not continue their education beyond high school. Many of these uninsured adults would have held union jobs in manufacturing that included health insurance twenty-five years ago. Having more education offered some buffer to these effects, but as we saw with Sam, Brian, Paul, and James, higher education is less of a guarantee of health insurance than it used to be. Today one in six adults who have taken some college courses and one in nine of those with a college degree are uninsured. These are greatly increased odds compared to 1979. Although the simple chances of being uninsured have not changed

Table 2.3 Ages of Non-Elderly Uninsured and Simple Probabilities of Being Uninsured, by Age Cohort, 1979 and 2004

Age Cohort	1979			2004		
	Number Uninsured (Millions)	Percentage of Uninsured	Simple Probability of Being Uninsured	Number Uninsured (Millions)	Percentage of Uninsured	Simple Probability of Being Uninsured
Younger than 19	10.784	39.3%	17.0%	9.034	19.9%	11.6%
19 to 24	4.974	18.1	21.5	8.001	17.6	33.4
25 to 34	4.112	15.0	12.2	10.174	22.4	25.9
35 to 44	2.438	8.9	10.0	8.108	17.8	18.8
45 to 54	2.349	8.5	10.8	6.257	13.7	14.9
55 to 64	2.818	10.3	14.0	3.934	8.6	13.3
Total	27.470	100.1	14.7	45.508	100	17.8

Source: March 1980 and March 2005 Current Population Surveys.

Table 2.4   Educational Attainment of Uninsured Nineteen- to Sixty-Four-Year-Olds and Simple Probabilities of Being Uninsured, 1979 and 2004

Educational Attainment	1979			2004		
	Number Uninsured (Millions)	Percentage of Uninsured	Simple Probabilities of Being Uninsured	Number Uninsured (Millions)	Percentage of Uninsured	Simple Probabilities of Being Uninsured
Did not finish high school	5.768	34.9%	20.3%	9.420	25.8%	41.9%
High school graduate	6.045	36.6	12.0	13.552	37.2	24.4
Some college or associate's degree	3.087	18.7	13.5	8.862	24.3	17.1
College degree	1.024	6.2	8.3	3.641	10.0	11.2
Postgraduate degree	0.605	3.7	7.2	1.000	2.7	6.4
Total	16.529	100.1	13.5	36.475	100	20.5

Source: March 1980 and March 2005 Current Population Surveys.

for people with a postgraduate degree, like Sam, there are today one million adults with a postgraduate degree who do not have coverage.

The fact that 37 percent of uninsured adults today have completed at least some college courses shows up in the incomes of the uninsured. As we saw earlier in table 2.2, compared with 1979, a slightly smaller proportion of the uninsured today have incomes below the poverty level. The policies to help the poor, especially children, explain the decline in poor people among the uninsured. For everyone else, the economic forces that have caused jobs to shift from the manufacturing to the services sectors, and from large firms to small firms, and the changes in employment relationships and marital status have taken their toll. People in every income group above poverty now have a significantly higher probability of being uninsured than they did in 1979.

The growth in the probability of being uninsured for people with incomes several times the poverty level can be seen also by looking at the annual family incomes of the uninsured (see table 2.5). In both years, almost two out of five (38 percent) of the uninsured had incomes less than $20,000 (in 2004 dollars). But the proportion with incomes above $60,000 has grown so that now almost one in five of the uninsured has an income above $60,000.

Since children account for far fewer of the uninsured today, it is important to look more closely at the incomes just for working-age adults between the ages of twenty-three and sixty-four. (Most people in this age group have finished their education and are not yet retired.) The working-age uninsured population more than doubled in size between 1979 and 2004; today almost one-fifth of all working-age adults are uninsured (see table 2.6). We can further simplify the income numbers by defining people as middle-class if they have an income in the upper half of all households' incomes (that is, above the median household income). The effects of the economic and demographic changes of the last twenty-five years on the simple chances of working-age adults' being uninsured are startling. The proportion of working-age adults with incomes below the middle-class threshold who were uninsured jumped, from 21 to 32 percent. But among middle-class working-age adults, the proportion who were uninsured also shot up, from 6.3 percent to 10.3 percent. Being without health insurance is now a bigger threat to people of all incomes.

IMPLICATIONS OF THE CHANGES IN WHO IS UNINSURED

The changes in the uninsured population require that we rethink the policies that are needed to help the currently uninsured and people who are at risk of losing their employer-sponsored coverage.

39

Table 2.5 Family Income of Non-Elderly Uninsured and Simple Probabilities of Being Uninsured, 1979 and 2004

Family Income Group (2004 Dollars)	1979			2004		
	Number Uninsured (Millions)	Percentage of Uninsured	Simple Probability of Being Uninsured	Number Uninsured (Millions)	Percentage of Uninsured	Simple Probability of Being Uninsured
Less than $10,000	5.000	18.2%	38.8%	8.016	17.6%	35.2%
$10,000 to $19,999	5.466	19.9	29.2	8.090	17.8	33.7
$20,000 to $29,999	5.091	18.6	22.8	7.898	17.4	28.9
$30,000 to median	4.236	15.4	13.9	7.759	17.1	20.5
Median to $59,999	3.391	12.3	8.9	4.836	10.6	14.4
$60,000 to $74,999	1.613	5.9	6.5	3.016	6.6	10.9
$75,000 or more	2.674	9.7	6.9	5.894	13.0	7.1
Total	27.470	100	14.7	45.508	100	17.8

Source: March 1980 and March 2005 Current Population Surveys.
Notes: 1979 family incomes were converted to 2004 dollars using CPI-U-RS index. Median household income in 2004 = $44,389. Median household income in 1979 = $42,700 in 2004 dollars ($17,710 in 1979 dollars).

Table 2.6   Middle-Class Status of Uninsured Twenty-Three- to Sixty-Four-Year-Olds: Family Income Relative to the Median Household Income, 1979 and 2004

Income Relative to Median Household Income	1979			2004		
	Number Uninsured (Millions)	Percentage of Uninsured	Simple Probability of Being Uninsured	Number Uninsured (Millions)	Percentage of Uninsured	Simple Probability of Being Uninsured
Below: not in the middle class	9.314	70.2%	21.1%	21.842	69.2%	32.1%
Above: in the middle class	3.953	29.8	6.3	9.707	30.8	10.3
Total working-age adults	13.267	100	12.4	31.548	100	19.4

Source: March 1980 and March 2005 Current Population Surveys.
Note: Family incomes relative to the median household income in each year: $17,710 in 1979 and $44,430 in 2004.

The Need for Publicly Funded Coverage or Large
Subsidies for the Poor and Near-Poor Uninsured

Although some of the poorest uninsured have been helped by expansions of Medicaid since the late 1980s, it is still the case that the 54 percent of the uninsured with incomes below two times the poverty level (approximately $30,000 for most people) cannot afford to buy health insurance on their own. If these 24.3 million people were to purchase individual policies, they would be spending more than 10 percent of their after-tax income on health insurance—something that very few Americans with employer-group coverage do. Premiums for individual coverage—frequently more than $300 per month for one person—are often close to what single people pay for apartment rents. Premiums for family coverage in the individual market are often more than $1,000 per month—again, close to or above many families' monthly housing costs.

Since two out of every three uninsured adults are employed, and another 8 percent are actively looking for work, there are good reasons to make it easier for people with ties to the labor force to purchase private coverage or for their employers to sponsor health insurance. As we have seen, many non-middle-class adults now work for service-sector firms. These employers are typically small, with fewer than fifty employees, often fewer than ten. The per-person premiums for small firms are substantially higher than those faced by large employers. Every small-business owner I spoke with expressed regret that he or she could not afford to sponsor health insurance for the people they hired (most of whom were paid wages below the middle-class threshold). A typical case is that of Ellen, who owns a successful interior design business. Ellen has high-income residential clients who are renovating or decorating their homes as well as business clients restructuring their office spaces. At one time she had seven people working for her, four of whom were employees and three of whom worked on a contract basis whenever Ellen had sufficient work for them. No one earned more than $40,000 a year. Until two years ago, Ellen sponsored health insurance for the four employees. But when the premiums shot up 50 percent, she felt that she could no longer justify the expense. Two of her employees quit, and the whole experience led her to restructure the relationship she has with the people who work with her. Today Ellen is the sole employee of her company, and everyone else has an independent contractual arrangement with her. For more employers like Ellen (and David) to sponsor health insurance, small-group health insurance premiums have to become more affordable. Likewise, if the people who work for small employers and earn more than $25,000 are to be able to purchase private health insurance, we need to reduce their premium costs—either through subsidies to them or to their employers.

The Need to Focus More on the Difficulties in
Gaining Access to Health Insurance

As noted earlier, many highly skilled middle-class people work in occupations where independent contracting is now the norm. They cannot find jobs with health insurance unless they give up their occupations. There is also a shadow middle-class group of uninsured people—people who in earlier decades had middle-class incomes but today do not. Many had high-paying jobs in manufacturing until the 1980s. Now, not only can they not earn middle-class salaries, but the jobs available to them do not provide health insurance and they cannot afford to purchase insurance on their own.

The middle class's increased difficulty in obtaining health insurance has much in common with the problems of lower-income people. The shifts in the economy from manufacturing to service sector jobs and the changes in employer-employee relationships have affected everyone. The difference is that people in the middle class have more income with which to purchase health insurance. So why are so many having trouble obtaining that insurance?

The explanation hinges on two puzzles. One has to do with the job market and how firms compete for workers. The other puzzle has to do with how insurers compete for people to insure and price premiums for different types of people. In the next two chapters, we explore these puzzles. The answers suggest ways in which the federal government might increase access to private health insurance, especially for the 30 percent of the uninsured with incomes above the median household income. Policies beyond subsidies are needed to help people with middle-class incomes obtain health insurance—and these policies need to address why such people are uninsured.

Chapter 3

Why Employer-Group Health Insurance Is Cheaper—and Why Those Who Have It Are Lucky

W hat is it about employer groups that insurance companies find attractive? How did it come to pass that the United States has an employer-based health insurance system? In 2004, 63 percent of Americans under age sixty-five obtained health insurance through their own or a family member's employer, down from 67 percent in 2000.[1] Only seventy years ago, almost no one had health insurance from an employer—so it is somewhat amazing that three out of five Americans have employer-sponsored health insurance today. Even so, this fraction is not as high as some envisioned fifty years ago, and it has been slowly declining over the past decade. The decline is reflected by the higher proportion of middle-class people who are now uninsured. One reason for the decline is the increased proportion (now 43.7 percent) of the workforce in establishments with fewer than fifty employees. What is it about larger employer groups that is not also true about small employer groups or individuals?

The proximate answer to these questions is that per-person costs in large groups are lower than in small groups or for individual coverage. The group size effect on cost is a major reason why some workers have health insurance and others—like Sam, Brian, and Susan Mitchell—do not. Why per-person costs are lower in large groups is the focus of much of this chapter. The reasons involve the complicated relationship between health insurance pools and the places where we work.

This chapter explains why people who work in large firms that sponsor health insurance are very lucky—and why people who work in small firms, are self-employed or are independent contractors, or work for temporary agencies are at a huge disadvantage when it comes to access to affordable health insurance. The growing percentage of workers who are in the disadvantaged group is a warning that the employment-based system of health insurance in the United States is in danger of failing.

HOW U.S. HEALTH INSURANCE BECAME EMPLOYMENT-BASED

Fifty years ago, there was a general expectation that American workers would be employed in large companies because large businesses offered economies of scale. Although that was indeed the case in manufacturing, few foresaw that manufacturing jobs would lose ground while various service industries would employ more of the labor force.[2] While some services can be produced at less cost by large firms—for example, banking or credit card billing—many are less amenable to large-scale production. Financial advice, interior design services, and even many forms of health care do not cost less in large-scale settings. Thus, the expectation that almost all Americans would have health insurance through the workplace has been foiled by shifts in the economy.

Health insurance has been part of the wage compensation package for a significant number of workers only since the end of World War II. It is widely believed that such coverage grew during the war because the National War Labor Board (NWLB) permitted its substitution for wage increases.[3] However, this view of the NWLB's role downplays the fact that also in 1943 the Internal Revenue Service (IRS) issued a ruling that employers' contributions to group health insurance policies were exempt from taxation. Indeed, Jennifer Klein makes a persuasive case for a different history of the NWLB's role in the expansion of employer-based health insurance.[4] Her reading of the NWLB's decisions yields two significant points: First, "it was not until April 1943 that the NWLB agreed to approve insurance plans, pensions, or sick leave plans if they did not exceed 5 percent of payroll." And second, "the board ruled against labor unions that requested new benefit plans or improvements in existing plans."[5] Although the NWLB consistently ruled that companies had to guarantee existing health insurance benefits, it would not order companies to establish new plans. Thus, the conventional wisdom seems implausible.

In the decade or so before World War II, large insurance companies were seeing a falloff in the popularity of the burial and accident insurance they sold to workers through their employers. In the mid-1930s, insurers began to experiment with hospitalization insurance to replace their waning business. They preferred indemnity hospitalization insurance—policies that paid a specific amount toward a hospital's charges—

because it was patterned on indemnity life insurance.[6] They also saw that selling such insurance through employer groups might open up a whole new market of business.

The choice confronting insurance companies before World War II was whether to market health insurance directly to workers or to sell it through employers. Several factors affected their decision to push for employer-sponsored policies. In the early part of the twentieth century, burial and accident insurance had largely been sold to individuals by insurance agents. But as workers began to move to the Midwest and West Coast in response to new job opportunities in manufacturing, insurance agents lost track of them, and sales of policies fell. Insurers began to realize that collecting premiums through an employer would be more efficient. Further inhibiting insurers' desire to sell policies directly to workers was the fact that union organizers in the 1930s had examined a number of the new forms of health insurance that were being tried, and they favored plans that today would be familiar as prepaid group health organizations—not at all what the insurers wanted to sell.[7] In addition, during the 1930s and especially after the war, many Americans viewed unions as having communist and socialist objectives. Business owners were reluctant to pay into union-organized health plans, particularly after the war ended. The large commercial insurers saw an opportunity for marketing their indemnity policies as an employer-sponsored insurance benefit, one that would enable the companies to sidestep any obligation to contribute to union-sponsored plans and avoid negotiations with unions about the content of the benefit.

In 1947 the Supreme Court ruled that Inland Steel could not exclude health insurance from the bargaining issues with the United Steel Workers union. It is regarded as the watershed case that set in motion the expansion of health insurance benefits as part of wage compensation packages. However, a great many unionized workers were already receiving indemnity hospitalization coverage by the time the Inland Steel case was decided. Immediately after the war, there was great demand for the products of the durable goods and heavy manufacturing industries, such as automobiles, electrical goods, household appliances, and steel. The companies needed capital to expand their production capacities—and the insurance companies had capital to lend. By the early 1950s, as Klein notes, the largest insurance companies and the leading manufacturing companies had many board of directors members in common. The close relationships among the leaders of these companies helped spread the idea that, by announcing that they were offering an indemnity health plan, the companies could take insurance off the bargaining table.[8] As a result, most unionized workers in the durable goods and heavy manufacturing industries had indemnity hospitalization insurance by mid-decade. Not surprisingly, the companies also offered their technical and management employees similar health benefits as part of their total compensation. By the end of the decade, it was commonplace for white-collar workers to have health insurance in their compensation packages.

Tax Code Incentives for Employer-Group Insurance

The spread of health insurance as a fringe benefit, especially among educated workers in high-paid occupations, also was aided by changes to the federal tax code. By enacting section 106 of the Internal Revenue Code of 1954, Congress eliminated confusion arising from a 1953 IRS ruling that had seemed to contradict its 1943 ruling that employer contributions to health insurance policies were tax-exempt.[9] Congress further amended the Internal Revenue Code in 1954 with section 3121, which clarifies that employer contributions to health and accident insurance are exempt from payroll taxes. Together, the 1954 amendments to the tax code strengthened the incentive for employers to offer compensation in the form of fringe benefits, since they did not have to pay payroll taxes (principally for Social Security) on the amount they contributed toward the benefits. Similarly, employees had an incentive to receive fringe benefit forms of compensation since they did not have to pay income taxes or payroll taxes on the dollar amount contributed by employers for those benefits. For people who had higher earnings, the tax advantages of receiving income in the form of health insurance provided strong incentives to welcome employer-sponsored health insurance as part of their compensation package.

After Medicare was created in 1965 and the payroll tax for the Medicare trust fund went into effect, the tax advantages for employers and employees of health insurance grew again. Over the 1970s and 1980s, general price inflation caused incomes to rise, and people "crept" into higher income tax brackets. Congress also raised the payroll tax rates for Social Security and Medicare a number of times after 1965 to meet rising costs for both programs. The increased tax advantages of receiving health insurance rather than wage increases during this period contributed to the expansion of the list of medical services covered by health insurance policies. As a result, the concept of health insurance shifted from indemnity hospitalization and surgery coverage to hospitalization and major medical coverage. Major medical policies covered far more medical services, including diagnostic tests. By the beginning of the 1980s, most employer-based health insurance policies had a major medical component.

Wages–Fringe Benefits Trade-Off

By accepting and sometimes encouraging a private-sector health insurance system based on employer groups, Americans agreed that health insurance is a form of compensation for work. They could be paid for their work through some combination of wages and in-kind benefits, health insurance and pensions being the most prominent.

The idea of health insurance as a form of compensation is a natural extension of company-provided housing, doctors, and stores where food and provisions could be bought. Company towns have a long history in Europe and the United States. Up through World War II, many workers employed in coal mining, oil extraction and refining, steel manufacturing, railroad building and production of railroad cars, and other industries lived in towns initially built by companies. They built the housing and other town buildings so they could attract workers to locations where transportation costs were low or raw materials were nearby. The costs of these company-provided benefits, however, were usually deducted from promised wages, so it was clear that they were provided in lieu of wages.

Two issues are notable about this arrangement. First, just as the deductions for company-provided housing and food from company stores were often mysteriously determined, the employer contributions for health insurance were not transparent. Workers never knew how much their wages would have increased in the absence of employer-sponsored health insurance. As Klein points out, companies frequently received premium dividends (or rebates at year end) from insurers, but they did not pass these savings along to the workers.[10] It was not clear in the 1940s and 1950s—and often is still not clear—what employer-group health insurance really costs an employer. Since the early 1990s, many employers have made the costs more transparent. It is not uncommon for paycheck stubs to list the separate amounts contributed by the employee and the employer for employer-sponsored health insurance. But with only a small proportion of the workforce belonging to unions, the vast majority of workers do not have the opportunity to bargain over whether they want less generous health insurance in return for increased wages. In countries where health insurance is universal, workers finance it with compulsory taxes on their wages.[11] The costs of health care and the health plan are transparent since they are translated into taxes. This is quite different from the American system of employers setting the terms of the trade-off of wages for fringe benefits and not giving employees more voice in how their nonwage compensation is spent.

The other notable aspect of substituting health insurance for wages is that the total premium per person in a company is the same regardless of the person. The *share* of the premium paid by the employee can vary if an employer chooses to subsidize lower-wage workers more than higher-wage workers. This subsidization often is in the form of a "tiered" system: people with annual salaries below some threshold pay a smaller share of the premium than do people with salaries above the threshold. Some tiered systems have more than two tiers. Also, an employee's share of the premium for single-person coverage is often lower than the fraction of the premium paid by the employee for family coverage. But across all people enrolled in a single-person policy or all people enrolled in a family policy, the *total* premium for each is independent of the person's income or health or any other factor.

This may have seemed fair in the 1940s and 1950s when the income distribution was significantly more equal than it is now. In the years after World War II, the top 10 percent of all tax-filing units (households) earned about 32 percent of all income in the United States, a share that remained stable until 1982, when it began to steadily rise. By 2000 the top 10 percent's share of all U.S. income had reached 42 percent.[12] The change in the income distribution can also be seen in the change in the ratio of compensation for the average chief executive officer (CEO) to the typical worker's pay. In 1965 CEOs earned about 24 times what the average worker made; in 2003 they earned 185 times as much.[13] Also, in the 1940s and 1950s, when health care costs were relatively low, so were premiums. Health care expenditures per person in 1960 were only $913 in 2004 dollars.[14] In those years there were fewer treatment options for medical problems. Little could be done to combat cancer or cardiovascular disease or diabetes. Since the 1980s the treatment options for a host of acute and chronic conditions have expanded exponentially. Life expectancy has risen, and survival rates from traumatic incidents, as well as chronic conditions, improve all the time. The result is that per capita health expenditures have grown from just over $2,535 in 1980 to $6,280 in 2004 (in 2004 dollars).[15] (To see how this change affects families, health care expenditures per capita were 6 percent of median household income in 1980—in 2004, they were 13.1 percent.) But in companies where everyone pays the same amount for a health insurance plan, or where employee shares of the total premium do not vary much by salary, low-wage workers are paying larger shares of forgone wages for health insurance than are their managers and executives.

When the rapid rise in health care expenditures is placed alongside what has happened to incomes, it is apparent why lower-income workers have been squeezed by the wage–health insurance trade-off. Since 1979 the average hourly wage of men with only a high school diploma has fallen from $16.75 to $15.47 in 2003 (all in 2004 dollars).[16] In fact, only people whose family incomes are in the top fifth of the income distribution have seen increases in their inflation-adjusted incomes. For people who have had to shift from manufacturing to service-sector jobs, where health insurance is not as prevalent a fringe benefit, it is easy to see why the wage–health insurance trade-off is not realistic. A high school graduate working in an automobile assembly plant might be able to make $25 to $30 per hour, which is equivalent to $50,000 to $60,000 per year (assuming 2,000 hours of work per year). A health insurance policy with an annual cost of $6,000 is the equivalent of $3 per hour in wages. After netting out the cost of the health insurance policy, the auto assembly worker still has a middle-class income. Now place that same person in a restaurant working for $12 per hour and reduce his wage by the same $3 per hour for health insurance. A $12 per hour wage generates an annual income of $24,000 and the $6,000 loss in income for health insurance is unsustainable. It is difficult to imagine anyone in good health accepting that trade-off.

Kristen offers another angle on the squeeze faced by lower-income workers. She is unable to afford health insurance because she cannot count on steady inflows of income as a freelance writer. Although Kristen has one contract that will pay her $18,000 this year for a series of articles, she does not have any other similar assignments with certain contracts. She worries that if she raises her fees enough to cover the premiums for an individual policy, she will be undercut by other freelancers willing to work for less. Kristen faces high rates for individual coverage because she is a forty-six-year-old single woman in a state that permits age-adjusted premiums for policies sold in the individual market.

It has become commonplace for researchers and policymakers to say that anyone who really wants health insurance will find a job that offers it. The not-so-subtle inference is that people who work and do not have health insurance must not want it enough. But the calculations above show how outdated that conclusion is. The employment-based coverage landscape has changed, along with the scope and costs of health care. There is no room for a trade-off between wages and health insurance when wages are barely enough to live on. Moreover, as we saw earlier, many occupations and careers now do not have the option of health insurance. Only the very best people in an occupation may have health insurance as part of their employment contract. The experience of Sam (whom we met in chapter 2) is typical of people in broadcast journalism. His goal is a position as a permanent employee, with health insurance, with one of the major networks. To achieve that, he has to distinguish himself in the cable broadcasts of local minor league sports and develop a distinctive angle on delivering polished play-by-play descriptions of games. In practical terms, Sam would have to give up his career as a sports broadcaster to gain a job with health insurance.

In addition, the suggestion that people who value health insurance will be willing to make the wage-insurance trade-off has perverse implications for the encouragement of innovation. Dynamic, growing economies need entrepreneurs to design new products and create new ways of producing goods and services at lower cost. The United States prides itself on having a dynamic market economy that is the largest in the world because of such innovations. But incentives to take risks and be innovative are constrained by concerns about exposure to the risks of health care costs. James, the thirty-three-year-old software engineer who has been involved in several Internet Web design start-up companies (see chapter 2), is not comfortable without health insurance. He talks about moving to Canada, where he and his fiancée could have affordable health insurance. James's dilemma points up the conflict between the outmoded premise that people who value health insurance will find a job that offers it and the American mantra that innovation and risk-taking should be encouraged. Often, people who start new companies do not earn enough money to purchase health insurance for themselves or to cover even a portion of the costs for their employees.

HOW GROUP SIZE AFFECTS PREMIUMS

James's calculation that he cannot afford health insurance as a co-owner of a start-up is quite common among small employers. As figure 3.1 shows, almost all firms with more than one hundred employees offer health insurance, and the proportion falls off markedly as the size of the firm gets smaller. A major reason for this is that premiums per person are much lower in large groups.

For both groups and individuals, premiums per person are based on two components: the average expected medical expenses for people in the group, and what is called a loading fee. The loading fee is determined by the costs of the administrative and marketing activities for the policy and the amount of money an insurer needs to be paid to bear the risk that the group (or an individual) might have higher expenses than the expected expenses. Since a person's expected medical expenses are the same regardless of whether he or she is in a large group or a small group, we need to focus on the loading fee to see why the size of a group affects per-person premiums. Three factors contribute to lower premiums as group size increases: efficiencies in administrative and marketing activities, lower risk of adverse selection, and declining risk that a high fraction of people will have very high costs.

Figure 3.1   Percentage of Private-Sector Firms That Offer Health Insurance, by Firm Size, 2003

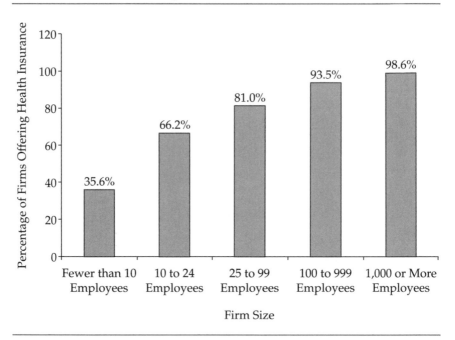

Source: Agency for Healthcare Research and Quality, Center for Financing, Access and Cost Trends, 2003 Medical Expenditure Panel Survey-Insurance Component, table 1.A.2.

Efficiencies in Administrative and Marketing Costs

Administering and marketing insurance policies involves a large proportion of fixed costs. For small groups—particularly twenty-five persons or less—these fixed costs represent a significant cost per person. As the number of people in an employer group increases, these costs per person decline. Consider the task of collecting premiums. It is far less expensive to collect money from one source for three hundred people than it is to collect from three hundred individuals or from ten independent groups of thirty—the insurer sends one bill to a company rather than bills to each of the three hundred people or to the ten small firms. The one employer is far more likely to be consistent in paying the premium bill on time too. Some individuals are chronically late, and some small firms have cash flow problems or even fail to pay; late and missed payments add to an insurer's administrative costs. Small firms also typically have higher employee turnover rates than do large companies. Removing or adding employees to the insurer's databases adds to administrative costs, and these costs are higher per insured person in small firms than in large firms.

Similarly, when an insurer markets its products to one large company, it deals with one person or, at most, a committee. The process of determining which benefits to include in the health plan and what the per-person premium will be takes about the same amount of time whether it is for a group of one thousand or a group of five or an individual. An insurer can further save on marketing costs if a single brochure can be produced for the one thousand people in the same company and the company takes on the distribution task.

The Risk of Adverse Selection

The amount of risk borne by insurers also declines as the number of people covered by a policy increases from one to many thousands. The primary risk for insurers is that actual spending for a person or a group will be greater than what the insurer predicted. There are two separate sources of this risk. One is the potential for adverse selection, and the other is the uncertainty around the predicted per capita (average) expenditure—in particular, that the individual or a high fraction of the people in a group will be outliers with very high costs. Each of these sources of risk declines as the size of a group increases. This reduction in risk is even greater if we compare groups to individuals.

The potential for adverse selection is relatively high among individuals and small groups that apply for insurance coverage when purchasing insurance is voluntary rather than compulsory. People who believe that they are unlikely to use much medical care are less likely to purchase health insurance. Conversely, people who expect that they might need expensive medical care are more likely to purchase insurance. The fact that a significant share of small employers do not offer coverage to their employees makes insurers suspect that small firms that do apply for coverage are doing so because the owner, a family member of the owner, or a beloved employee may have a serious medical problem. The same suspicion arises when individuals apply for coverage in the individual market. In contrast, concern about adverse selection is almost nonexistent among large employers. Among private-sector employees who were offered health insurance by their employers in 1996, 84.4 percent of those in establishments of more than one hundred employees enrolled in the health plan. But in establishments of fewer than twenty-five employees, only 74 percent enrolled.[17] Even when employees turn down employer-sponsored insurance, it is because most of them have coverage through a family member's plan (usually a spouse's employer-sponsored plan).[18] Those who do turn it down and remain uninsured are most often younger than twenty-five. Thus, the risk of adverse selection is large for individuals and very small groups and falls dramatically once the size of a group exceeds one hundred.

The Risk of Bad Predictions

When insurers write a policy for an individual or group, they project an average expenditure, but they also recognize that their prediction contains an element of uncertainty. Consider, for example, these two predictions:

- *Policy A*: Predicted average expenditure per person: $300, with a 95 percent chance that the true (or actual) average expenditure will lie between $250 and $350.

- *Policy B*: Predicted average expenditure per person: also $300, but with a 95 percent chance that the true average expenditure will lie between $100 and $675.

Although both policies have the same predicted average expenditure, policy B involves greater uncertainty and a correspondingly greater risk of a particularly bad outcome for the insurer. In practice, the uncertainty surrounding a prediction and the risk of bad outcomes decline as the number of people covered by the policy increases.

To see this, imagine a scenario in which everyone in the population has a 10 percent chance of being sick; the risk of becoming sick is random, and a person's characteristics have no bearing on the risk. Each of those who become sick needs $10,000 of medical care. If an insurer covers one person, it has a 10 percent chance of paying out $10,000. Now suppose a two-person group purchases an insurance policy. The insurer's concern is that both people will become sick and it will have to pay $20,000. But the probability that this will happen is not 10 percent but $0.10 \times 0.10 = 0.01$ (that is, 1 percent). For a three-person group, the probability that the insurer will have to pay out $10,000 for each of them ($30,000) is $0.10 \times 0.10 \times 0.10$, which equals 0.001 (1/10 of a percent). With every additional person added to a group in this example, the risk for the insurer of having to pay out $10,000 for *every* insured person falls by a factor of ten. The probability of the worst possible outcome—that everyone in the group will become sick—falls as the group size increases. Since insurers are primarily concerned about incurring unexpectedly large losses to a large number of people needing expensive medical care, it is easy to see why they prefer large groups: the risk of such an event becomes infinitesimally small as the group gets larger.

In sum, because there are efficiencies in administrative and marketing activities in larger groups, and because insurers' risk declines as group size increases, the loading fee component of health insurance premiums falls rapidly as the size of the group increases. Thus, people who do not have access to large groups that sponsor health insurance—typically employer-sponsored groups—are at a distinct disadvantage when it comes to the cost of health insurance.[19] The premiums for people in small groups or whose only source of coverage is the individual market are substantially higher.

WHY PREMIUMS VARY AMONG COMPANIES OF THE SAME SIZE

Of course we know that many medical expenses are not truly independent of people's characteristics. There are distinct patterns of medical care use that are correlated with age. Table 3.1 shows how per capita medical care expenditures varied by age, gender, and race-ethnicity for people in the United States in 2002.

Many factors have some bearing on a person's use of medical care: education, income, presence of a spouse for older adults, health status (including whether or not one smokes, gets regular exercise, or has chronic conditions such as diabetes or hypertension), mental health status, family history of certain conditions (especially cancers or cardiac-related conditions), race and ethnic background, ability to speak English, and whether one lives near a good center of medical care. As a result, actuaries, statisticians, physicians, and economists have developed models to predict ranges of expected medical expenses for people with different socioeconomic and demographic characteristics.[20] (However, the models intended to predict a particular person's likely medical expenses in the next year are not yet very accurate.)[21]

The Impact of the Relationship Between Characteristics and Costs on Pooling

Regardless of the current ability of the models to predict expenditures, the knowledge that medical care use is not independent of personal characteristics alters the economic incentives for people to join insurance groups to pool their risks. The pooling advantage breaks down if some people can be identified as having higher risks than others. Low-risk people perceive that they can pay lower premiums if they can be pooled

Table 3.1   Health Expenses by Various Demographic Characteristics, 2002

	Total Expenses (Millions)	Average Per-Person Expenses	Percentage with Expenses
Age			
Younger than 6	$ 28,204	$1,364	88.8
6 to 17	50,786	1,228	83.6
18 to 44	195,017	2,233	78.5
45 to 64	264,451	4,321	90.0
65 and older	272,266	7,797	96.3
Sex			
Male	$351,351	$3,116	80.1
Female	459,373	3,461	90.1
Race-ethnicity			
Hispanic	$ 62,330	$2,223	70.7
Black	84,635	3,124	77.7
Asian	16,836	1,906	77.0
Other race	646,923	3,564	89.8

Source: Agency for Healthcare Research and Quality, 2002 Medical Expenditure Panel Survey-Household Component.
Note: Average per-person expenses are only for those with an expense.

only with other low-risk people. Higher-risk people, of course, also prefer to pool their risks with low-risk people.

For people who have employer-sponsored group health insurance, being high-risk or low-risk is immaterial if the employer offers only one choice of coverage. Everyone is pooled in the same group. There may be grumbling among the young and healthy workers that they are subsidizing the older or sick workers. But if the employees expect to remain with the firm and be members of the insurance pool during years of expected high and low expenditures, the insurance takes on the aspect of a life-long contract rather than a year-to-year decision made on the basis of the premium. The annual premiums can be expected to grow only at the rate that medical care costs grow if the firm has a steady flow of new, young employees replacing retirees. In this case, the average risk level of the employer-sponsored pool remains constant. But if the employer does sponsor more than one choice of insurance policies, and it is possible to create a policy that attracts only low-risk employees, then premiums for the different plans will reflect the relative risk levels of the different pools of people in each plan. High-risk employees will have to pay more for their coverage simply because there are few, if any, low-risk employees in their plans.[22]

The Impact of Workers' Characteristics on Employer Costs

Because medical care use is related to people's characteristics, the health insurance costs of every company are affected by the characteristics of the people in its workforce (and of their dependents). As a result, firms that are the same size in the same industry in the same locale can face different premiums. A firm with an older workforce will have a higher total premium than a firm with a higher proportion of young workers. Or a small firm that has one worker with a very expensive medical condition can face a much higher premium than its competitors.

These differences in health insurance premiums directly affect competition within an industry. When an industry is characterized by intense competition among firms, the firms cannot individually determine the price at which their product or service is sold. The market determines the price. Their profit level depends on the difference between the price and their own per-unit production costs. In highly competitive industries, there is little forgiveness for differences in costs that lower profits. So if a company finds that its labor costs are higher than its competitors' costs because the health insurance premiums are higher, it will try to reduce the costs.

The Effects of Employers' High Premium Costs on Potential Employees

Thus, there are strong incentives for companies to try to identify which of the people applying for a job opening are high-risk. When employers discriminate against such people, it is especially difficult for them to obtain health insurance if they do not already have it. They may face difficulties not only when they apply to companies that offer a health plan but also when they try to buy individual coverage. These difficulties need to be acknowledged when discussing why some people do not have health insurance. In addition, we should be more aware that our ability to predict accurately which people are going to have low or high medical expenses is problematic. Characteristics that are hard to observe or measure play a role in why some people become ill or seek medical care when others do not. Further, people generally do not continue to have very high medical expenses after one year of high expenses. There is evidence from observing the same people over many years that health care expenditures follow a pattern of regression to the mean.[23] People with very high expenses in one year may incur above-average expenses associated with a diagnosed chronic condition the next year, but generally their expenses do not become very high in successive years. Nonetheless, these people frequently have difficulties obtaining employment with health insurance, especially in industries characterized by small employers.

EMPLOYER-BASED HEALTH INSURANCE NEEDS HELP

Intense competition throughout the economy is forcing employers to look for ways to reduce their labor costs. In some cases, the economic pressure comes from lower labor costs overseas. In other cases the pressure is from investors and Wall Street analysts who focus on labor costs, especially the costs of pensions and health insurance, as a measure of a company's competitiveness.[24] As a result, some creative ideas about restructuring the workforce have emerged. As discussed in chapter 2, a newly accepted way of reducing labor costs is to hire workers on a temporary basis or as contractors who work on specific projects. Another is to outsource noncore parts of the business (such as payroll). This removes the employee relationship, thereby eliminating the workers' compensation liability and any need for funding benefits packages. The business service firms, which specialize in a variety of specific services, including executive-level professional services, provide the services at lower cost—in part because they focus on one or two particular services and do not have to maintain balance across a large number of classes of workers. They pay lower wages and often do not offer fringe benefits.

Outsourcing has become the norm for many business services. Companies with familiar household names offer such services either directly or through franchise arrangements with smaller companies. Pinkerton provides security services; Marriott and ASA provide cafeteria or dining room services; Pitney Bowes is among a number of companies that supply mail room staff and services. Employment in professional and business services grew 48 percent between 1990 and 2003.[25] (Only education and health services employment grew more.) After all, why would a company choose to deal with the vagaries of hiring kitchen staff (and the proverbial temperamental chefs) for a company cafeteria or employ full-time human resources recruiters with the expertise to screen and hire security people? Smaller firms, especially in technology-related businesses, have also contracted with personnel services companies to take over their entire human resources operations and serve as the employer of record. Such personnel services companies (contract houses) then lease back the employees to the original companies, in the same way as business service companies lease equipment to companies. Although many of the personnel services companies offer group health insurance to their employees, they usually require continuous employment for a substantial period of time. The worker leaseback arrangements allow a company to hire workers at lower wages and create a different class of worker within its workforce. These arrangements also reduce a company's obligations for pension and health insurance benefits, making the financial bottom line more attractive to investors.

Employment-based health insurance has declined even further since the economic recession of the early 2000s, which intensified companies' efforts to reduce labor costs. Increasingly, employers are creating an inner core of jobs for which health insurance and other fringe benefits are common and an outer ring of jobs that are outsourced or filled by temporary workers. It is apparent that we are in a new era—we cannot continue to count on large companies and an expanding economy to provide employment-based health insurance to a larger proportion of the population. As health care treatment options expand and premiums in the small-group and individual markets continue to rise faster than those in the large-group market, the availability of an adequate health insurance benefit has become a critical factor in the career decisions made by workers and their families.

The shift to smaller companies and the greater use of individuals in the contingent workforce require that public and private policymakers pay greater attention to the small-group and individual health insurance markets as sources of coverage. We need to understand how insurers compete with each other in these markets to avoid adverse selection. The forms of competition make it much more difficult for some people, especially those who are older or have a history of medical problems, to acquire health insurance. Moreover, the mechanisms to avoid adverse selection drive up the costs of insurance so that it is unaffordable for middle-class working families. How insurers compete with each other in the small-group and individual markets is the focus of the next chapter.

Chapter 4

How Health Insurance Markets Work

Health insurance is different from most of the goods and services we buy each week. The price of a half-gallon of milk or a sweater does not depend on who buys it. But the costs of producing and purchasing health insurance depend in large part on who buys it and who belongs to a group that buys it.

A major factor in determining premiums is the amount of medical expenses a person or group is expected to have. As described in chapter 3, premiums equal the expected spending of a person or group plus a loading fee. Expected medical expenses depend on the age of a person (or the ages of people in a group) and the health status of the person (or the people in the group). Increasing age and the presence of prior medical problems are especially associated with greater spending on health care. So a group with a large share of people over the age of fifty will have higher expected expenses per person than a group that consists almost entirely of people under forty. As also described in chapter 3, the larger the group to which a person belongs when purchasing insurance, the smaller the loading fee portion of the premium. Thus, the price one pays for health insurance is lower if it can be purchased through a group that is predominantly young, healthy, and large.

The pricing of insurance clearly involves uncertainty, since neither insurers nor their potential customers know how much medical care a particular person will need in the coming year. But insurers can make predictions based on past experience with people who have the same observable characteristics or for a given person based on his or her past spending. What complicates the pricing of health insurance, however, is that the insurers and the people wanting insurance do not have access to the same information that is useful in predicting expenses. Consumers often know quite a lot about their family medical history or their own predisposition to seek medical attention, facts that insurers cannot know or discover without effort.

This asymmetry in the information available to consumers and insurers would not be a problem if everyone were required to purchase health insurance and, moreover, if everyone had the same insurance policy. But because health insurance is a voluntary purchase, people who do not think they will become sick are far less likely to buy coverage and protect themselves from the low-probability risks they face. Conversely, people who have higher expectations of needing medical care are more likely to want to buy insurance. Because of these two factors—the voluntary nature of insurance and the asymmetry of information—insurers believe that a larger fraction of people wishing to buy individual and small-group health insurance are going to have high expenses than would be observed in the general population. This is known as adverse selection. An insurer that cannot block it will underestimate expenses, charge premiums that are too low—and lose money.

Insurers' fear of incurring adverse selection is the elephant in the room when it comes to understanding why people without employer-based health insurance find it very difficult to obtain health insurance in the individual market. It also is one of the reasons many small companies face high premiums if they try to obtain group coverage for their employees. Ultimately, the issue of adverse selection must be addressed if we are to continue to rely on private insurers for all but the poorest and the oldest. In this chapter, we focus on how health insurance is sold in the United States, how insurers compete with each other, and how that competition leaves many people unable to buy health insurance. We begin by looking more closely at the people insurers most want to avoid.

VERY HIGH-COST PEOPLE: ARE THEIR COSTS PREDICTABLE?

To understand why insuring a disproportionate number of high-cost people causes heartburn in insurance executives, look at the distribution of annual total U.S. health care spending across all Americans. Figure 4.1 shows the distribution for the entire U.S. population, but it could just as easily be for any large segment of our population. It is immediately obvious that health care spending is very concentrated—only 10 percent of us are responsible for 70 percent of all expenses in a year.[1] The 50 percent of the population with the highest medical expenses account for 97 percent of all health spending. The sum total of medical expenses for the other half is only 3 percent of all U.S. medical spending.

The distribution of American health care spending shown in figure 4.1 has remained remarkably stable over the past eighty years, and has been repeatedly shown to hold in a variety of different groups of people.[2] The 1996 and 1997 Medical Expenditure Panel Surveys (MEPS) have been used by Alan Monheit to estimate the threshold levels of spending that mark the top 50 percent, 30 percent, 20 percent, 10 percent, 5 per-

Figure 4.1   Distribution of Health Care Expenditures, 1996

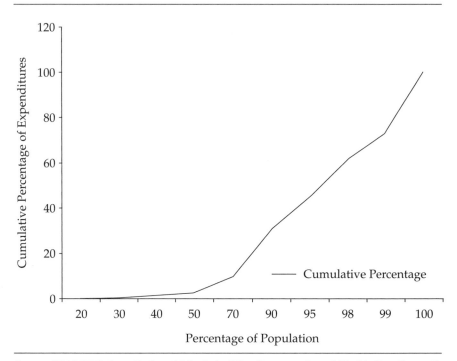

Source: 1996 MEPS, from Berk and Monheit, "The Concentration of Health Care Expenditures, Revisited."

cent, 2 percent, and 1 percent of the population.[3] However, since 1996 to 1997, we have experienced price inflation and changes in the way medical care is practiced. We can adjust for the price inflation, but it is difficult to know how the changes in the practice of medicine have affected the overall distribution of health care spending. New and expensive pharmaceuticals and diagnostic imaging techniques have become more widely used since the late 1990s, for example, and we know that since 1997, health care spending in total has increased 41 percent after adjusting for general price inflation.[4] In what follows, I have adjusted Monheit's estimates of the thresholds for the top percentiles of the expenditure distribution by first accounting for price inflation. Then I have benchmarked those numbers to 2004 data on the distribution of health care spending in the individual and small group markets of one state. My estimate, then, is that $50,000 is the threshold for the top 1 percent of health care spending in 2005. I will use that number throughout the book. Similarly, $30,000 is my estimate of the threshold for the top 2 percent of the expenditure distribution.

People in the bottom half of the expenditure distribution spend very little on health care; many have zero expenses. As noted in chapter 1, people in the bottom half had total spending that was no more than just over $500 in 2005. Even the people whose medical spending puts them between the seventieth and ninetieth percentiles in spending do not have radically high expenses. Annual health expenditures among such people who were younger than sixty-five were between $2,000 and $10,000 in 2005. Many of the people in the bottom half (and some of those in the fiftieth to eightieth percentiles) no doubt think of themselves as healthy. Insurers worry that some unknown fraction of these people will not want to purchase health insurance, while people who have reason to believe that they are in the top half of the distribution, and especially the top tenth, will all want coverage. For insurers, the heartburn comes from concern that the insured will include a disproportionate number of people with medical spending in the top tenth of the distribution. If this happens, their losses might well force them out of business.

People with annual expenditures greater than $10,000 in 2005 would be in the top tenth of the expenditure distribution. Anyone who has some form of cardiac surgery, an organ or bone marrow transplant, spinal surgery, or surgery for cancer is going to have medical expenses that place them in the top tenth of the population's expenses. According to Alan Monheit's analyses of the 1996 and 1997 expenditure distributions, 62 percent of the people in the top 10 percent in 1996 were not in the top 10 percent in 1997.[5] Nonetheless, insurers remain very concerned that someone who has had high costs in one year will remain a high-cost person in subsequent years. In particular, it is the people in the very top 1 percent—those with annual medical expenses greater than $50,000— who cause insurers the most anxiety.[6]

People who make it into the top 1 percent are very sick in that one year. Some have chronic conditions that flare up, requiring extremely high acute-care costs. Once the acute problem is dealt with, the medical costs often return to manageable levels that are more typical of some high-cost chronic conditions—above $6,000 per year. Other people in the top 1 percent never have a hospital inpatient stay but need extraordinarily high-priced medications to stay alive. People in this group may well persist in the top 1 percent for several years until either the medications drop in price or an alternative (surgery or another medication) is developed—or they die. Still others may experience acute, life-threatening episodes, such as strokes or some forms of cancer. In subsequent years, many of these people may have medical expenses that place them in the top 20 percent of the population (costs above $4,000) but not the top 10 percent.

Insurers know from experience that people with some chronic conditions have high probabilities of landing in the top 1 percent group. But they cannot predict who among those with these chronic conditions will in fact reach that level in any given year. People in the other two categories—suffering from a rare disease or undergoing an acute, life-threatening episode—are virtually impossible to identify in advance.

Examples of Extremely High-Cost Cases

Five examples of the types of medical problems that cause people to be in the top 1 percent of the distribution for health care spending illustrate why it is difficult to characterize such people:

- *People who need costly pharmaceutical treatments*: Hemophiliacs who cannot take the usual blood-clotting factor product may be prescribed a new one that currently costs more than $100,000 a month. Similarly, the drug of choice for treating Gaucher's disease (a relatively rare metabolic liver disease) costs more than $150,000 a year. Multiple sclerosis, a disease that is more prevalent in the population, also is treated with very expensive prescription drugs. These drugs help patients avoid even more costly hospital stays. People who need these new high-cost drugs to stay alive are likely to remain in the top 1 percent of the expenditure distribution until the production costs of the new drug or a substitute fall markedly—which could take years.

- *Premature babies*: Babies who are born at very low birthweights easily can spend three months in a neonatal intensive care unit (NICU). Premature babies' time in NICUs can cost anywhere from $300,000 to more than $1 million. (And since many premature babies are twins or triplets, the costs for a health plan multiply accordingly.) Some premature babies go home after their NICU stay and thrive; they are not very high-cost in subsequent years. But many leave the hospital with developmental disabilities or chronic illnesses that keep them in the top 10 percent for five years or longer.

- *Victims of spinal cord injuries*: Treatment for spinal cord injuries is usually exceptionally high in the months following the accident. After the initial year, the costs of care are lower, but they often remain at a level that is in the top 10 percent of the expenditure distribution.

- *People with intermittently very high costs or medical costs that will tend to go up over time:* People with poorly controlled diabetes, coronary heart failure, or coronary artery disease often experience acute episodes of very expensive medical care. For example, diabetics can experience kidney failure or need amputations of toes (or limbs) because of their poor circulatory system. The cost of other rare, chronic diseases, such as cystic fibrosis or ALS (amyotrophic lateral sclerosis, or Lou Gehrig's disease), increase toward the end of the victim's life, and these costs can become extremely high. In such cases, it can be hard to manage the care and costs because trying to predict when the crises that lead to these extremely high costs will occur is very difficult.

- *Very intense, acute problems*: Examples of intense acute problems are cardiac events, organ transplants, strokes, and some types of cancer. The initial costs of the intense, acute episode can be extremely high, and then the costs may persist at levels that put them in the top 20 percent of the expenditure distribution for years. For example, treatments for certain types of cancer often last six to twelve months and can easily cost more than $50,000. But if the treatment sends the cancer into remission, the patient's pattern of medical care use is usually normal in subsequent years, with additional testing only to determine whether the cancer is still in remission. These costs may put such patients in the top 20 percent of the distribution but nowhere near the top 1 percent.

These examples show why it is difficult to predict, based on diagnosis or age, who will have medical expenses in the top 1 percent of the distribution. In addition, people's responses to treatments and therapies differ. Finer gradations of diagnoses may enhance the ability to predict who might be in the extremely high-cost percentiles, but we are not there yet. Nonetheless, insurers try very hard to avoid insuring anyone who might need extraordinary levels of medical care. They do this by trying to avoid insuring (and sometimes refusing to insure) anyone who might have expenses in the top 20 percent of the expenditure distribution.

THREE DISTINCT MARKETS FOR
HEALTH INSURANCE

Health insurance is sold in the United States in three distinct markets. They are loosely consistent with the fact that insurers' risk of misestimating predicted average costs declines markedly as the size of a group increases. Thus, we have the *large-group* market, generally for any group with one hundred people or more; the *small-group* market, usually for groups of less than one hundred people or fewer than fifty employees; and the *individual* market (also known as the nongroup or direct-pay market in some states), which is for individuals purchasing coverage as individuals (or for their families) and without a group.[7]

The evolution of the three different markets reflects the history of how nonprofit and commercial firms got into the business of selling health insurance. Large commercial insurers have generally favored selling insurance through large companies. Other, typically smaller commercial insurers formed and entered the market when they realized they could create a profitable niche for themselves by selling to small companies. The nonprofit insurers—principally the Blue Cross and Blue Shield Plans and many of the original health maintenance organizations and managed care plans—started by selling policies to individuals in a community as well as to specific employee groups, such as teachers. Because the Blues set premiums on the basis of community rating (everyone who purchases the same policy pays the same premium regardless of age, health status, or other characteristics), commercial insurers realized they could attract younger and healthy people if they used experience rating to set premiums. Experience-rated premiums are determined by the recent spending experiences of only the people within the group. (When setting the initial premium for a new group, it is determined by the recent experience of groups of people with very similar characteristics.) For employers, experience rating avoids pooling their own employees' spending patterns and risks of unexpected spending with those of employers that have less healthy employees. The development of experience-rated health insurance policies by commercial insurers after World War II was a primary reason three insurance markets developed rather than one.

The partitioning of the markets has permitted insurers to specialize in ways of avoiding adverse selection, given that health insurance purchases have always been voluntary. When large commercial insurers first began to sell policies through large companies, they convinced most of the firms to provide it as a benefit removed from collective bargaining.[8] Moreover, because of concerns about adverse selection, insurers often required that at least 75 percent of a firm's employees be enrolled in the health insurance plan or the insurer would withdraw the plan. Under these circumstances, large companies simply included all employees in the health plan—removing the issue of health benefits from collective bargaining and the threat of adverse selection simultaneously. By contrast, the threat of adverse selection is much greater in the small-group and individual markets, where small numbers and information asymmetry increase insurers' risk.

States Regulate Health Insurance Markets

The fact that the three separate markets relate to insurers' ratings of risk by group size is not a coincidence. The insurers and their large corporate customers lobbied state legislators and regulators to develop the three market divisions. The commercial insurers' large customers understood that they could gain lower premiums if the regulations governing insurance sold to large groups were different from those for insurance sold to small groups or individuals. They lobbied state rather than federal policymakers because states regulate the insurance business. The Tenth Amendment to the U.S. Constitution is the basis for the power of state governments—not the federal government—to regulate the sale of insurance within their borders.[9] The McCarran-Ferguson Act of 1945 affirmed that "the business of insurance, and every person engaged therein, are subject to the laws of the states which relate to the regulation or taxation of such business."[10]

Since the history of business regulation and the development of health insurance differ from state to state, the distinctions between the three markets are not consistent across states. Thus, although we talk about three different markets for health insurance, we really have three such markets in every one of the fifty states (plus the District of Columbia). Some of the differences between states' regulations of their individual and small-group markets are trivial, while others are sizable. For instance, Texas and Illinois allow insurers great leeway in setting premiums in the individual market. New York, New Jersey, and Massachusetts require community rating of premiums (everyone pays the same premium for the same policy regardless of age or gender). In some states, the small-group market is open to self-employed individuals, while in other states self-employed individuals can obtain insurance only through the individual market. Such a distinction may seem small until one considers that self-employed people are probably healthy. They certainly cannot afford to take much time off to pursue every ache and pain, and typically they use fewer health care services than the rest of the population. If a state requires insurers to community-rate premiums in the individual market, the self-employed face higher premiums in that market than in the small-group market. Self-employed people can obtain group rates by joining business organizations such as the local chamber of commerce or associations of people in the same profession. States also differ markedly in mandated benefits—the medical services that must be covered. Florida and California have about thirty such mandates, while Delaware and Idaho have only a few. Mammography screenings and treatment for alcoholism are very common mandated benefits, while mental health care is mandated in only thirty-two states, and coverage for disabled dependents is mandated in only thirty-four.[11]

The differences in state regulations and mandated benefits affect insurers' decisions about where they will sell insurance in the small-group and individual markets. When an insurer has made the investment in becoming knowledgeable about one state's regulations and several other states have the same regulations, there are no additional learning costs for selling in the other states. In contrast, if a state has regulations that are quite specific to its individual or small-group market, insurers may be reluctant to enter those markets. Some states have active insurance departments or legislatures that often change the regulations. Under these circumstances, unless a state has a population that is so large that it cannot be ignored, insurers may choose to stay out of the state and conduct business in states that are friendlier to their interests.

Some states also require insurers to sell policies in the individual market if they want to be in the large-group or small-group market. However, when these states also regulate their individual markets so that an insurer cannot refuse to insure an applicant or premiums for individual policies must be community-rated, some insurers will not sell any health plans at all in the state. Many insurers do not have sufficient assets to take on the larger risks involved in the individual market. Thus, in 1997 almost 700 insurers sold individual policies in the United States; by comparison, 2,450 insurers sold policies in the large- and small-group markets.[12] In spite of this difference, only a small number of insurers sell at least half of the total number of policies sold in each of the three types of market in each state.[13]

In addition, the federal Employee Retirement Income Security Act of 1974 (ERISA) reaffirmed the right of states to regulate health insurance, but it also opened the door to the widespread use of self-funded insurance by companies.[14] Employers that self-insure do not purchase health insurance policies from insurance companies but instead pay for a share of the medical care costs of their employees and dependents. The employers bear the financial risk that the medical care costs may exceed the amount they anticipate. Since that risk declines as the number of people in a group increases, companies with fewer than two hundred employees rarely self-insure. Employers that self-insure pay a fee to a third-party administrator, often an insurance company, to process the claims and handle the disbursement of funds to medical providers. In many cases, self-insured firms contract with a third-party administrator to gain access to the insurance company's network of physicians and other medical providers and the reimbursement rates negotiated by the insurer.[15] ERISA encouraged the growth in self-insured companies because a short section of the act stipulates that employers that self-insure are exempt from state mandates on services to be included in health insurance policies and also exempt from any state taxes on premiums for health insurance policies. With the recession of the early 1980s, many companies were desperately looking for ways to reduce their benefit costs. ERISA provided incentives to self-insure, and companies, especially large companies with more than one thousand employees, responded.[16] Today it is more common than not for companies with more than five hundred employees to self-insure.

Moreover, almost all firms that self-insure also purchase reinsurance to protect themselves from unexpectedly high spending by their employees. We focus on reinsurance in chapter 6.

Market Specialization by Insurers

In part but not solely because of the differences in states' regulations, insurers differ in their degree of market specialization. A few national insurers sell products in all markets. But many national insurers operate almost exclusively in the large-group markets. Other insurers have developed niches within the small-group markets, specializing, for example, in particular industries, particular sizes of firms (such as the so-called baby groups of fewer than five), or the self-employed. As noted earlier, self-employed people who belong to a local chamber of commerce are able to obtain small-group insurance, and among the companies that offer policies to chambers of commerce, a small number even have "Chambers" in their name.

Few insurers specialize in the individual markets. However, because insurers usually sell other types of insurance or financial services to individuals, many also sell individual health insurance policies. In addition, some states require or pressure insurers to sell policies in their individual markets. Some states require insurers that are health maintenance organizations (HMOs) or managed care organizations to offer standardized insurance products in the individual market. Some states have what is known as an "insurer of last resort" that must provide insurance to any individual who applies for coverage during an open enrollment period. The insurer often has to sell such coverage at a community-rated premium. In exchange for providing last-resort insurance for the state's residents, the insurer is granted lower tax rates. At one time, most of the states in the Northeast and Midwest, as well as California and several states in the West, had nonprofit Blue Cross and Blue Shield Plans that were designated as the insurer of last resort. However, since the early 1990s many of these plans have become for-profit companies and have sought release from their "insurer of last resort" status.

The behavior of insurers in any one of the three markets is often linked to strategies that permit them to accomplish a larger objective, such as expanding their share of the total health insurance market and increasing profits through economies of scale. Insurers that specialize in the small-group market, for example, rely heavily on agents and brokers to sell their coverage.[17] Even though many insurers would prefer not to be in the individual market at all, some are willing to incur small losses on individual policies if those policies enable their agents and brokers to sell more small-group policies. For example, a small-business owner may wish to purchase a group policy for his employees and a better individual policy for his own family. In effect, the individual policy is the loss leader for the more profitable business in the small-group market. An insurer also might sell individual policies only under limited conditions (such as when they are packaged with other types of insurance or with a group policy) to protect itself from larger losses.

Bundling with Other Insurance and Financial Products

The three segments of the health insurance market also are often connected to markets for other, non–health insurance products. The larger insurance companies frequently prefer to sell bundled insurance offerings that include life, long-term care, and perhaps insurance specific to the firm, such as fire or catastrophe. Bundling insurance offerings like this reduces insurers' risks. It lowers the potential for adverse selection because it avoids the situation where the only people who purchase a particular type of insurance are those who know they will have related expenses.[18] Also, the risks involved in each of the component insurance types are not highly correlated, so the company actually has less exposure to risk if consumers buy the bundle of insurance products.[19] As a result, it has become customary for insurers to bundle the insurance products that employers like to offer as fringe benefits to their employees.

Large companies that self-insure the health care expenses of their employees also often want to offer life insurance or other forms of insurance. Insurers that sell their services as third-party administrators to self-insuring companies frequently sell non–health insurance products to the companies' workers. Insurers that specialize in the small-group markets also offer other insurance products with one price for a bundled package. Bundling the health insurance with other insurance offerings is particularly attractive to the insurer because it reduces the threat of adverse selection. Managed care plans are at a disadvantage in this type of bundling of products since almost all of them are only in the business of providing health coverage.

States' regulation of the markets, insurer specialization in different markets, and bundling of insurance products are three important aspects of today's health insurance market. Market specialization and the bundling of insurance products help insurers avoid adverse selection. At the same time, they also make it more difficult for individuals and employees of small firms to gain access to health insurance. We turn next to the information problems that consumers and insurers have in negotiating these markets.

CONSUMER INFORMATION PROBLEMS IN
HEALTH INSURANCE MARKETS

Consumers' information problems compound those of insurers. When it is difficult to learn about health insurance options, healthy people, who are least worried about being covered, will not pursue options and buy coverage.[20] By comparison, those with family medical problems or those with a predisposition to seek medical care will be more persistent in trying to find coverage. Consumers' information difficulties contribute to the adverse selection environment of today's health insurance market.

The Role of Agents and Brokers

Agents and brokers are matchmakers between consumers and insurers.[21] Generally, the distinction between agents and brokers is that agents sell products offered by just one insurer while brokers sell products for a number of competing insurers. It would seem that an agent would have strong incentives to act in the interest of the insurer for which it is selling products, while a broker would have a greater desire to act in the interests of the consumer. However, the distinction between agents and brokers is not always clear, nor is it transparent whose interests they represent. Many states have one licensing exam for both roles.

As matchmakers, agents and brokers provide information about alternative insurance products and help consumers compare the value and appropriateness of these alternatives. They also assemble packages of insurance products (including life, homeowner's, and auto) for their clients. Most individual purchasers and small firms that sponsor health insurance use agents and brokers, and they usually buy more than one type of insurance product. The decision to purchase health policies is facilitated by a history of trust between the consumer and the agent—trust that the agent is providing good information and looking out for the consumer's interest. At the same time, agents and brokers must maintain relationships with the insurers from whom they earn commissions. (Commissions generally equal a percentage of the premium and continue in subsequent years when policies are renewed.) Since more work is involved in closing the initial sale than in renewing a policy, agents and brokers want to arrange policies that are easily renewed after the initial year. It is in their interest to know which insurers are more likely to accept applications from clients with particular needs or health histories and to steer business accordingly.

The most common way individuals obtain individual coverage is through an insurance agent. Most people with homeowner's insurance, life insurance, or auto insurance purchase such coverage through an agent, and if they need health insurance, they turn to the same agent for assistance. Agents and brokers are a frequent source of help for people who are self-employed and for contract workers and consultants—in part because they have ongoing relationships. It is fairly typical for people who switch to working as a contingent contractor or consultant to maintain the former employer's group health insurance for eighteen months under COBRA (a practice often referred to as "cobra-ing") and then turn to an insurance agent or broker for help in finding a suitable policy. Unfortunately, many people who might be the most confused by all the information they would have to sift through to obtain health insurance are often the least likely to have relationships with agents. They may not drive or own a home, or they may be immigrants from countries where private health insurance is not available. If agents and brokers perceive some customers as not worth the time it takes to educate them and sell them policies, they may shy away.

Expanding Other Sources of Information
for Consumers

Many states have tried to increase access to health insurance in the individual and small-group markets by making it easier to learn about choices in these markets. State efforts to expand available information have largely focused on websites, public service announcements, and 800 phone numbers. Consumer advocacy groups also provide comparative information. Such efforts may be interpreted as bypassing agents and brokers, and perhaps as attempts to reduce the commissions paid to them. But in general such efforts are meant to help consumers compare policies and ask the right questions of insurers and their agents.

The problems that consumers have with gathering and understanding information about their insurance choices can be considerable. A large proportion of young adults are in this group, and as noted earlier, if healthy people are already less inclined to buy health insurance, information problems make adverse selection a more likely outcome.

INFORMATION PROBLEMS FOR INSURERS:
THE IMPORTANCE OF ADVERSE SELECTION

Insurers have a significant information problem as well. They cannot perfectly identify the subset of people, among all their applicants, who will have high medical expenditures in the next year. This problem is compounded in a voluntary system of health insurance purchases, because people who expect to incur high medical costs are more likely to buy insurance than people who expect to have low medical costs. As a practical matter, adverse selection has not been an issue in large-group markets, since almost everyone in a large employer group enrolls in the insurance plan.[22] As a result, the proportion of enrollees who are low-cost will be consistently large enough to generate sufficient premium revenues to cover the expected expenses of the entire group. But for the small-group and individual markets, fear of adverse selection drives insurer behavior.

Adverse selection is a very real problem—it can result in the loss of so much money that an insurer has to declare bankruptcy. The downward spiral begins when an insurer's expenditures outpace its projections and close examination of claims reveals that the insurer has a disproportionate number of high-cost enrollees. It then raises its rates for the following year in order to generate enough revenues to cover anticipated higher expenses (and perhaps some of the previous year's shortfall). When people who believe they are at low risk for incurring high medical expenses subsequently view the higher premium as beyond their expected costs and drop their coverage in the second time period, the insurer's remaining pool of enrollees then includes a larger share of high-risk people—and the insurer again will have higher-than-projected expenses. The insurer will lose money and be compelled to raise premiums again. This sequence is often referred to as a "death spiral," since it can eventually drive an insurer out of business.

In most businesses the drive to maximize profits involves price competition and efforts to minimize costs of production. Competition in insurance markets is characterized by efforts to reduce adverse selection and the risk of covering people with very high costs.[23] This leads to competition both in strategies to avoid risk altogether and in the design of models for predicting expected costs so that revenue from premiums will be sufficient.

Competition in the Use of Medical Underwriting

Medical underwriting is the process by which insurers set the premium for an applicant based on that person's expected medical care costs.[24] In states that permit premiums for groups and individuals to be set according to calculations of expected medical expenses, insurers compete largely in terms of the accuracy of their underwriting models. These models are based on actuarial tables of probabilities of the use of different amounts of medical care by many different demographic and socioeconomic characteristics. Insurers set a "standard" premium for a policy based on the results predicted by their actuarial models. The underwriting models are used to determine how much a policy's standard premium should be increased (rated up) for particular individuals or firms. If a firm is predicted to have a high probability of large medical expenses in the next year because several people had high expenses in the previous year—for example, in a small firm, two employees were treated for cancer—the insurer may agree to renew the policy only if the firm pays a higher premium. The additional premium amount underwrites the basic premium for the policy. In some states, underwriting of premiums is not permitted because it is viewed as a selection mechanism that discriminates against people who are perceived to have high risks of expensive medical care. When underwriting is not permitted or its use is restricted, insurers turn to other selection mechanisms to avoid insuring high-risk people.

Competition with Selection Mechanisms

Adverse selection fears in the small-group and individual markets have led insurers to use selection mechanisms to screen out high-risk applicants.[25] These include refusing to issue a policy, creating market niches, redlining certain industries and occupations, excluding coverage of services for preexisting medical conditions, and differentiating their policies from their competitors' by generously covering some types of services (such as preventative screening for types of cancers or cardiovascular disease) while limiting other services (such as substance abuse treatment).[26] Thus, competition in the small-group and individual markets focuses on how well insurers use mechanisms to identify which firms or individuals might be high-risk versus low-risk. As Joseph Newhouse points out in the context of risk adjustment models, an insurer needs to be only a little better than its competitors in the use of selection mechanisms to make a larger profit.[27]

Refusing to Issue a Policy Some states permit insurers to deny coverage to applicants without providing a reason. Karen Pollitz and her colleagues found in their study of seven hypothetical consumers making a total of 420 applications for coverage that they were rejected 37 percent of the time.[28] Where insurers cannot deny applications, they often are allowed to set premiums without significant constraints. Although it might seem fair to charge high premiums to insure people who are very likely to incur high medical expenses, it would be unfair if the models used to predict a person's risk of high expenses were not accurate. In fact, these models are not accurate. But they continue to be used, and very high premiums constitute an important barrier to coverage for people who are identified as high-risk.[29] This is especially true in states where insurers cannot refuse to issue policies but are allowed to underwrite premiums. Pollitz and her colleagues found that, among the 63 percent of applications that were accepted, insurers placed benefit restrictions, premium surcharges, or both on more than half.

Market Niches and Redlining   Insurers have developed monopolistic market niches in the small-group and individual markets as another mechanism for avoiding adverse selection.[30] In the individual markets, for example, some insurers specialize in marketing to individuals who have left the armed services, while others offer policies that are attractive to very small firms of professionals (for example, lawyers or financial advisers) or to individuals who are self-employed. It is also fairly common practice to avoid insuring people in certain occupations or firms in specific industries—a practice referred to as redlining. For example, hairdressers and florists have difficulty obtaining health insurance because it is thought that a disproportionate share of them are at risk for HIV/AIDS. Similarly, taxi drivers have a difficult time obtaining coverage because actuarial data indicate that they frequently suffer from back troubles. Nonprofit small firms can have problems finding insurance because they are thought to employ disproportionate numbers of people who have had physical or mental conditions. The result of this type of market niche specialization and avoidance of specific occupations or industries is that few insurers actively compete for business among all consumers seeking individual policies. People who are perceived as high-risk have few, if any, options open to them.[31]

Exclusion of Coverage for Preexisting Conditions   With very few exceptions, states permit insurers to set a period of time during which they may exclude coverage of medical expenses related to preexisting conditions, such as cancer, osteoarthritis, or allergies.[32] Without such preexisting condition exclusions, people would not purchase health insurance before they were diagnosed with a medical problem. Some states detail which conditions may be included in the preexisting condition exclusions, while others leave it to the insurers. Most states limit the exclusion period, typically to twelve months. As a result, insurers often simply deny an application from a person who has had serious conditions, such as angina or a myocardial infarction.[33] They would rather avoid insuring the person altogether than risk facing the high medical expenses connected to a preexisting condition after the waiting period expires. (Pollitz and her colleagues found that insurers responded to applications by hypothetical people with preexisting medical conditions with "substandard" offers or denial of coverage most of the time.)[34] Since diagnostic techniques have become more sophisticated and more people are surviving episodes of cancer or living with chronic conditions, the issue of how insurers regard preexisting conditions has taken on great significance.

Differentiating Policies' Benefits   A frequently used mechanism for subtly encouraging insurance applicants to reveal themselves as high-risk versus low-risk is to offer a variety of policies that differ in covered medical services or required cost-sharing. If an insurer is able to identify a health care benefit that is particularly attractive to low-risk people, it can design benefits packages that cause people to disclose their status without directly asking them. For example, if an applicant knows that colon cancer runs in his or her family—which the insurer does not know—that person might choose a policy that has high upper limits on covered expenses, provides for cancer screening tests, and includes first-rate cancer centers in the list of providers. The insurer will interpret this choice as a reflection of the applicant's expectation of needing expensive medical care.

Insurers also have found that different levels of cost-sharing or choice of physicians can be used to group people with similar levels of expected medical costs. People who view themselves as healthy and unlikely to use much medical care generally choose policies with high deductibles (more than $2,500 per year for an individual and $5,000 per year for a family) because they have lower premiums than policies with much lower deductibles. Or, in the case of managed care plans, low-risk people prefer plans with limited lists of physicians and hospitals in exchange for lower premiums. In contrast, people who have chronic health problems or expect to need treatment from specialists are more likely to select plans with lower deductibles or a greater choice of providers.

Toward this end, insurers have invested a great deal of effort in designing benefits and cost-sharing packages that are intended to attract low-risk people to some packages and high-risk people to others. A simple example of a benefit thought to help attract healthy, active people is subsidization of membership costs for health clubs. A subtle subtext operates here: if a person is not active, he or she may feel out of place belonging to the health plan. So the benefit is both attractive to people expected to be low-risk and less appealing to high-risk people. Health policies that offer low premiums and limited numbers of inpatient hospital days might strike a recent college graduate as reasonable and adequate. Paul, the computer software engineer we met in chapter 2, might find this type of policy quite appealing, but Kristen, the freelance writer we met in chapter 3, might think it inadequate given her age and increasing odds of having serious medical problems. With this health plan, the insurer has thus produced a subtle screening mechanism that permits it to sort people.

The use of different benefit designs to induce people to reveal their level of risk has become quite sophisticated. These efforts also indicate how difficult and expensive it is, however, to create policy designs that perfectly accomplish the objective. It is even more difficult to design policies that accurately separate low- to medium-risk people into finer gradations of risk classes. Newhouse has argued that these difficulties are the reason insurers still pool low- and high-risk people together, even if they would prefer to enroll only low-risk people.[35] In spite of the costs and complexity, insurers appear to be quite actively using variations in benefits packages as a selection mechanism and a way to compete with other insurers.[36]

Efforts to Block Selection Mechanisms

The differences in state regulation of the insurance markets permit the greater or lesser use of the strategies to avoid insuring high-risk people. States that have attempted to block insurers' use of selection mechanisms, particularly in the small-group or individual markets, have only partially succeeded. States almost always block the use of only one or two of these mechanisms. For example, a state might mandate that all policies cover substance abuse treatment, inhibiting insurers' ability to avoid people with substance abuse problems by not including such treatment services among policy benefits. Quite a few states have enacted regulations requiring insurers in the individual market to accept all applicants (a policy known as guaranteed issue) so that an insurer cannot turn down an applicant it views as high-risk.

If a state has only one or two of these regulations in place, however, the insurers can use other mechanisms to accomplish the objective of avoiding enrolling high-risk applicants. A common example is a state requiring guaranteed issue but not regulating how premiums are set. We observe a predictable outcome: high-risk people are indeed offered coverage, but at an extraordinarily high premium. Also, when states require community rating of premiums but do not standardize the benefits to be covered in policies, insurers can use differences in benefits to try to separate high-risk firms from low-risk firms (or people). Because every policy (defined by a set of benefits and specified cost-sharing) has its own community-rated premium, the premium depends on who else enrolls in the policy. This creates strong incentives to use different benefits and cost-sharing requirements to attract low-risk people to new lower-cost policies and high-risk people to higher-premium policies.

The Health Insurance Portability and Accountability Act of 1996 (HIPAA) contains some restrictions on the use of these selection practices in the individual insurance market. HIPAA provides portability of coverage and protection from some selection practices for a limited group of statutorily defined "eligible individuals"—people who had prior group coverage for at least eighteen months, have exhausted COBRA benefits, and lack current access to group coverage or public programs.[37] HIPAA does not, however, prohibit insurers from applying selection practices to the great majority of people who seek coverage in the individual health insurance markets.

Competition Based on Avoiding Adverse Selection

The usual competitive market forces that cause companies to seek profits by reducing their costs are more complicated in the insurance industry. The cost of producing insurance very much depends on health care expenditures for the people covered. To keep the cost of insurance low, insurers need to minimize their outlays for the medical expenses of their enrollees. The best way to do this is to insure as many people as possible who are likely to use very little medical care. The problem for insurers is that they do not have perfect information with which to predict applicants' medical expenses. As a result, the competition among insurers is focused on efforts to obtain the highest proportion possible of people expected to have low medical expenses. To achieve a high proportion of low-risk enrollees, insurers use the selection mechanisms already described. The competition is fierce, but it needs to be understood as driven by the lack of perfect information. The need to avoid adverse selection dominates insurers' actions because they cannot maximize their profits without keeping their costs low.

The competition keeps premiums low for companies and people who are predicted to be unlikely to have high medical expenses, but it severely limits the options for small firms and, particularly, individuals who are perceived to be high-risk. As noted earlier, not many insurers actively compete in the individual markets, and people whom insurers perceive as high-risk have few, if any, options for obtaining health insurance.[38]

HEALTH INSURANCE MARKET FAILURE DUE TO INFORMATION PROBLEMS

Markets with information problems are known among economists as market failures. Consumers or companies make choices that are less beneficial than the choices they would make with more complete information. When markets fail, government intervention or public policies that address the cause of the failure are justified if such actions could improve the functioning of the market.

Haphazard Regulations

States have rarely used their regulatory power over insurance markets to fashion cohesive policies that would relieve fears of adverse selection or even reduce the use of risk selection mechanisms.[39] Most regulations focus on maintaining the financial solvency of the insurers, directing how premiums may be set, and providing access to coverage for people who cannot obtain group insurance.

Almost all states require insurers to have sufficient financial reserves to pay medical claims. This requirement helps reduce the likelihood of insolvency, which would leave enrollees without coverage. The financial reserve requirement is also an effective method of blocking the entry of companies that are not large enough to bear risk.

Many, but by no means all, states have regulations pertaining to how premiums can be set or increased. Insurers are often required to seek permission from a state insurance department to raise premiums. However, they are usually free to offer new policies with slightly different benefits packages, which effectively enables them to separate people on the basis of their underlying risk of needing expensive medical care. An insurer might offer a new policy at an initially lower rate than an existing policy, believing that lower-risk people will switch to the new policy. The loss ratio (the payments for benefits divided by the premiums for the people enrolled in the policy) for the first policy then would rise, and the insurance department would permit the insurer to raise the premium. Being able to offer new policies with different benefits packages in effect end-runs regulatory efforts to restrain the growth in premiums.

Some states also have regulations to ensure that policies are available for people who do not have access to group insurance plans. Until the early 1990s, in many of the Northeast states where Blue Cross and Blue Shield plans were the dominant insurers, the Blues were required to be the insurer of last resort in exchange for preferred tax rates as part of their nonprofit status. These plans had an advertised open enrollment period every year when individuals could apply and could not be turned down. But beginning in the late 1980s, a number of the Blues converted to for-profit status and requested relief from the status of insurer of last resort. As discussed in more detail in the next chapter, thirty-three states also have created high-risk pools for people who have been turned down for coverage because they had high medical expenses in the past and they are expected to continue to have high costs.[40] However, the high-risk pools serve a small number of people compared to the number once served by the insurers of last resort.

Blocking Selection by Standardizing Policies

By the early 1990s, state insurance regulators had become intrigued with Alain Enthoven's argument that it would be more efficient to have managed competition in the private sector.[41] In particular, he argued that if all insurers had to offer standardized benefits packages, consumers would choose an insurer based on the quality of its service relative to its premiums. Enthoven advocated standardized benefits packages in the context of other changes in the management of competition among insurers, and he was not arguing that standardized benefits should be used to assist high-risk people. However, his proposal drew attention to the idea that insurers were using differences in benefit package designs to separate people based on their underlying risk, and this caught policymakers' attention. The result was that a handful of states required that insurers selling policies in the small-group and individual insurance markets offer standardized policies.[42] The assumption was that such a policy would block insurers' ability to restrict access to coverage by high-risk people. Standardizing policies would also force insurers to pool low- and high-risk people together since there could no longer be benefits differences to separate them. Policymakers also justified the standardization of policies as a way to help individuals and small employers judge premium differences between insurers—a response to the consumer information problems described earlier.

If state insurance regulators and policymakers saw the standardization of benefits packages as a way to reduce insurers' fear of adverse selection, it received little attention. Yet when benefits packages in health insurance policies are standardized, insurers are not subject to adverse selection based on perceptions that their policies cover more (or certain types of) medical services than other insurers' policies. Instead, the insurers have been returned to a level playing field. Note, however, that the playing field is once again one with asymmetry of information between consumers and insurers. Insurers cannot counter the information asymmetry by using different benefits packages to encourage people to reveal their own estimate of their risk of high medical expenses.

The standardization of benefits packages has usually been implemented along with community rating of premiums. The combination has had an unexpected outcome—high premiums. In states like New Jersey and New York, premiums for individual coverage have become quite expensive. As of the fall of 2005, premiums are above $400 a month for an individual policy and more than $1,200 a month for a family policy.[43] The first impression of analysts is that adverse selection has set in, and the only people still buying individual coverage are those who have high costs of medical care and have sufficient income to pay the premiums.[44] But another interpretation of the events preceding the high premiums is that insurers are using the high premiums to limit their exposure to adverse selection. If the insurers cannot use mechanisms to separate people who are likely to be high users of medical care from those who are not, high premiums will discourage most people from applying for coverage.

It is true that high premiums discourage low-risk people from purchasing coverage, but they largely cover the costs of high-risk people who do purchase coverage. The unanticipated—but nevertheless predictable—outcome of the high premiums is that fewer people obtain health insurance in the individual markets.

Thus, states' regulatory efforts to date have not been directed at insurers' fear of adverse selection and the information asymmetry that is the root cause of market failure in the individual and small-group markets. As a result, competition in these markets consists of creating and refining mechanisms to avoid people who might be high-cost. This has restricted access to insurance for people who are perceived to be high-risk. In states where regulations prevent insurers from using some of their more effective risk selection mechanisms, high premiums are now the norm. The high premiums also have the effect of reducing access to health insurance—both for low-risk, low-income people and for people who might be perceived to be medium- to high-risk for using expensive medical care. To make these markets more accessible to people who are thought to be high-risk, government intervention must address the adverse selection problem.

IMPLICATIONS FOR SMALL COMPANIES AND PEOPLE WITHOUT EMPLOYER-BASED INSURANCE

As already noted, people with access to employer-based coverage, especially those in large employer groups, are lucky—insurers do not worry about adverse selection in the large-group insurance market. But for people without employer-based coverage and small companies that would like to offer their employees a health plan, the story is very different and sobering. Desperate to avoid adverse selection, insurers compete through their use of selection mechanisms. Depending on states' regulations, this competition leads to low premiums for low-risk people. But for people perceived to be high-risk, the competition leads to high premiums, limits on the types of covered services, or outright rejection. Thus, people like Susan Mitchell find themselves being rejected for coverage or quoted premiums of $1,000 a month or more.

With the U.S. economy rapidly shifting to one in which more people are employed in small firms or work as independent contractors or through temporary firms and contract houses, there is an urgent need for increased access to small-group and individual insurance markets. But given the problems that small firms and individuals have in finding information about insurance options and the asymmetry of information between consumers and insurers, insurers in these markets are quite correct to worry about adverse selection. Although regulations to block in-surers' ability to risk-select have not been widely used, those that have been tried have not so far had the intended effect of increasing access to these markets, and in some cases they have led to higher premiums. Subsidies to encourage people to purchase insurance do nothing to alle-viate insurers' concerns about adverse selection; if anything, insurers may well believe that subsidies exacerbate adverse selection by drawing in poorer people with medical problems.

If we want private health insurance to continue to be the basis of our health insurance system, and if we want it to be widely available to small firms and individuals, we need to address insurers' fear of adverse selection. We need to give them incentives to lessen their use of selection mechanisms and reduce their premiums so that low-risk people can pur-chase coverage. Accomplishing this is the focus of the next two chapters.

PART II

Public Policies to Make Private Insurance More Available

The need for government policies to help small firms and individuals obtain health insurance is urgent. But policies focused only on providing subsidies to help people purchase private insurance are inadequate because they fail to address the way insurers respond to adverse selection in the individual and small-group markets. In this part of the book, we shift our focus to examine three approaches that the federal government or state governments could take to reduce insurers' fear of adverse selection.

In chapter 5, we look closely at two of these approaches: formal high-risk pools and an equivalent of high-risk pools that requires insurers to pay fees that are then redistributed to any insurers that experience adverse selection. High-risk pools, which have been in existence since 1976, are now operated in thirty-three states.[1] A variation of high-risk pools is an assessment mechanism that compels insurers to share the costs of high-risk people. Often these assessments, which are managed by a state's insurance department, operate as complements to high-risk pools rather than as substitutes. The concept of assessing insurers to share the burden of high-cost people within a state is well established for a wide variety of other insurance products, most notably auto insurance.

In chapter 6, we examine government-sponsored reinsurance as the third approach to reducing insurers' concern about adverse selection. Reinsurance is insurance for insurers—it provides them with protection against the small risk of enrollees' medical expenses exceeding expectations by more than some stated amount. The idea of government reinsurance for the private health insurance market is not new. It was seriously considered fifty years ago and emerged again as a little-noticed part of a national health insurance reform proposal almost twenty-five years ago.[2]

Reinsurance as we know it today is more sophisticated than it was fifty or even twenty-five years ago. Private market reinsurance is available for a wide variety of insurance products and possible events. Risk can be shared between the buyer and seller of reinsurance in a dazzling array of imaginative and complex ways. Private market reinsurance is available for many types of devastating situations because the government has become the ultimate rescuer when huge losses occur or potential losses threaten to cause economic dislocation. The concept of government rescue is now well established—witness the government's role in the savings and loan crisis of the 1980s and the assistance given since 1978 by the Federal Emergency Management Agency (FEMA) to regions that have suffered destruction from natural disasters. More recently, in November 2002, the federal government assumed responsibility for catastrophic losses due to terrorist attacks. The Terrorism Risk Insurance Act calls for the government to pay 90 percent of the costs of any terrorist attack after losses exceed $10 billion. As a result of this legislation, the markets for liability insurance and catastrophe reinsurance are functioning again and offering terrorism coverage.

The shifts in the economy that are causing so many workers to lose access to employer-group health insurance are laying the seeds for a social disaster unless we can make it easier and cheaper for people to purchase insurance in small groups or as individuals. The largest obstacle to this is insurers' fear of adverse selection. Short of requiring everyone to purchase coverage, government shouldering of responsibility for the highest-cost people would significantly lessen the consequences of adverse selection. The three approaches we examine in the next two chapters differ in their incentives for insurers to continue to use selection mechanisms and in how monies are allocated to insurers. But as a group, they have more potential for making private coverage accessible to workers and their families than proposals to provide tax credits. They reduce insurers' risk from adverse selection while tax credits and other subsidies do not.

Chapter 5

Two Approaches: High-Risk Pools and Assessments to Cover High-Risk People

W e need to devise a policy approach that substantially reduces insurers' risk of extremely high expenditures. The costs of using selection mechanisms will then exceed their advantages for insurers. Moreover, if the expenses of very high-cost people are spread among the total population, low-risk people will not face significantly higher premiums when they are pooled with high-risk people. So long as low-risk people can find low premiums, they will buy health insurance, ensuring that the overall level of expected medical expenses in the risk pool will not rise dramatically with the addition of high-risk people.

Two policy approaches that have gained attention are state high-risk pools and assessment funds that reallocate monies from insurers with low costs to insurers with high costs. Both types of approaches have been used by states for more than twenty-five years. As mentioned earlier, high-risk pools exist in thirty-three states (and a thirty-fourth state, Idaho, has an arrangement for high-risk individuals that is quite similar).[1] However, it is not appropriate to review the states' enrollment experiences with the objective of projecting how expanded versions of such pools would work as a vehicle for enrolling substantial numbers of the uninsured. At least originally, the state high-risk pools were not intended to be a source of health insurance for large numbers of people. Instead, they were designed to be limited programs that guarantee access to health insurance for people who cannot obtain it, primarily because of preexisting conditions or chronic illness. The high-risk pools were supposed to be very small complements to states' individual markets rather than programs offering substitutes for policies sold in the individual market. Nonetheless, most studies of the states' experiences with high-risk pools have judged them from the perspective of their numbers of enrollees and the extent to which their premiums exceed standard individual premiums.[2] We will examine the states' experiences with the risk pools to understand why their designs may prevent them from being a mechanism for spreading the risk of many people with very high costs to a broader population. The insurer assessment programs have not been systematically analyzed, so less is known about how well they work in terms of equitably spreading the costs of high-cost people among insurers.

Both approaches to the adverse selection problem have the common feature of identifying people who are *likely* to have extremely high costs. Their health care expenses can then be shared among insurers and the general population. They are no longer the responsibility of just one insurer. But the drawback to labeling individuals "high-risk" based on a prediction of having very high costs in the future is that it does nothing to eliminate the strong incentive to continue to select only people expected to have low costs.

HIGH-RISK POOLS FOR HIGH-COST PEOPLE

Minnesota and Connecticut established the first high-risk pools in 1976. The idea was slow to catch on. It was not until the early 1980s that Wisconsin and North Dakota implemented the next two high-risk pools. By 1989, nine more states had created high-risk pools, and then the momentum picked up.[3] Eleven states established pools between 1990 and 1995, and five more followed between 1996 and 2001. In 2002, as part of the Trade Adjustment Assistance Reform Act (Trade Act), Congress approved a Bush administration request for $100 million to be spent in fiscal years 2003 and 2004 to expand the use of state high-risk pools: $20 million was reserved to establish new pools, and the remaining $80 million was to offset the operating losses of qualified existing pools. To put this in perspective, the $40 million for fiscal year 2003 equals 7.4 percent of the total estimated losses of the state pools in 2003. As of mid-2005, six states had received $4.2 million to create (or study the feasibility of creating) a high-risk pool, bringing the total to thirty-three states with pools.[4] Nineteen states had received Trade Act funds totaling $65.7 million to help defray their operating losses. (New Hampshire is the only state to have received both types of grants.)[5] The remaining $14.5 million to defray operating losses was to have been awarded by the fall of 2005, and nine states (including five that have yet to receive any of the funds) are eligible to receive parts of the $14.5 million. Although Congress has not yet authorized further funding for the pools, efforts continue to include and possibly expand funding for them over the next five years.[6]

High-risk pools provide subsidized, comprehensive health insurance to individuals who, because of preexisting conditions or chronic illness, have been denied coverage by private insurers, offered restricted policies, or offered coverage only at high premiums.[7] This is a restricted group of people who are often referred to as "uninsurable." No one has a reliable estimate of the number of people who are uninsurable; two figures bandied about are 1 percent of the uninsured population or 1 percent of the total population—it has never been quite clear.[8] If we think the 1 percent refers to 1 percent of the uninsured (45.5 million in 2004), then 450,000 people might be uninsurable. An alternative estimate of the number of uninsurables is the 1 percent of the population without public coverage or large-group health insurance. At most, this amounts to about one million people (1 percent of 100 million people). As of a mix of end-of-year 2003 and some June 2004 reporting, more than 181,000 people were enrolled in one of the high-risk pools.[9] Thus, given the two estimates of the number of uninsurables, the high-risk pools are covering between 18 and 40 percent of the potential group of enrollees.

For some analysts and policymakers, the current enrollment is a disappointment. They would like to see the pools cover far more of the uninsured.[10] Since the purpose of the pools is not to cover the uninsured but rather to pull the very small number of uninsurables out of standard individual markets, this disappointment is misplaced. Moreover, the percentage of the estimated number of uninsurables who are enrolled in the pools is low in part because three of the most populous states, each with high numbers of uninsured, do not have high-risk pools or have pools that serve very few people. New York, with the third-largest population in the country, does not have a high-risk pool, and Florida, with the fourth-largest population, has a pool that has not been open to new enrollees since 1991. California significantly restructured its pool in September 2003; 9,230 people were enrolled as of January 1, 2006, but the cap on enrollment had just been raised to 10,227.[11]

Given the interest in using high-risk pools to shift the risk of very high-cost people from insurers to a broad population, we need to understand how they have been structured. In particular, we need to see whether they provide insurers with incentives to reduce their use of selection mechanisms so that more people could obtain coverage in the individual and small-group markets. However, since the primary reason for the pools' creation was to provide access to insurance for people who have been denied coverage or offered it only at very high rates, it is important to interpret their structural features in this light. The stringent eligibility criteria, relatively high premiums, and high cost-sharing are deliberate features to make sure the pools are used only by uninsurable people. The states do not want the pools to become dumping grounds for people who have had high medical expenses and whom insurers or self-insured employers might want to move out of their insurance policies. The states want to guard against the use of the pools to share the costs of very high-cost people who have group insurance coverage.

Who Is Eligible?

As noted earlier, the eligibility criteria are deliberately restrictive. The point is to maintain the pools only for people who truly cannot obtain coverage elsewhere; if people can obtain coverage elsewhere, they should. The states with high-risk pools vary in their criteria, but two common themes emerge. First, suffering from a serious illness or condition is not sufficient to qualify. Second, people who are eligible for any other state or federal program (such as Medicare, Medicaid, or access to group insurance under COBRA) do not qualify. People who may be covered fall into one of three categories: the medically uninsurable (that is, they have been denied coverage based on their current or prior medical history, or they can get coverage only at rates higher than those available through the high-risk pool or with riders restricting the covered services); those eligible for guaranteed issue of individual coverage under HIPAA; and Medicare beneficiaries who have been denied a supplemental policy because of their medical history.

People who are medically uninsurable account for the largest of the three types of possible enrollees in most state high-risk pools. One estimate is that the medically uninsurable constitute 72 percent of pools' enrollees on average.[12] However, since the definition of uninsurability is not consistent among the states, the percentage of a state's high-risk pool enrollees who are medically uninsurable varies considerably.

HIPAA prohibits insurers from denying individual coverage to people who lose group coverage after leaving employment. However, states are permitted to use high-risk pools as an "acceptable alternative mechanism" for providing such people with individual coverage. Twenty-eight states use their high-risk pools to meet the HIPAA requirement. In fact, Alabama's high-risk pool is only for HIPAA-eligible individuals, and South Dakota's pool (established in August 2003) is only for HIPAA-eligibles and other high-risk people in the individual market who have twelve months of creditable coverage.[13] Eleven states enroll Medicare beneficiaries who are not able to obtain supplemental coverage because of their medical history. (Illinois and Wyoming allow only disabled Medicare beneficiaries to enroll in their high-risk pools.)

States with high-risk pools require insurers to notify people denied coverage that the pool exists, but notifying someone is not the same as advertising. If people are unaware of their state's pool or believe that it is not accepting new enrollees, they do not apply.[14] The public's lack of information is especially unfortunate since nearly all of the states permit year-round enrollment.

Premiums and Cost-Sharing

In addition to tight restrictions on eligibility, the premiums are expensive by any measure. The high premiums are designed to dissuade people from regarding the high-risk pools as an alternative to other forms of coverage to which they have access. The pools are not intended to compete with the private markets, and the easiest way to make this point is to have high premiums.[15] By and large, this strategy has worked. Premiums run between 105 and 200 percent of the average standard premium for policies sold in the states' individual markets; most high-risk pool premiums are around 150 percent of standard individual premiums. Minnesota and Oregon have the lowest premiums; by statute, their premiums cannot go above 125 percent of the standard individual market premium. In recent years, Minnesota's premiums have been 105 to 108 percent of the standard premium, and Oregon's premium for people converting under HIPAA to individual coverage has been 100 percent of the standard rate.[16] That both states have the highest enrollments among the state high-risk pools strongly suggests how much price matters to people. By contrast, other states' premiums are much higher and their enrollments much lower. One study of six states' high-risk pools found that the premiums to cover one person were greater than 10 percent of the states' median household incomes.[17] In states where age rating of premiums for people in the high-risk pool is permitted, premiums are even more expensive. People in their late fifties and early sixties may face premiums greater than $10,000 annually unless they choose policies through which they pay the first $1,500 (or more) of medical expenses before the insurance policy begins to pay.

The cost-sharing requirements of the pools' options also add to the total cost of the policies. The two primary cost-sharing mechanisms in health insurance are deductibles and coinsurance rates. A deductible is the amount of medical expenses that a policyholder pays before the health insurance begins to pay anything. Not all medical expenses are covered by the high-risk pools' policies (just as with regular health insurance policies), and the deductible applies only to covered medical care. For instance, chiropractic services and dental and vision care are not included in covered services in many states. All states that use their high-risk pools to meet the HIPAA portability requirements must offer a choice of at least two plans. Most states comply by simply offering alternative deductible levels for a basic indemnity policy. Some states offer a choice of an HMO or PPO (preferred provider organization), sometimes without an indemnity policy option. The indemnity and PPO plans generally include a $500 deductible, though most of the states have set the deductibles at $1,000 or more (some are at $2,000, $5,000, and even $10,000).[18]

A coinsurance rate is the percentage of medical costs that a person pays after meeting the deductible; for example, a coinsurance rate of 20 percent means that the insured person pays twenty cents of every dollar of covered medical expenses above the deductible. The coinsurance rates for the high-risk pools' policies range between 20 and 50 percent depending on the medical service and whether the medical provider is in the insurer's network of providers. Policies with higher deductibles and higher coinsurance rates have lower premiums because the policyholders have to pay greater amounts of their costs of care; typically the people who enroll in such policies use less medical care.

In addition to the premium and cost-sharing requirements, states can use dollar limits on lifetime coverage to further discourage people from thinking of the high-risk pools as alternatives to regular insurance. Most states' high-risk policies have a maximum lifetime benefit of $500,000 to $1 million—an amount that can be exceeded in just a few years by individuals with serious illnesses. Indeed, the rapid growth in health spending in the last five years makes these limits look miserly. Six states have lifetime benefits limits of less than $1 million, and three states have *annual* limits on coverage of less than $250,000. Most of the people who exceed these limits end up having part of their costs covered by Medicaid, which is advantageous to the state since the high costs are then partly paid by the federal government. (Medicaid is financed jointly by the federal and state governments.) Some people who are eligible may decide that enrolling is futile since they expect to exceed the lifetime limits. People with serious mental health problems may not enroll because most states have stringent limits on coverage of mental health services and prescription drugs. However, the expectation is that someone with extremely serious mental health problems is either eligible for Medicaid or a dependent of someone who has private health insurance. Either way, the person should have access to another source of insurance and is not a prime candidate for the high-risk pool.

The high-risk pools have been criticized for having high premiums. It is true that the premiums and cost-sharing responsibilities together account for a sizable proportion of the incomes of the vast majority of enrollees.[19] Eight states have special programs to assist low-income people with the costs of the premiums and/or the cost-sharing that is required.[20] Although state funding of these financial assistance programs has not met the estimated need,[21] it is important to bear in mind that the high premiums and cost-sharing responsibilities are features that are designed to discourage the migration of high-cost people from employer-sponsored policies or from individual policies.

How States Finance the Difference Between
Premiums and Costs

Uncertainty surrounding state funding of the shortfall between high-risk pools' premium revenues and their costs is a third factor that keeps the programs small. All of the states' high-risk pools collect premiums from the enrolled individuals, but the premium revenues never cover the policyholders' medical costs. The ratio of premiums collected to claims incurred in 2003 ranged from 34 percent in Washington to 78 to 79 percent in Alabama and Iowa; most states ranged between 66 and 75 percent.[22] The claims incurred per enrollee in each state can change significantly from year to year, as they did between 2002 and 2003.[23] This further complicates state efforts to project the funding that will be needed from enrollee premiums and from the state.

States finance the difference between premium revenues and spending in various ways. General revenue funds are subject to all the uncertainties that surround tax receipts, as state policymakers have been sharply reminded these last few years. Just as importantly, the allocation of general revenue funds is subject to political favoritism—and small programs, like the high-risk pools, do not typically have large constituencies and therefore strong support among politicians. In the early 2000s, state tax revenue shortfalls put pressure on governors and legislatures to reduce the use of general revenue funds for the high-risk pools.[24] Although state tax receipts have increased in the last three years, cuts in federal monies going to the states have continued to place general revenue funding at risk for high-risk pools.

Illinois, Louisiana, and Utah rely primarily on general revenue funds to help finance their high-risk pools.[25] Louisiana also collects a service charge on all hospital inpatient admissions and outpatient procedures. The surcharges are collected from a broader population base and are analogous to the assessments on insurers' earned premiums. Wisconsin uses general revenues to supplement assessments on insurers.[26] Four other states use sources of state funds that have been earmarked for the high-risk pools, but during the last few years pressure to use these funds for education and Medicaid has increased. California sets aside $40 million per year from its State Cigarette and Tobacco Products Surtax Fund. Colorado uses its unclaimed property (such as wages and deposits on utilities) and unclaimed insurance funds (from policies for which the beneficiaries cannot be found). Kentucky was the first state to use money from the master tobacco settlement agreement funds. In 1998 and again in 1999, Minnesota allocated a portion of the state's Health Care Access Fund on an emergency basis; the fund raises money from a 1.5 percent tax on hospital and provider charges to obtain monies.

Twenty-nine of the states fund all or part of the difference by assessing each insurer that sells health coverage in the state in proportion to its share of all health insurance premiums.[27] Twelve of these states permit the insurers to offset their corporate income tax liability by the full or a partial amount of their assessment. This is equivalent to using state general revenues to finance the high-risk pools, but the equivalency is not easily discerned by the public.

Using High-Risk Pools to Cover More of the Uninsured

The relatively small number of people enrolled in the pools is a result of the deliberate restrictions on eligibility, the use of high premiums and cost-sharing as hurdles to discourage enrollment, and the uncertain financing of the shortfall between premium revenues and expenditures.[28] The states have succeeded in maintaining a program reserved only for uninsurable people, and the numbers show this. Only five of the states have more than 10,000 enrollees; half have enrollments between 1,000 and 5,000.[29] Among the thirty-three states with high-risk pools, only three cover more than 1 percent of the small number of people with individual insurance. Minnesota's enrollment (33,705) is the highest of any state; it equals about 6 percent of those with individual coverage. The high-risk pools in Oregon (9,885 people) and Nebraska (6,087 people) cover about 3 percent.[30] The enrollment in these three states' high-risk pools approaches 1 percent of each state's population without public or large-group insurance who might have very high costs.

In spite of much misunderstanding of the objective of the high-risk pools and the low enrollments, it has been suggested that they could cover more of the uninsured. In particular, the suggestion is that the pools cover people who do not meet the definition of uninsurable but are still viewed by insurers as likely to have high costs. These people might well be offered policies if they apply for coverage, but their premiums are medically underwritten, so they pay higher than standard rates for their coverage. Implicit in the suggestion is the notion that the high-risk pools would be used to spread the risk of high-cost people more broadly. It would not be just the individual and small-group markets (and perhaps also the large-group market) that bore the risk of high-cost people. The state's entire population would bear the risk and help pay for the expenses of people deemed high-risk.

If the high-risk pools were to be used more aggressively to cover the uninsured, the eligibility criteria, management, and financing of them would have to change substantially to meet this new and broader objective. The recent experience of California may be a model for other states. California revised its high-risk pool strategy and is trying to use it as an "incubator" for high-risk people for thirty-six months. After three years, people will have to disenroll but will be offered guaranteed-issue coverage in the individual market.[31] The hope is that insurers will be relieved of the costs of high-risk people for three years, and then the people's expenses will return to lower levels that are within the "normal" expenditure ranges of people in the individual market.

The Incentive to Use Selection Mechanisms Remains

Since the high-risk pools are available only for people who are predicted to be high-risk, expanding their scope would maintain incentives for insurers to use selection mechanisms. The people most likely to be newly eligible would be uninsured people who have trouble obtaining coverage because they are perceived to be high-risk. Susan Mitchell might be in this category because she is in her early fifties. In fact, expanding the use of the pools actually might increase insurers' incentives to use selection mechanisms since they would prefer not to enroll people they believe will have expenses greater than premiums. This goes against the objective we started with—trying to find a policy approach that will substantially lower insurers' concerns with adverse selection.

ASSESSMENTS OF INSURERS TO SHARE THE COSTS OF HIGH-RISK PEOPLE

The assessment mechanism used by most states to help finance their high-risk pool offers a second approach for minimizing insurers' risk of high expenditures due to adverse selection. Assessments are commonly used by states to share the very high costs among all insurers in a market (such as auto or homeowner) in order to maintain it. An assessment is the equivalent of a tax on insurers that is used to reduce the costs of a few insurers in cases where costs are higher than would have been predicted, given their share of insured people. Essentially the insurers with the higher-than-predicted costs are partially reimbursed. This is similar to the risk-adjustment mechanisms that have been implemented in California, Minnesota, Colorado, and Washington, among others, to compensate health plans that enrolled high-risk individuals.[32]

The assessments, though seemingly imposed on insurers, are passed through to anyone who pays for a health insurance policy or has coverage from a self-insured employer, depending on how the assessments are structured. If the assessment is based on the number of people an insurer covers (covered lives), it spreads the costs of high-risk people over a broad share of the population. The assessment also is independent of the premiums, which means that those who purchase more expensive policies are not incurring a proportionately higher assessment. In contrast, with an assessment based on premiums (earned premium), insurers that sell more comprehensive benefits packages—which typically are sold at higher premiums—have higher assessments.[33] Insurers that have more high-cost enrollees, either because they sell more comprehensive benefits packages or because they have been affected by adverse selection, also have higher premiums and therefore higher assessments. In addition, assessments based on premiums are passed through to policyholders of any type of insurance policy related to health, including stop-loss and reinsurance policies. These types of policies provide self-insured firms with protection against high total expenses or high expenses for any one individual. As a result, an assessment based on premiums "captures" companies that self-fund their employee health plan and permits states to go around the ERISA provision that exempts self-insured firms from state taxes on health insurance policies per se.[34] Thus, assessments based on premiums enable the state to spread the burden of very high-cost people to almost all of the population with private health insurance.

Insurers are quite familiar with the loss assessment mechanisms used to spread the costs of high-risk people beyond a particular insurer and its enrollees. Assessment mechanisms also avoid the need to establish a formal high-risk pool. Since people who have high medical costs in a particular year often do not continue to have them in succeeding years, creating a mechanism that temporarily assigns them to a high-risk group is a more transparent method of sharing very high costs.

Insurer assessments also are frequently used for what are known as residual market mechanisms (RMMs), which themselves are a model for high-risk pools. RMMs are another source of insurance coverage—though not for health-related insurance—for people who are not able to purchase coverage, typically because insurers stop offering it. Insurers will stop offering coverage for specific types of losses when they believe they have too many insureds in a geographic area who would be affected by the same potential disaster, such as a hurricane or earthquake.[35] If such a disaster were to occur, an insurer would be exposed to a level of risk greater than its financial ability to pay for the losses. States have responded to these insurance availability crises by creating RMMs that are run by the insurers.

RMMs offer a warning on the limits of using the assessment mechanism for addressing the access problems of high-risk people. If losses among the insurers become large because a high proportion of people are high-cost, the RMM assessment mechanism will not function to provide coverage to high-risk people. The assessments will simply overwhelm the market and drive premiums to the point where a death spiral for the market ensues. This is what has happened to property insurance for 2005 hurricane damage along the Gulf Coast. Florida, Mississippi, and Louisiana are among the states that have used RMMs to provide property insurance for people in areas at high risk for hurricane damage. Florida's RMM insurer, Citizens Property Insurance Corporation, went from a surplus of $1.3 billion to a deficit of $516 million before the 2005 hurricane season—and in 2005 Florida was hit by Hurricanes Dennis, Katrina, and Wilma, the costs of which were still being tallied in the fall of 2005. Even before the 2005 hurricane season, Citizens was adding as many as thirty thousand new policies a month as the large private insurers began pulling out of the state.[36] Thus, creating RMMs and using such assessments should be seen as a solution only for situations that involve a small number of high-cost people.[37]

New Jersey's Individual Health Coverage Program

New Jersey used a variant of the assessment mechanism to distribute the costs of high-cost individual enrollees among all the insurers selling health coverage in the state. The state revised its individual insurance market regulations in August 1993 in order to create the Individual Health Coverage Program (IHCP).[38] The IHCP required all insurers selling health coverage in the state to participate in the program, either by actively selling a target number of policies or by paying a loss assessment that reimbursed the insurers that did sell policies and incurred losses. The target number of policies to be sold and the loss assessments were based on each insurer's share of total net-earned premiums. By using net-earned premiums, the state included payments for stop-loss and reinsurance policies purchased by self-insured firms.

An insurer could avoid paying its share of the total losses incurred by other insurers selling policies in the IHCP if it enrolled its assigned target number of people. Insurers that otherwise would have to pay large assessments had a clear incentive to meet their target enrollment numbers. In fact, the expectation was that the half-dozen insurers with the largest shares of the market would be the insurers forming the individual market under the IHCP.[39] The IHCP regulations also contained an incentive for the insurers to be efficient in providing individual coverage. They allowed an insurer that was meeting its target enrollment number to not seek reimbursement for its own losses. In exchange, an insurer was exempted from paying for any of the total losses submitted for reimbursement by other insurers. Clearly, an insurer would choose to not seek reimbursement if its own losses were expected to be less than its expected share of the total IHCP losses.

Unfortunately, this incentive encouraged a small number of small insurers with very tiny market shares to enter the market.[40] Each of these insurers must have realized that if it did incur losses, its own share of the losses would be small because its share of the total market was very small. Between eight and ten small insurers perceived the incentive to come into the market and then suffered significant losses (a total of $76 million over a two-year period from 1995 to 1996) that were shared among the other insurers in the state.

One lesson from New Jersey's experience with using a loss assessment mechanism to spread the costs of high-risk people is that it is crucial for policy analysts to think through how the assessment mechanisms are set up. Otherwise the assessments can have unexpected effects.[41] The point of mechanisms to shift the costs of very high-risk people from insurers to a broader population base is to reduce insurers' incentives to risk-select enrollees. At the same time, however, we do not want a system that provides incentives for insurers with insufficient capital reserves to offer coverage they cannot deliver and thereby cause other insurers to bear the losses.

Do Insurers Have an Incentive to Stop Using Selection Mechanisms?

Like the high-risk pools, the assessment approach relies on predicting people's likely medical costs. The amount that an insurer receives back from the fund depends on the difference between the insurer's total actual costs and the total expected costs of the people it insured. But the insurer is not guaranteed an assessment fund payout that equals the full difference. Rather, its share of the fund equals its share of the total "overrun"; the overrun is the net amount of actual costs minus the expected costs of all insurers in the state market. Unless the assessments are set to make the fund equal the total overrun of costs, the insurers will not receive full reimbursement of their unexpected costs. Thus, the approach does not discourage insurers from using selection mechanisms to avoid high-cost people. In fact, depending on how the assessments for the funds are designed, insurers may have more incentive to use selection mechanisms. Just as with high-risk pools, the potential for the assessment approach to reduce insurers' concerns about adverse selec-

tion is hindered because insurers will still see it as advantageous to identify people likely to have very high costs.

DETERMINING WHETHER SOMEONE IS
HIGH-RISK OR HIGH-COST

We began with the idea that if insurers' concerns with adverse selection
can be allayed, they will significantly lower their use of selection mechanisms and more people will gain access to insurance. The high-risk pools
and assessment approaches help redistribute the costs of the people
likely to have high medical expenses. But neither approach reduces insurers' incentives to use selection mechanisms, because at the heart of
each approach is the need to predict who is likely to have very high
medical expenses in the coming year.

Any approach to addressing insurers' fear of adverse selection has to
shift most of their risk of very high costs to a broader population. A
critical choice in any such approach is deciding whether to use estimated
or actual costs. When costs are estimated, they are predicted with models
that take into account observable characteristics of the person (including
perhaps the person's medical expenses in the prior year). If the models
estimate that someone's annual costs will be greater than some level, the
person is identified as high-risk. Alternatively, some models are used to
predict the *probability* that a person will have health costs above some
level, and if the predicted probability is greater than 0.5 (or some higher
probability), the person is labeled high-risk. In contrast, identifying
someone as actually having incurred very high costs requires knowledge
of a person's medical expenses after the year is over.

Estimating a person's medical expenses requires information on personal characteristics that are highly correlated with predictable expenditures. As we saw in chapter 4, predictable expenses are those that are to
be expected in a given year—for example, a physician visit for an ear
infection in a child or an ob-gyn visit for a forty-five-year-old female.
Unpredictable expenses come from random events such as being hit by
a bus or having a heart attack without any cardiac risk factors. Insurers
rely on models that include characteristics such as a person's age, sex,
education, income, occupation, and health information to estimate his or
her predictable expenses. The same types of models also are used in risk-
adjustment methods to risk-adjust premium payments to managed care
plans or payments to providers. Such models are not very accurate for
individuals. At the very best, they explain 30 percent of the variance in
a person's predictable expenditures.[42]

In contrast, when people are classified on the basis of actual claims experience, then we are identifying high-cost individuals rather than high-risk individuals. The uncertainty present in the models used to predict someone's costs is eliminated. Most important, using actual costs to identify people as high-cost lowers insurers' incentives to use selection mechanisms.

The Netherlands's Experience

The implications of identifying people either as high-risk or as high-cost have been studied in the Netherlands since several health care reforms were introduced there starting in 1988. The most recent reform, which went into effect in January 2006, was necessitated by the continuing coordination of social systems under the European Union. Everyone in the Netherlands automatically is entitled to coverage for long-term care and nursing. However, as of January 2006, everyone in the country (except active-duty military personnel and conscientious objectors to insurance) is required to have health insurance that covers the costs of "care with a view to cure."[43] (Before the latest reform, health insurance coverage was voluntary for about one-third of the population who had higher incomes.) There is only one standardized package of benefits, but the insurance is sold by private insurance companies known as "care insurers." Insurers have to accept anyone who applies, and they must offer them the same terms and conditions of coverage. Funding for care insurance comes from premiums and income-related contributions. Premiums are community rated, so those who choose a particular insurer pay the same amount; people send their premium payments directly to the insurer. The Dutch equivalent of the IRS determines the income-related contribution, and employers are required to reimburse their employees in full for the income-related contributions. The income-related contributions go to the Health Insurance Fund, as does a government contribution equal to the premiums for children younger than eighteen. Children are not enrolled as part of a family plan; health care costs of children are considered the responsibility of the country as a whole. The Health Insurance Fund then uses a "risk equalization" model to pay each insurer additional amounts based on the health risks of the people who enroll with the insurer.

The new system of risk equalization builds upon the Netherlands's experience with risk adjustments gained since 1988. Prior to 2006, people with incomes below certain limits were in a mandatory insurance system of "sickness funds" that were private insurance companies. About two-thirds of the population were covered by such insurance. The compulsory system was run by a Central Insurance Fund, which collected revenues based on payroll taxes shared between employers and employees (with employers generally paying a substantial share).

Starting in 1992, the system of fully reimbursing the funds for enrollees' expenses was changed so that the funds received a risk-adjusted capitation payment.[44] The risk-adjusted payment equaled the national predicted per capita costs in the risk group to which a person belongs. The initial risk-adjusted payments were based on very simple risk adjusters: age and sex. It was widely understood that they were too simple to capture much of the variation in predictable expenditures. Over time, as more risk adjusters were added, the sickness funds were at risk for increasing percentages of the difference between actual and predicted costs. Between 1993 and 1995, the Dutch funds were put at risk for only 3 percent of the difference between their actual costs and the age- and sex-predicted costs for the pool of people they each covered. The other 97 percent of the difference in costs was reimbursed retrospectively by the government. By 2003 the risk adjustments included five new adjustment factors (including a pharmacy cost adjustment added in 2002) and in 2004 diagnostic cost groups (DCGs) were added as another risk adjuster. In 2004 the sickness funds were at risk for 53 percent of total expenses; they were at risk for almost all of outpatient expenses (96 percent) and 26 percent of inpatient expenses.[45]

It is important to note that the Dutch have not gone so far as Switzerland or Germany, where demographic risk-adjustment models are used and the insurance funds are at risk for 100 percent of total expenses. Risk selection is a very serious problem in those two countries.[46] Some combination of the deliberate incremental improvements to the Dutch risk adjustments and the fact that the Dutch government still is responsible for almost half of the risk has enabled the Netherlands to avoid a serious risk selection problem. As three Dutch researchers put it, "Good health adjustment not only reduces the predictable losses from high-risk consumers, but it also increases the sickness funds' costs of risk selection as well as the uncertainty about their net benefits of selection."[47] In addition, there are four further explanations for the "absence of serious selection problems": very few people switch funds; the benefits covered by the funds are standardized; because of a physician shortage in the Netherlands, there is very little selective contracting by the funds with physicians; and a "social" culture within the sickness funds strongly disapproves of using risk selection mechanisms.[48]

In part because few people switch sickness funds, and in part because there is such a strong ethical bias against using risk selection mechanisms, the Dutch funds now have a great deal of information about people's expenses over time. They seem to have used this to better manage their enrollees' medical care. All along, concerns were raised that if the funds were not fully at risk, they would be less efficient, particularly in how they managed the extremely high-cost people. Analyses suggest just the opposite. The studies found that *identification* of high-cost people (rather than *predictions* of high-risk people) provides more incentives for efficiency in producing health care.[49] Management of costs is more likely to be a priority when managers focus on people who actually are experiencing high costs, some of which the insurers are at risk for. This may be particularly true in situations where few people switch plans and therefore the insurers know they will continue to be at risk for future costs. The Dutch changes may have created the incentive to better manage the costs of people who very clearly were on track to be high-cost.

SUMMARY

To address insurers' fear of adverse selection and its consequences, we need to shift the risk of extremely high costs from the insurers that enroll uninsured people to a broader population base. The state high-risk pools and the assessment approaches appear to provide options for doing this. However, each of these relies on identification of high-*risk* people rather than high-*cost* people. The identification depends on models that predict a person's expenses: if the predicted expenses are greater than a predetermined amount, the person is said to be high-risk. The high-risk pools and assessment mechanisms prolong insurers' incentives to use selection mechanisms. With high-risk pools, the insurers still want to predict who is likely to be high-risk so that they can try to send the person to such a pool. And under the assessment approach, since insurers are unlikely to be fully reimbursed for the losses they might incur, they want to minimize those losses by minimizing the number of people they insure who are high-risk. These approaches do not address the information asymmetry between insurer and insured that is the core problem in the small-group and individual insurance markets.

An alternative approach is to have the government provide reinsurance to insurers in these markets. Reinsurance relies on identifying people who actually have extremely high medical costs rather than identifying people who are high-risk. In the next chapter, we examine how reinsurance works and how a government reinsurance program might be designed as a federal policy to increase access to small-group and individual insurance markets.

Chapter 6

A Third Approach: The Government as Reinsurer for Small-Group and Individual Markets

Almost all insurers purchase reinsurance to protect themselves from low-probability but very costly events that could force them into bankruptcy. The hurricane seasons of 2004 and 2005 provide good examples of financial disasters that occasionally befall property and casualty insurers with a large proportion of their business in Florida and along the entire Gulf Coast. In 2004 the federal government, through the Federal Emergency Management Agency, provided more than $10 billion to reimburse hurricane-related losses in Florida that were not covered by private-market business property and homeowner's insurance. In 2005, after Hurricanes Katrina and Rita (and before Wilma), Congress authorized more than $60 billion for aid and reconstruction in Texas, Louisiana, Mississippi, and Alabama. The total of federal funds for these states' hurricane losses is expected to be higher. In addition, FEMA spent hundreds of millions of dollars more for losses sustained in Florida after Hurricanes Dennis and Wilma, in states where tornadoes struck, and in New Jersey and New Hampshire after flooding in October. Some of the FEMA funds assisted owners of damaged properties that were not insured, and a substantial fraction defrayed losses that exceeded the coverage limits of policies.

Just as important as its assistance to the people devastated by these disasters, however, is FEMA's provision of de facto reinsurance for the insurers that sell the policies in the first place. Without the federal government's implicit promise to reimburse the extreme losses, catastrophe reinsurance would not be available from the private market. In turn, this would cause insurers to stop selling homeowner's and business property insurance in hurricane-prone areas.

The federal government could assume a similar role in the small-group and individual health insurance markets. This approach would shift the risk of individuals with extremely high costs from the insurers to the broad population and greatly reduce insurers' fears of adverse selection. It would benefit those trying to obtain private coverage in two ways: insurers could reduce their use of selection mechanisms that now prevent some people from obtaining coverage, and insurers could significantly reduce their premiums. Since the costs of people with extremely high medical expenses are traditionally built into insurance premiums, a government reinsurance program would help lower them considerably. Both effects would reduce the number of uninsured by enabling more people to purchase private health insurance. This is exactly the effect of FEMA on homeowner's and business property insurance and the catastrophe reinsurance markets.

Reinsurance is insurance for insurers. Just as people want car or homeowner's insurance and companies want liability or property insurance to reduce their exposure to risks, insurers want protection against risks that pose potential financial disasters. Insurers that sell health coverage to large groups typically purchase reinsurance through reinsurance companies or financial syndicates. (Among the best known of these syndicates is Lloyds of London.) But reinsurance for health insurance policies sold to small groups and individuals is more expensive since reinsurers have the same concerns about the potential for adverse selection in the small-group and individual markets.

Reinsurance is structured very much like standard indemnity insurance products. There is a threshold level, or deductible, of expenses that must be incurred before the reinsurance takes effect, and there is the equivalent of a coinsurance rate that the original insurer pays for expenses above the deductible. By still having to pay a fraction of all costs above the deductible, the original insurer retains some risk for those costs. Also, like most insurance policies, reinsurance is sold for a limited amount of coverage—it is not open-ended. In contrast to the high-risk pools and insurer assessment programs (described in chapter 5) that rely on predictions of which people are likely to be high-cost, reinsurers reimburse only for actual expenses. A considerable advantage of a government-sponsored reinsurance program is that by using actual expenses, it significantly reduces insurers' incentives to use selection mechanisms.

This chapter starts by describing the variety of ways in which reinsurance can be structured, then discusses the components that would need to be part of a government reinsurance program and assesses its costs.

THE TYPES AND STRUCTURE OF
REINSURANCE POLICIES

Until about twenty-five years ago, reinsurance was sold almost exclusively to insurance companies. Since then, companies that self-insure their employees' health expenses and hospitals that have insurance-like specialty-care contracts have become buyers of reinsurance. For example, in some joint ventures between hospitals and insurers, the hospitals agree to capitated payments for the care of patients with cancer or cardiac or orthopedic conditions. Such joint ventures put hospitals at risk for costs exceeding expected costs, but hospitals accept the risk because they hope that their expertise and efficiency will keep costs below the payment and they will keep the difference. However, they typically arrange for reinsurance to reduce their risk exposure. Reinsurance has become the equivalent of a very high deductible or catastrophic insurance policy for businesses that bear risks in a variety of situations. Sellers of reinsurance are generally large syndicates of investors (such as Lloyds of London) or insurance companies that specialize in it. (Swiss RE and AIG are two of the biggest.) An important feature of reinsurance is that the reinsurer protects itself from moral hazard and adverse selection by requiring the original insurers to bear the risk for a portion of the possible losses.[1]

Reinsurance serves two key functions. It protects insurers against events that, though very unlikely to happen, would ruin the insurer financially. It also helps insurers when their business is not diversified enough to bear their different risks. An insurer may sell policies primarily in one geographical region, leaving it vulnerable to a natural disaster that could strike the region. Or an insurer could specialize in health coverage (as do managed care organizations) instead of selling a variety of insurance products that involve independent risks. If the small-probability but costly event occurs, or the nondiversified risks all come to pass, reinsurance provides a safeguard.

The other key role of reinsurance is to enable insurers to expand their business. By purchasing reinsurance, an insurer shifts the risk of a low-probability event to the reinsurer and is thus able to reduce the amount of capital it has to hold in reserve in case a small-probability but very costly event occurs. With less capital tied up insuring an initial set of people, the insurer can expand the number of policies it sells. Similarly, a company that self-insures its employees' health costs can, by purchasing reinsurance, reduce the amount of capital it needs to hold in reserve; it can use the capital instead to invest in new equipment or buy down debt.

In the last two decades, the use of reinsurance expanded markedly. As it evolved into a product sold not just to insurers, it came to describe insurance that covers any situation where the purchasing company is at risk for particular types of losses.[2] The non-insurance companies that buy reinsurance also could reduce their exposure to the risk of substantial losses by using other financial instruments, including hedge funds or derivatives. But such alternatives require that the companies employ experts in the financial markets. Reinsurance is a more straightforward and less expensive method for transferring risk.[3]

Forms of Reinsurance

There are three common types of reinsurance arrangements or contracts:

- Quota share (sometimes called proportional reinsurance)
- Aggregate stop-loss
- Excess-of-loss

In *quota share reinsurance* arrangements, the original insurer and the reinsurer share the risks from all the policies sold in connection with a particular benefits package (often referred to as a "book of business"). Unlike insurance policies with a flat premium, the reinsurer is paid a share of the premiums from the original policies in exchange for taking on a share of the risk that the policies may incur net losses. The "quota share" of premiums paid to the reinsurer partially determines the proportion of the losses covered by the reinsurer. Typically, the share of premiums paid to the reinsurer is smaller than the share of the losses for which the reinsurer is at risk.[4] The reason for this is that the original insurer continues to be responsible for the administrative expenses associated with the policies, including the claims-processing costs for all of the possible losses. Quota share reinsurance arrangements are particularly useful for insurers that are trying to expand their business or reduce the concentration of their risk exposure. For example, some insurers may want to shed risk from having a high proportion of small employer groups in the same industry as clients. If a common problem were to hit small employers in the industry, the insurers' portfolio of risks might not be diversified enough to offset the concentrated losses due to the common problem.

Quota share reinsurance is not as prevalent in connection with health insurance as aggregate stop-loss or excess-of-loss reinsurance.

Aggregate stop-loss reinsurance protects the original insurer from very large aggregate (total) losses from a book of business, or all the policies sold to a large group. The reinsurance goes into effect when total losses exceed a threshold known as the stop-loss level. (The stop-loss level is equivalent to a deductible.) Generally, aggregate stop-loss coverage is used to limit the original insurer's financial risk from all the possible combinations of probabilities of losses and magnitudes of losses. For instance, it provides protection for the original insurer against an unexpectedly large number of people with small losses or an unexpected increase in the small number of people with losses that are high but not catastrophically so. The threshold level that activates the stop-loss reinsurance may be either a specific dollar amount or a loss ratio equal to the percentage of premium income that is paid out in claims. Thus, a stop-loss might be set at $50 million for a self-insured employer with a total of ten thousand employees and their dependents. Or it could be set at a loss ratio of 95 percent, indicating that the insurer had paid claims by medical providers that were at least equal to 95 percent of premium revenues.

Excess-of-loss reinsurance arrangements are generally created on a per-policy basis for an entire group or a book of business. This type of reinsurance is designed to protect the original insurer from very large losses that might occur with separate policies rather than from total losses from all the policies in a group or book of business. The reinsurance goes into effect and pays expenses once any individual has expenditures above a threshold amount. The original insurer might have only one person or a large number of individuals with annual expenses eligible for reinsurance. The lower the threshold level, the more likely it is that people will have expenses above it. Not surprisingly, the premium for excess-of-loss reinsurance increases as the threshold level is lowered.

The Structure of Reinsurance

Three parameters or contract specifications determine the premium for a reinsurance policy. Because all three are variable, the premium is negotiated by the purchaser and the supplier of the reinsurance. The first specification is the number of people in a policy or set of policies for which the purchaser wants reinsurance. As the number increases, the premium also increases. The other two specifications are the range of expenses to be covered and the fraction of the expenses in that range that will be the purchaser's responsibility (equivalent to a coinsurance rate). These last two determine the structure, or design, of a reinsurance policy.

Reinsurance is typically sold in "layers" of coverage for specified ranges of expenses. For example, an insurer might want excess-of-loss reinsurance for annual expenditures that exceed $50,000 per insured person. In this case, it might purchase a reinsurance policy that covers the layer, or "corridor," of expenses between $50,000 and $100,000, and then purchase another policy for the layer of expenses between $100,000 and $200,000 (see figure 6.1). Aggregate stop-loss reinsurance contracts are written so that the layers refer to the sum of losses for the group or book

Figure 6.1 Layers of Reinsurance

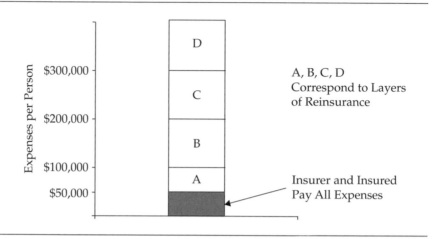

Source: Author's illustration.

of business. A company that self-insures the medical expenses of all its employees and their dependents and expects total costs to be below $25 million, might seek a sequence of reinsurance layers—each of $1 million to $5 million—to reduce its risk of total expenses being between $25 million and $35 million.[5]

The premium of each layer is determined by how large it is, how much of the underlying risk of extremely high costs is covered by the layer, and the fraction of the expenses within it that the reinsurance purchaser will continue to pay. As we saw in chapter 4, the distribution of annual health care expenses is quite skewed: half of the population has expenditures below about $500 per year, and at the other end of the spectrum, 10 percent of the population is responsible for 70 percent of all expenditures. Now suppose an insurer wants to purchase an excess-of-loss reinsurance policy to cover expenses above the threshold for people whose spending is so high that they are in the top 1 percent of the population. In 2005 this threshold was $50,000. As the layer of reinsurance gets higher and higher above $50,000, the probability that a random person will have such extremely high costs decreases. So the premium for a layer of reinsurance just above $50,000 will cost more than the same-size layer starting at expenditures of $250,000. The premium will also cost more the larger the size of the layer, regardless of where the layer is relative to the threshold.

Sellers of reinsurance for health insurance always require the pur-

chaser to retain some risk in order to provide an incentive for the purchaser to manage the medical expenses. Since the purchaser must pay
some fraction of medical expenses above the threshold level, it has a
strong motivation to design policies with benefits packages that encourage efficient use of health care.[6] For example, policies that have no co-
payments for mammograms encourage women to seek timely screenings
to increase the chances of detecting cancer early, reducing the treatment
costs. The fraction of risk that a purchaser of reinsurance bears can vary
across the layers it buys. Thus, it could be responsible for 25 percent of
the costs in the first layer, 15 percent of the costs in the next layer, and
only 5 percent of the costs in the third layer. (Figure 6.2 illustrates this
scenario.) If the purchaser retains responsibility for a larger fraction of
the costs in a given layer, the premium for that layer of reinsurance will
be lower.

When the purchaser and supplier of a reinsurance policy negotiate
the premium for the policy, they consider the number of people to be
covered, the range of expenses to be covered by the layer and where that
layer is in the distribution of expected expenses, and the fraction of the
risk that the purchaser will bear for expenses in the layer. If the population to be covered consists of people with unknown or uncertain expenditure patterns, the reinsurance premium will be higher because the reinsurer will view the risk connected to the population as greater. For instance,

Figure 6.2   Risk Sharing by Layers of Reinsurance: Percentage of Risk Retained by Insurer

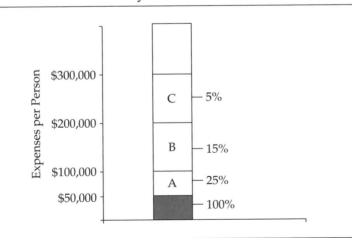

Source: Author's illustration.

public-private insurance programs designed to attract low-income work-ers may draw healthy, young workers or they may draw older workers with chronic conditions. Reinsurers will charge more for reinsurance for such a program until the expenditure patterns of enrollees become clear and are consistent over some amount of time.

Excess-of-Loss Reinsurance and Reductions in Insurers' Use of Selection Mechanisms

Although both aggregate stop-loss and excess-of-loss reinsurance offer protection against financial losses that have a small probability of hap-pening, there are two reasons why the excess-of-loss type of reinsurance is preferable for the purpose of reducing insurers' use of selection mech-anisms. It directly addresses insurers' concerns about covering people with extremely high costs. It also is much easier and less expensive to administer—there are far fewer very-high-cost people compared to the number with costs that are above average but not high. Since the choice of type of reinsurance is important, it is worth expanding on these reasons.

Recall that adverse selection is said to occur when an insurer has higher than expected costs for a group or a book of business. The higher expenses could happen because a substantial fraction of the people has expenses above the expected average but no one has extremely high costs. Alternatively, the higher expenses could be the result of a larger number of people than expected having extremely high costs. Either way, an insurer could lose money, since the sum of the medical costs of the enrollees exceeds the premium revenues, which are calculated on the basis of expected costs for the group.

As we saw in chapter 4, insurers in the small-group and individual markets are most concerned about the losses they face when they have a larger-than-anticipated number of enrollees with extremely high costs. To reduce the chances of this happening, insurers use selection mecha-nisms to avoid insuring people who might have very high medical ex-penses. The appeal of excess-of-loss reinsurance contracts is that they address the risk of losses due to an unexpected number of enrollees with very high costs. Excess-of-loss reinsurance significantly reduces the ben-efits of using selection mechanisms. In contrast, aggregate stop-loss rein-surance addresses higher costs due to reasons beyond adverse selection. When total costs are higher than expected for a book of business but not many people within the book of business have very high costs, the high total could reflect new, more expensive treatments, or a general increase in medical providers' charges, or perhaps even that an epidemic has broken out. But these factors would affect all insurers and are not related to an unexpected number of enrollees with extremely high costs. Aggregate stop-loss reinsurance would reimburse insurers for these expenses, however, and therefore would address more than adverse selection. In addition, on average, insurers should be able to manage the claims expenses of people with above-average costs that do not reach the top 5 or even 10 percent of costs. People in this range had total annual expenditures below $15,000 in 2005.

The second reason for preferring excess-of-loss reinsurance is far more pragmatic. It is easy to set an expenditure threshold that defines who has extremely high medical expenses—it could be the threshold that captures the top 1 percent of the expenditures' distribution. Fewer people's claims would have to be submitted for audit by a government reinsurance program than would be the case if the reinsurance were designed as an aggregate stop-loss contract. An aggregate stop-loss form would require the auditing of a large number of claims, increasing both the administrative costs and the potential for fraud.

Excess-of-loss reinsurance directly addresses insurers' primary risk— that a greater-than-expected number of people with very high costs will be enrolled. This type of reinsurance is also much more practical and less expensive to administer—two critical issues for government-provided reinsurance programs.

THE DESIGN OF A FEDERAL REINSURANCE PROGRAM

"The devil is in the details" when considering how a government reinsurance program for the small-group and individual health insurance markets might be structured. Many design details could be raised as issues, but they should be addressed as aspects of the overarching goal of government-sponsored reinsurance: to cause insurers to lower premiums and reduce their use of selection mechanisms. To do this, the reinsurance must be structured so that insurers believe the program significantly reduces their risk of adverse selection. With this in mind, the major design details can be separated into issues related to the operations, costs, and financing of the program.

Operations Issues

Addressing three major operational issues is essential to any reinsurance program:

The Need for Transparency as to Why Some People Have High Expenses A reinsurance program will encourage insurers to reduce their use of selection mechanisms only if it is clear that the people whose expenses activate the reinsurance were indeed extraordinarily sick. The incentives for fraud are huge unless it is crystal clear that the individuals whose expenses are reimbursed are in the top percentiles of the population or had expenses above a threshold level that activates the reinsurance. However, the need for transparency about extremely high medical costs inherently conflicts with Americans' desire for choice when it comes to insurance policies. This makes decisions about how to achieve transparency difficult.

To see why transparency and choice conflict, consider that the simplest way to achieve transparency is to standardize policies' benefits packages and cost-sharing. Standardizing avoids having to determine whether someone had high expenses because his or her insurance policy was generous and covered every imaginable medical service or had low levels of cost-sharing. "Cadillac" policies invite high use of health care and increase the likelihood of expenses in excess of the threshold for the reinsurance. Creating uniformity in cost-sharing also sidesteps the problem of deciding which out-of-pocket expenditures should be included when calculating a person's total spending. A policy with a low deductible or low co-payments not only encourages more use of health care but also has higher insurer-paid expenses than a policy with a high deductible. In addition, standardizing the benefits and cost-sharing reduces the ability of insurers to use particular benefits or deductible levels to either attract low-risk people or discourage high-risk people.

Standardizing benefits and cost-sharing is at odds with offering choice to consumers. Insurers (and some consumers) argue that consumers want choice because they are not identical when it comes to preferences, either for the types of medical services covered or for levels of cost-sharing. They contend that it is unfair to consumers to require standardized policies. Whether they would continue to make this argument in the face of a program that offered them substantial relief from the risk of adverse selection is unclear. Moreover, it is not clear what choice means in the context of health insurance. About half of employees who are offered employer-based health insurance have a choice of health plans through their employer, and only about half of these employees can choose among the products of different insurers.[7] Medicare has been hugely popular with beneficiaries, and until the mid-1990s most beneficiaries did not have managed care plan alternatives to traditional Medicare. The Medicare Modernization Act of 2003 (MMA) authorized an increase in the payments to managed care plans in an effort to expand the number of participating plans. In spite of the greater availability of choices, the vast majority of beneficiaries (87 percent) continue to choose traditional Medicare, which has one set of covered benefits and cost-sharing requirements.[8] Retiree health plans and MediGap supplemental policies provide additional coverage to people for the costs that Medicare does not pay, but even here, the choices of such plans are constrained.

Given that many people seem to want a limited choice of health plans rather than dozens of alternatives, it ought to be possible to experiment with having a choice of two or three standardized policies. However, there are problems with this. Imagine a choice of two policies. One is quite generous in the medical services it covers or has very low enrollee cost-sharing, while the other is relatively lean. We might expect people who have been sick in the past or who expect to have high expenditures in the future to choose the more generous policy, even though it has a higher premium. The leaner policy, on the other hand, would be more likely to attract people who expect their medical spending to be low in the next year. This type of self-selection is known as risk selection, and it is well documented among employers that offer different policies to their employees.[9] Insurers take advantage of this phenomenon, as we saw in chapter 4, to try to attract low-risk people and avoid potentially high-cost people. Yet, with the same reinsurance threshold activation level, the lean policy would require far more out-of-pocket spending by an individual than would the more generous policy. This no doubt would discourage health care use. It also raises issues of fairness. Should the reinsurance reimbursements go to the insurer without any compensation to the individual for the out-of-pocket expenditures? On the other hand, people who choose a leaner policy would also be paying a lower premium, so they are already beneficiaries of lower out-of-pocket premium expenses.

If a choice of different levels of generosity of policies were permitted, the reinsurance activation thresholds could be different for the policies—the leaner policy having a lower threshold. But setting different reinsurance threshold levels for different policies turns out to be complicated. The different threshold levels should be set to correct for the self-selection that a choice of policies would produce; it would take at least a year after the choices were made to determine the expenditure levels of the people who made them. This could lead to delays in setting the threshold levels, and any additional complexity might lead to distrust of the thresholds.

Requiring that policies have equal actuarial value is another way of dealing with differing levels of generosity of policies—but actuarial equivalency will not achieve the transparency objective. Actuarial equivalency means that under actuarial assumptions about the population being covered and prices, one health policy is equal (or greater) in value to another policy even though they may differ in cost sharing required of enrollees or services that are covered. This would encourage people with high likelihoods of using expensive medical care to choose more generous policies—leaving us again with the outcome that more generous policies are more likely to attract people with extremely high costs.

There is a conflict between the desire for transparency in why someone has extremely high medical costs and the wish for choice of policies. The only way to create transparency is to have a standardized policy. Providing choices of policies should be done with the recognition that we are making a trade-off: reducing transparency in exchange for more choices of benefits packages and cost-sharing. Such a trade-off, however, requires that we recognize the potential for gaming and abuse of the program. Program administrators have to be granted the power and resources to investigate possible gaming by the insurers and charges of improper reimbursements. Whether the loss in transparency and the need for close monitoring of expenses submitted for reimbursement are worth the gains from choice of policies is ultimately a political decision. Nonetheless, these trade-offs need to be recognized.

From a practical standpoint, achieving standardization of one, or even several, insurance policies bumps into the fact that states supersede the federal government in regulating insurance products. States determine the standards regarding which medical services will be covered by the health insurance policies sold within their borders. A federal reinsurance program could overturn this, just as the federal government did in 1990 with the Omnibus Budget Reconciliation Act (OBRA '90), which established ten different MediGap policies (or supplemental insurance policies) that can be bought by Medicare beneficiaries. OBRA '90 left it to the states to decide whether all ten MediGap policies or just a subset of them could be sold within their borders. Alternatively, a federal reinsurance program could sidestep the state primacy issue by making the reinsurance available only for insurance policies that cover a specified set of medical services with specified cost-sharing requirements. This would effectively force the states and insurers to converge on one or several standardized insurance policies.

The Need to Restrict Risk Selection Mechanisms   By significantly reducing insurers' risk of covering people with extremely high costs, a government-sponsored reinsurance program will reduce the benefits to insurers of using selection mechanisms. Because it is very difficult to distinguish between people who will have higher-than-average costs and people who will have just-below-average costs, it would cost insurers more than they would gain from continuing to use selection mechanisms.

Nonetheless, some insurers still may believe that they can gain a competitive advantage if they are able to deny coverage to people they believe will have higher-than-average expenses but not extremely high expenses. This raises a question about government leverage. The prime motivation for creating a government-sponsored reinsurance program is that it will enable more people to purchase private insurance. Such a program does this by reducing insurers' risk—by having the government take responsibility for most of the costs of people with extremely high expenses. Under these circumstances, it seems appropriate for the government to restrict insurers' use of selection mechanisms that allow them to deny coverage to some people. In particular, requiring that insurers accept all applicants (guaranteed issue) and renew all existing policies (guaranteed renewal) will greatly reduce the remaining incentives to use selection mechanisms. HIPAA went a long way in this direction by requiring insurers in the small-group market to guarantee-issue any products they offer to all small groups and to guarantee renewal of their products.[10] HIPAA only required insurers in the individual market to guarantee renewal of policies. If the government does not use this leverage, the program will not be able to fully achieve its goal of enabling more people to purchase private coverage.

Require Community Rating of Premiums   Similarly, community rating of premiums by each insurer selling small-group and individual policies will help prevent insurers from discouraging consumers by charging high premiums. Premiums could continue to be set for states, or for substate areas, as they are now, since most insurers operate in limited geographic areas (states or counties). Having community rating of premiums within currently accepted geographic areas also recognizes that there are different reimbursement rates for hospitals and physicians and other medical providers in different parts of the country and that premiums generally reflect these differences.

The need for different premiums for different groups or individuals will be mitigated by the reinsurance program. But just as the government should use its leverage to restrict insurers' use of selection mechanisms, the government also should require community rating of premiums to restrict insurers' use of high premiums that discourage people from purchasing coverage.

Design Issues That Determine Costs

A number of design decisions have a direct bearing on the cost of a government reinsurance program. The threshold level that activates the reinsurance and the fraction of the expenses that the reinsurance would pay for can vary; thus, the total costs will depend on the distribution of medical expenses, the threshold level, and the fractions for the layers of reinsurance that determine how the reinsured expenses will be split between the reinsurance program and the insurers.

Threshold for Reinsurance   The reinsurance program could be set up to cover most of the costs of people whose medical expenses place them in the top 1 percent (or some other percent) of the distribution of expenses. From a practical standpoint, however, it will be easier to announce a threshold level of expenses above which costs in the small-group and individual markets will be eligible for reimbursement each year. This could be done initially by using the Medical Expenditure Panel Survey (MEPS) data to calculate the national distribution of expenses and then the threshold level that marks the top 1 percent. An alternative to using the MEPS would be to collect data from many insurers with large numbers of enrollees and similar benefits packages. This larger sample of medical expenses could yield more information about the medical problems that cause some individuals to incur high costs. If desired, the threshold for the top 1 percent could be set at the state level (or substate area) to account for differences in costs of care across the country.[11] Setting different thresholds would require the gathering of data from many insurers, because the MEPS is not large enough for calculating such state-specific levels.

The threshold does not have to be set at the spending amount that marks the top 1 percent of the distribution of expenses. It could be set to capture whatever percentile is both practical and affordable. Of course, the affordability of the program depends on both the threshold level and the fraction of the expenses above the threshold that the reinsurance will pick up. It is possible to have the same total cost for a program with different combinations of threshold levels and fractions of cost-sharing between the original insurers and the reinsurance program.

From a practical viewpoint, we need to be aware that it would be impossible to have data that are less than two years old for determining the threshold. Insurers do not close a calendar year's medical bills and claims until April 1 of the year following the calendar year. This allows for the processing of bills for care delivered in the last three months of the year. Of course, it will take time beyond April 1 to combine all the insurers' data on their expenditures and audit the data for inconsistencies or errors. Thus, the per-person expenditure data needed for estimating the expenditure distribution will most likely lag two years behind the current year. An estimate of the increase in health expenditures in the interim two-year period will be needed. And the estimate will have to take into account any significant changes in disease patterns or medical treatment protocols.

The Structure of the Layers of Reinsurance and Cost-Sharing   As noted earlier, the overriding principle of reinsurance is that the original insurer should continue to bear the risk for some of the costs of the insured individuals. Reinsurers do not want to encourage originating insurers to stop worrying about people who have high costs.

Private reinsurance for health has become quite sophisticated in structuring cost-sharing between the originating insurer and the reinsurer. A federal reinsurance program for extremely high medical expenses should be similarly sophisticated, with different cost-sharing fractions for each layer of reinsurance. Experts on structuring reinsurance should be involved in the design of the layer and cost-sharing structure. An important goal of the design should be to provide incentives for insurers to manage the care of high-cost people.

The Administration of the Reinsurance Program   There will need to be sufficient funding to administer the program so that insurers are discouraged from engaging in fraud or abuse. We need to be prepared to spend enough money to run the program well. The reinsurance program should be managed by a new office or agency within the U.S. Department of Health and Human Services. The program should have the authority to obtain aggregate data on health care expenditures in the individual and small-group markets across the country in order to set each year's threshold level.

Finally, the administrator of the program must have the authority to audit claims submitted for reinsurance. This is a critical task, since the integrity of the program will depend on reimbursing only the expenses of people with the very highest expenses. The recent financial difficulties and bankruptcies of some of the country's largest auditing firms are pertinent reminders of the importance of strong audits.

Financing Issues

Reinsurance enables insurers to shift risks to the reinsurer in exchange for a set payment. Private-sector reinsurance is generally priced so that the total premium revenues collected over a five-year period equal the amount that would have to be paid if the loss being insured against occurred once in the five-year period. Given this expectation, the purchase of reinsurance does not greatly alter the total amount of premium money that the originating insurer collects. The system is "closed" in that the funds for reimbursing the unlikely risky events come from the originating insurer and the people covered by its policies. The reinsurance simply smooths out the risk. Moreover, the insurer retains strong incentives to continue to use selection mechanisms to avoid covering high-cost people.

A government-sponsored reinsurance program for the small-group and individual insurance markets has different goals than smoothing out risk. The primary goal is to reduce insurers' concerns about adverse selection so that more people can obtain private health insurance. In exchange for taking on the risk of enrolling people with extremely high expenses, the government expects the insurers to reduce their use of selection mechanisms and to lower premiums. Both of these moves will increase the number of people who then purchase private insurance.

Note that these moves depend on an infusion of new funds into insurance markets. If insurers have to pay for the reinsurance, the situation reverts to a "closed" system in terms of the financing, and the incentives to continue the use of selection mechanisms remain. Because the insurers would need to pay for the reinsurance out of premiums, they would not substantially lower their premiums.

Thus, a government-sponsored reinsurance program has to contain new funding if it is to succeed in reducing insurers' use of selection mechanisms and lowering premiums. Given that the events that cause people to incur the top 1 percent of medical expenses are random and any of us could be struck by such a catastrophe, it is appropriate that the reinsurance be financed by as large a share of the population as possible. Two ways of financing the program meet these criteria. One is to rely on the tax base for general revenue funds for the government, including personal income taxes and corporate income taxes. The second is to take advantage of exceptional sources of funds, like the tobacco settlement funds, or to create a new tax specifically dedicated to the program.[12] In the current period of high federal budget deficits, the idea of using general tax revenues to pay for reinsurance may not seem to make sense. But with the rising number of middle-class uninsured, it is likely that Americans would support a program that enables their family and friends to purchase private health insurance. Without such a program, personal bankruptcies, hospital bad debt, and charity care will all rise significantly—and everyone pays for these outcomes.

The high federal budget deficits will cause some people to call for funding the program by assessing a fee on all insurance policies and companies that self-fund their employees' health care. Such a fee would be passed along to all the people currently covered by private health insurance—just like a tax. However, the changes in employer-employee relationships that have increased the number of "1099" workers, many of whom work without health benefits, suggest that the number of people for whom this fee might apply is already shrinking. Further, such fees will raise the price of insurance, which will cause more firms to drop insurance benefits and reduce the likelihood that individuals will buy coverage. Finally, requiring insurers to pay for the reinsurance program indirectly through such a fee returns us to the problem of the closed system.[13]

The financing of the reinsurance program will require a strong commitment to using public funds to improve the ability of people to obtain private health insurance. Too many younger adults age twenty-five to forty-four are uninsured and have job prospects that do not suggest they will gain employer-sponsored coverage in the future. Moreover, since one in ten working-age middle-class adults is now uninsured, middle-class families are increasingly concerned about their children's ability to obtain health insurance when they finish college. A government-sponsored reinsurance program for the small-group and individual markets would go a long way to allay these concerns.

ESTIMATING THE COST OF A FEDERAL REINSURANCE PROGRAM

Depending on the extent of the high-cost expenses covered, a federal reinsurance program for the small-group and individual insurance markets will cost between $5 billion and $20 billion per year. The cost estimates vary so much because they depend on the design of the program—the threshold level that activates the reinsurance, the cost-sharing required of the insurers for different layers of reinsurance, and how much premiums will decline as a result of the reinsurance program. Assuming that premiums decline significantly, we should expect the demand for individual and small-group health insurance to grow. A sophisticated simulation model, such as that used by the Congressional Budget Office or those used by research organizations, such as the Lewin Group and the Urban Institute, is needed to estimate the costs of the program.

Two Urban Institute researchers, Linda Blumberg and John Holahan, estimated the costs of several variations of a federal reinsurance plan.[14] They used the MEPS data from 1998 to 2000 and did not specify any actuarial equivalent of a standardized benefits policy. One problem with using the MEPS data is that the sample does not include many people with individual (nongroup) coverage. In one case, Blumberg and Holahan used a $50,000 threshold to activate the reinsurance and restricted their estimates to people who worked for small firms (defined as fewer than one hundred employees) and had employer-sponsored coverage. The simulation had only one layer of reinsurance, but they varied the fraction of costs that the government would pay for expenses above the threshold. If the government paid 75 percent of the expenses above $50,000 for these people, the cost to the government was estimated to be $5.2 billion per year (in 2004 dollars). If the government paid 90 percent of the expenses above the threshold, the annual cost to the government was estimated to be $6.2 billion. These estimates are important for telling us what the costs might be with 1998 to 2000 enrollments in small-group and individual insurance. As Blumberg and Holahan acknowledge, however, the estimates do not adjust for behavioral responses to the program. For example, their estimates do not tell us what the costs might be if more people were to buy coverage in the small-group or individual markets as a result of reduced premiums brought about by the reinsurance.

Blumberg and Holahan, joined by other researchers at the Urban Institute and Alan Weil of the National Academy of State Health Policy, also estimated the costs of a reinsurance program that is part of their proposal for reducing the uninsured population in Massachusetts.[15] That proposal is the basis of legislation that was being taken very seriously by the Massachusetts House and Senate in November 2005, and some version of it was expected to be enacted. Blumberg, Holahan, and their colleagues proposed that the state establish a reinsurance pool that would reimburse insurers for 75 percent of the annual expenses above $35,000 (in 2005 dollars) incurred by persons covered in the individual and small-group markets. Firms with fewer than one hundred employees would be eligible to purchase coverage in the small-group market or through a new purchasing pool that would be open to individuals (and their families) and small employers. Insurers would not have to offer policies through the pool, but there would be strong incentives for them to do so. The reinsurance would apply to policies purchased through the pool or in the individual and small-group markets. Blumberg, Holahan, and their colleagues estimate that the annual cost of the reinsurance pool would be $446 million if the state maintains the current voluntary system of purchasing health insurance. If a requirement that individuals purchase coverage were included, the cost of the reinsurance would rise to $484 million, and if a requirement that employers with ten or more employees sponsor coverage also were included, the cost of the reinsurance would be $632 million (in 2005 dollars). In 2005 about 270,000 people were estimated to have individual coverage in Massachusetts; under the proposal, this number would almost double to 536,000 people.

The Lewin Group, led by John Sheils, provided estimates of the costs and effects of 2004 Democratic presidential candidate John Kerry's health plan.[16] The reinsurance part of the Kerry plan called for the government to pick up 75 percent of medical expenses of employees with annual costs above $30,000 (starting in 2006). The reinsurance was not restricted to the small-group or individual markets, so many more people would have been eligible for it.[17] Sheils and his colleagues estimated that the reinsurance part of the Kerry proposal would cost $51.1 billion in 2006 and $725.7 billion over the ten-year period of 2006 to 2015 (both figures in 2004 dollars). In comparing this cost estimate to those of Blumberg and Holahan, it is important to distinguish between estimates that include large employers and those that are just for small firms and individuals. The Kerry plan did not call for reinsurance for small employers and individuals—they were to be given tax credits to purchase coverage through a pool within the Federal Employees Health Benefits Program (FEHBP). Also, the Lewin Group made some assumptions about how people and employers would respond to the tax credits and about the expansion of Medicaid that Blumberg and Holahan did not. These assumptions about behavioral responses seem reasonable, but as Sheils and his colleagues are careful to note, people may not respond as expected.

My own rough estimate is that a government-sponsored reinsurance program restricted to the small-group and individual insurance markets could cost $18.5 billion to $19.5 billion per year (in 2005 dollars).[18] This calculation is based on estimates of the number of people with small-group coverage and the number with individual coverage, a threshold level that defines the top 1 percent of the population ($50,000 in 2005), and government cost-sharing of 85 to 90 percent of costs above the threshold. This estimate does not account for the expected growth in the number of people who would find it easier and cheaper to obtain coverage in these markets. Like the estimates by Blumberg and Holahan and by Lewin, my calculation has many caveats and relies on simplifying assumptions. A microsimulation model should be used to arrive at a more sophisticated estimate. A microsimulation model also could be used to show how different threshold levels and cost-sharing requirements across differently defined layers of expenses might affect the distribution of expenses between the insurers and the reinsurance program.

The bottom line about the cost of a reinsurance program is that it depends on the scope of the program. As these cost estimates illustrate, if the reinsurance program is available to insurers of large employers as well as in the small-group and individual insurance markets, the costs will be substantially higher. Since our interest is primarily in making small-group and individual insurance coverage more widely available, the estimates of $5 billion to $20 billion per year for reinsuring these markets are plausible starting points. For comparison, the cost of eliminating the estate tax has been estimated to be about $1 trillion over the first ten years of extending it (2012 to 2021).[19] And FEMA spent more than $5.2 billion in Florida as of May 2005 for the recovery efforts from the four hurricanes in 2004.[20]

BENEFITS OF A GOVERNMENT-SPONSORED REINSURANCE PROGRAM

A government-sponsored reinsurance program would confer very large benefits in exchange for its costs:

- Premiums in the small-group and individual markets would decline, enabling more people to buy insurance.

- Unnecessary medical expenses would be restrained.

- Such a program would create the right incentives for insurers to reduce their use of selection mechanisms.

- Private insurance markets would be bolstered.

Lower Premiums

The fact that the top 1 percent of the population accounts for about 28 percent of all medical expenses suggests that premiums would be lowered substantially in the small-group and individual markets. Not all of the 28 percent of expenses will be covered by the reinsurance since it does not pay for expenses below the threshold, nor for some fraction of the expenses above the threshold. At the same time, premiums reflect insurers' risk of costs, and insurers are very averse to the risk of extremely high costs. The reinsurance program might therefore induce insurers to lower their premiums by more than the percentage of expenses that the reinsurance will cover.[21] Reduced premiums would make health insurance affordable for many currently uninsured people. Lower premiums are essential for making health insurance affordable to younger adults and healthy people who now do not buy health insurance because they feel that the premiums are expensive relative to their likely needs for care. Attracting more such people to the market also will keep premiums lower.

Restraints on Unnecessary Medical Expenses

More attention will be focused on people whose care or diagnoses appear to be potentially very expensive. Often people with extremely high medical costs have received poorly managed care, which contributes to the high costs.[22] While profit incentives ought to inspire insurers to assign managers to coordinate the care of people whose claims exceed some dollar amount or who have specific diagnoses, many insurers do not do this. If the government were the reinsurer in these markets, it could require insurers to institute management programs or face higher cost-sharing.

The Right Incentives for Insurers to Reduce Their Use of Risk Selection

The attraction of a government-sponsored reinsurance program is that it directly addresses insurers' fears of adverse selection in the small-group and individual markets. When most of the highest costs are shifted to a reinsurance program, it greatly reduces incentives for insurers to use selection mechanisms. A reinsurance program reduces the risk of extremely high-cost people in the small-group and individual markets to a level comparable for large groups. At that point, the benefits from using the mechanisms will be less than the costs, and insurers will reduce their use. Note too that when the risk of paying for the top 1 percent of people is shifted, well-run insurers should be able to cope with the expenses of other enrollees in their estimates of expected total expenditures. The expenditure threshold for people being in the top 1 percent was $50,000 in 2005. The threshold was $30,000 for people in the top 2 percent, and it was $15,000 for the top 5 percent. The threshold for people in the top 20 percent is $4,000.[23] These numbers suggest that insurers can bear the risk for the costs of people who are in the top 20 percent but not the top 1 percent. Thus, spending resources on trying to identify people who might be in the top 20 percent is more costly than the potential benefits.

Reinsurance contains a key incentive for insurers to reduce their use of selection mechanisms: it is based on people's actual expenditures. Because reinsurance does not rely on prospective models of a person's probable costs, it removes the incentive to try to predict whether someone's medical care will be extremely high-cost. In contrast, high-risk pools and assessment programs depend on models that estimate a person's likely medical expenses. As we noted in chapter 5, these models are only predictive—and to date they have provided poor estimates of a person's expenses.

A Boost to Private Insurance Markets

Government-sponsored reinsurance is a simple concept, even though one can become absorbed in technical details about how to design it. The beauty of reinsurance is that it would strengthen the ability of the private market to meet the insurance needs of the increasing number of people who do not have access to employer-sponsored health insurance. Of the current 45.5 million uninsured, at least one-third—those in the middle class—would be helped by a reinsurance program. They have high enough incomes to afford private insurance if the premiums were reduced and insurers did not select against them. In addition, single people and people without children who have incomes below the middle-class threshold of $44,400 but above $35,000 might also purchase coverage if the premiums were reduced substantially. Thus, the total number of uninsured people who might become insured if a reinsurance program were in place could be closer to half of the uninsured.

The costs of a reinsurance program—estimated at between $5 billion and $20 billion per year—are a challenge. These costs need to be compared with the current tax-favored treatment of employer-sponsored health insurance and individual insurance purchased by the self-employed. The tax code treatment of employer-sponsored health insurance and the self-employed's purchase of coverage were recently estimated to cost the U.S. Treasury about $140 billion.[24] Since approximately 165 to 170 million people under the age of 65 have either employer-sponsored coverage or are self-employed and purchase their own coverage, this tax subsidy equals $825 to $850 per person covered. If 15 to 20 million uninsured people can be covered by insurance because of a reinsurance program that costs $15 to $20 billion, the subsidy per person amounts to about $1,000. The cost of the reinsurance program would be of the same order of magnitude as the current subsidization of employer-group coverage and the self-employed's purchase of individual coverage.

The reinsurance program would enable the small-group and individual insurance markets to expand so that more people could have private health insurance. The appendix contains four examples of government assuming responsibility for the worst risks in certain situations, thereby enabling private-sector markets to flourish and more people to have the benefits provided by the markets. Bolstering the private market for health insurance surely is consistent with these precedents.

PART III

Getting from Here to There

Chapter 7

The Need for a New Health Insurance Structure

T he American system of health insurance is in trouble. Since at least the 1950s, the country has had a health insurance structure that relies on the vast majority of people having insurance as part of employment compensation. The expectation has been that as the economy grew and the country prospered, more and more workers and their families would gain employer-sponsored coverage. After 1965, anyone who could not work would get help from Medicare or Medicaid, filling out the rest of the system. Changes in the economy and in employer-employee relationships over the last twenty-five years, however, have upset that expectation. It is no longer the case that good jobs automatically come with health insurance as a fringe benefit. The new reality is that many employers want to get out from beneath the post–World War II expectation that they will provide health insurance as part of compensation. They already have reduced their role as the source of health insurance for most Americans. If we want to retain a voluntary private health insurance system, we need to create a new structure that enables people who work in small firms, are self-employed, or work as nonpermanent employees to obtain affordable insurance.

EMPLOYERS WANT LESS RESPONSIBILITY FOR HEALTH INSURANCE

The primary reason employers want to reduce their assumed responsibility for health insurance is its cost. Annual premiums for employer-sponsored insurance averaged $4,020 for single coverage and $10,884 for family coverage in 2005, a 9.2 percent increase from the premiums a year earlier.[1] Even with employees paying on average 16 percent of the cost of single coverage and 26 percent of family coverage, the total costs are significant.[2] Just as important, the costs of health insurance have been rising much faster than the rate of worker productivity or inflation. Between 2000 and 2005, health insurance premiums on average went up 73 percent.[3] During this same time, the consumer price index (a measure of consumer prices for a wide range of goods and services) increased 15 percent, and between 2000 and 2004 (the most recent year), worker productivity in the nonfarm business sector rose 16.6 percent.[4] The difference between the rates of growth in worker productivity and health insurance premiums is not sustainable.

Similar large differences between rates of increase in premiums and inflation and productivity existed in the late 1980s and early 1990s. Employers tried to slow the rate of increase in health insurance costs then by shifting employees to managed care plans. They succeeded mainly in altering the types of health insurance most workers had. Among full-time workers in the private sector with employer-sponsored health insurance, 74 percent were enrolled in fee-for-service, indemnity insurance plans in 1989–90; by 2000, 91 percent of such workers were enrolled in HMOs or preferred provider organizations (PPOs).[5] For a short time, this seemed to have an effect on the rate of increase in premiums. Between 1989 and 1996, health insurance premium increases slowed considerably. Starting in 1997, however, premiums began to grow at increasingly higher rates, peaking in 2003 with an annual rate of 13.9 percent and then growing by 11.2 percent in 2004 and 9.2 percent in 2005.[6] The slower annual rates of increase in premiums in 2004 and 2005 reflect the shifting of more out-of-pocket costs onto enrollees when they use medical care.

In hindsight, it seems clear that managed care was not the sole reason for the decline in the growth of health insurance premiums between 1989 and 1996. Medicare was paying hospitals relatively generously during the mid-1990s, enabling them to negotiate lower reimbursement rates with large insurers for their enrollees. However, the Balanced Budget Act of 1997 lowered the rate of previously projected increases in Medicare payments to hospitals and physicians. Hospitals in particular began to demand higher reimbursements from insurers for non-Medicare patients after 1998. A large number of new pharmaceuticals also started coming to market in 1996. The rate of increase in prescription drug spending has been a major driver of increased health care spending since then.[7] Employers and health policymakers were not fully aware of the impacts of the decline in Medicare payments and the new drugs coming to market in the late 1990s, a time when the economy was booming and employers were feeling the effects of tight labor markets. Employee outcries over managed care plans' restricted choice of physicians and hospitals led to the loosening of restrictions on eligible providers—just when providers were demanding higher fees and prescribing the newly available prescription drugs more often.

The rapid increase in health insurance premiums after 1997 coincided with increased competitive pressures due to globalization and the loosening of trade barriers. In particular, the explosive growth in Internet capabilities enabled companies to exchange information and coordinate orders and supplies much more easily. This added to competitive pressures by expanding the sites where goods and services could be produced. By the late 1990s, the rapid increases in health insurance costs, and the lack of any obvious way to control that growth, were focusing employers' attention on the need to reduce their role in the American system of health insurance coverage. The situation became more urgent after 2000. Between 2000 and 2004 (the most recent year for which we have data), national health expenditures increased by 38 percent. Although spending growth slowed in 2004, the 7.9 percent increase between 2002 and 2003 is still higher than the slow-growth years between 1993 and 2000.[8]

In the last five years, increasing globalization has increased competitive pressure, from firms both here and abroad, on all kinds of service companies, not just on manufacturing companies. To succeed in this new era, American businesses and employees need to maintain high productivity and keep their labor costs as low as they can. One way to control such costs is to focus on core business activities and outsource everything that is not essential—in other words, to shed employees who are not involved in core business activities.

Competition increases the pressure on companies to respond swiftly to changes in demand for their products. Companies' demand for business services and consumers' demand for services such as entertainment, restaurants, and landscaping, and even for health-related services is sensitive to economic fluctuations. As we saw in chapter 3, many service companies prefer to work with independent contractors or to hire temporary workers when the demand for their services grows; and then if demand shrinks, they can reduce their labor costs more quickly. It is almost a mantra now that companies must be nimble in expanding and shrinking production—and therefore employment—in response to shifts in demand for their goods or services. Overlaying this state of affairs is the fact that new service companies are typically small firms. As we saw in chapter 2 with James, the entrepreneur, start-ups and new small businesses usually do not have the cash flow to provide health insurance to employees. Many of the lower-wage uninsured workers in the service sector are employed in small and new companies.

As a result of all of these trends—outsourcing, greater use of nonpermanent employees, the increase in employment in smaller companies—a much higher fraction of workers are outside the system of large employer–sponsored health insurance than was the case twenty-five years ago. Almost 44 percent of private-sector workers are employed at establishments with fewer than fifty people. Low-wage workers between twenty-three and sixty-four years old are now faced with a one-in-three chance of being uninsured. These changes also have increased the chances that a middle-class worker will be uninsured—one in ten now lack health insurance.

President Bush's use of the "ownership society" theme in the 2004 election campaign shifted attention away from workers losing access to employer-sponsored coverage. He tapped into a popular sentiment with the phrase: it conjures up a vision of rugged individualism that is ever popular in American lore, as well as a vision of entrepreneurial individuals who gain more of the profits generated by the economy. The phrase also plays on the commonly held notion that one should take responsibility for one's own life rather than rely on government programs. Implicitly, the "ownership society" places responsibility for obtaining health insurance (as well as saving for retirement and other activities) on individuals. The result is that people who have been forced to become independent contractors or nonpermanent employees, as well as people who have become small-business owners or self-employed, now find it even more difficult to appeal for help in obtaining coverage: such appeals would be out of step with the spirit of independence implicitly valued in the "ownership society."

YOUNGER AGE COHORTS ARE AT RISK

The people who have been most affected by the changes in the economy and in employer-employee relationships are younger adults between the ages of twenty-five and forty-four. In 2004 more than 18 million of them were uninsured. A significant minority of these people are earning middle-class incomes.

The fact that high fractions of younger adults are uninsured is sobering. More than one in four adults age twenty-five to thirty-four and almost one in five adults age thirty-five to forty-four are uninsured. One in three nineteen- to twenty-four-year-olds also is uninsured. These high proportions are a concern for several reasons. Because these are the age groups most likely to be parents of young children, there are implications for the health care of children. There is some evidence that when parents do not have health insurance, they do not bring their children in for timely medical care.[9] The disenfranchisement of large numbers of the younger population from the system of health insurance is a significant difference from twenty-five years ago. It is more difficult to reach people without health insurance who have risk factors for diseases before the disease strikes and the costs become quite high. Finally, when this many people who are very likely to be healthy stay out of the health insurance system, the insurance risk pools contain a higher mix of risks than would otherwise be the case. Viable insurance systems need risks to be pooled among people of many different ages. If we do not bring more younger adults into the system, it may collapse.

Younger adults already are facing unprecedented pressures on their incomes. They can expect to pay higher taxes and/or receive reduced benefits under Medicare and Social Security. Many are heavily in debt for college expenses, and the costs of housing relative to average incomes for people in these age groups are forcing many to forgo homeownership. These financial pressures may be part of what is behind the recent rapid increase in the median age at first marriage. Sam and James both mentioned that, among their friends, not having health insurance made them wonder whether they were ready for marriage. For some younger adults, having health insurance may be a sign of being able to financially support a marriage in a way that was not even a consideration a decade ago.

The fact that younger adults who are twenty-five to forty-four years of age (as well as very young adults age nineteen to twenty-four) are most likely to be uninsured points up a vicious cycle. When high fractions of younger adults do not buy health insurance, the risk level of health insurance pools is higher than it would be if they were covered. Insurers respond by setting high premiums, particularly because in this situation they fear adverse selection. This leads to a catch-22: healthy younger people believe the higher premiums are far above what their health care costs might be, so they do not buy insurance; the people who do purchase coverage are indeed higher-risk people and have greater expenses, so insurers raise premiums; healthy young people decide again that the premiums are too expensive, and so forth.

The challenge is to make it much easier for younger adults to obtain health insurance coverage. Many younger workers are low-wage workers and need to be subsidized if they are to afford coverage. But since so many younger uninsured adults are working in small firms and as independent contractors or temporary employees, the small-group and individual insurance markets must become more affordable and accessible. At the same time, more efforts need to be made to impress upon younger adults why they need to value health insurance, especially in the changed economy that we are now living in.

People in their late forties to early sixties make up the second age group that has been significantly affected by the economic changes of the last twenty-five years. More than ten million uninsured adults are in this group. They face somewhat different problems in obtaining health insurance. Many lost their access to employer-sponsored health insurance when they were forced out of manufacturing jobs and into service-sector jobs. Many work in small firms or as self-employed or temporary workers and do not have access to group coverage. But they differ from the younger adults in two ways. First, they are old enough for health problems to begin to show up. For example, heart disease, cancer, gynecological problems, and arthritis are much more prevalent among people over the age of fifty. Second, the higher prevalence of diseases and medical conditions among middle-age adults causes insurers to charge them higher premiums and, as we saw in chapter 4, to try to screen out anyone whom they suspect will have very high expenses. If middle-aged (or younger) adults are diagnosed with almost any medical condition, it is difficult for them to obtain health insurance. Thus, they are at a disadvantage that even a middle-class income cannot overcome. Those with low incomes also need subsidies to be able to afford the premiums that reflect their higher probability of having above-average expenses.

ACTIONS TO INCREASE ACCESS TO HEALTH INSURANCE

Actions along three lines would help the 36 million uninsured adults between the ages of nineteen and sixty-four gain access to health insurance:

- Provide incentives for small firms to offer health insurance coverage to workers and independent contractors who work with the firm. Included in the incentives should be financial assistance for small employers with low profit margins and subsidies to low-wage workers.

- Work with professional or occupational associations to obtain group insurance policies for members who are self-employed and work as consultants, independent contractors, and freelancers. Currently, there are some state-level professional associations that help members obtain coverage (for example, architects and dentists), but other associations (such as the National Writers Union) have had problems retaining insurers willing to provide policies.

- Increase access to individual insurance markets, especially for middle-aged adults and people who have had episodes of chronic conditions, and provide subsidies to people whose premiums would exceed between 5 and 10 percent of their income.

Actions to reduce premiums and increase access to insurance through small employers, professional associations, and individual markets would offer significant help to the vast majority of uninsured adults. Since many of these adults are parents of the 9.1 million uninsured children, these moves also would provide coverage to many of the uninsured children.

Government-Sponsored Reinsurance and Earlier Precedents

These measures cannot succeed, however, without a fourth. Insurer concerns over adverse selection and the risk of covering people with extremely high medical costs must be reduced. Unless this happens, insurers will not significantly cut their use of selection mechanisms or substantially reduce premiums. The most efficient way to reduce insurers' risk of covering people with very high costs is to have a government-sponsored reinsurance program. All of us would help pay for the costs of the few people who, by random bad luck, were extremely sick in a particular year.

The idea that private insurance markets can exist and operate more efficiently if the government takes responsibility for the worst risks is not new; there is a rich history of precedents (described more fully in the appendix).[10] In many cases, without government acting as the reinsurer and backstopping the market, we would not have private insurance markets for lower levels of risk. In turn, those private markets greatly increase the efficiency with which our economy operates because they enable people and companies to pay to reduce risks significantly.

Among the many precedents of government assuming the worst risks, two are striking: the catastrophe reinsurance market and the secondary mortgage market. It is interesting to note that in 1954 both of these markets were given boosts by decisions that increased the federal government's responsibility for identifying risk by geographic area. The catastrophe reinsurance market is integrally related to flood loss insurance; in the early 1950s there was a strong push to create flood loss insurance.[11] One of the key impediments was the lack of knowledge about flood risks in different locales around the country. There was a proposal that the federal government lead the effort to identify the risks of flood loss in communities and small geographic areas of the country. It was a novel idea to use federal powers to accomplish what individual states had not been able or willing to do in a consistent manner. In a coincidence of timing, 1954 was also the year when the ability of the country to increase funds for home mortgages was greatly expanded by the rechartering of the Federal National Mortgage Association (FNMA, or Fannie Mae). FNMA was established in 1938 to create a secondary mortgage market with mortgages guaranteed by the Federal Housing Authority (FHA). The new charter of FNMA created restrictions on maximum insurable loan amounts, which varied with the geographic region in which the loan was made. Thus, by 1954, in two quite different situations, the powers of the federal government were being used to identify risks by geographic locale.

It cannot be a coincidence that, also in early 1954, the Eisenhower administration proposed the health reinsurance bill (83 HR 8356).[12] Title II of the proposed legislation called for the federal government to determine the incidence of various diseases and identify sources of sickness in the population. Clearly, there were people in Washington who understood that to boost insurance markets the risks to be covered had to be identified first—and then perhaps the federal government could assume the worst risks in the market.

The federal government's interactions with catastrophe reinsurance and the secondary mortgage market are revealing examples of the role the federal government can play in markets to reduce risk to a level acceptable to the private sector. Four other government programs, three at the federal level and one at the state level, also involve the government acting as reinsurer. At the federal level, Medicare has provided a system of payments to hospitals for very expensive cases (known as outliers) since 1983. Medicare pays a hospital for 80 percent of its costs above the threshold that defines an outlier case. The Medicare prescription drug benefit (Medicare Part D) established risk corridors such that if an insurer has an individual with expenses in excess of a complicated formula of costs, the Centers for Medicare and Medicaid Services provide a reinsurance payment.[13] The primary risk in the Part D benefit is due to potential adverse selection. Prescription drug use is relatively predictable: people who have chronic conditions are more likely to use prescription drugs than those who do not. Thus, without some protection from the risk that a disproportionate share of enrollees would be people with high costs, it was not clear that many insurers would enter the market and sell prescription drug policies to seniors. By the time the enrollment period began, however, more than forty options were available to beneficiaries in most states.

The third federal program with reinsurance is a result of the Terrorism Risk Insurance Act of 2002. The Terrorism Act calls for the government to pay 90 percent of the costs of any terrorist attack after losses exceed $10 billion. As a result, insurance companies are willing to sell liability insurance for losses due to terrorist attacks.

At the state level, New York State's Healthy New York program was the first in the country to rely on an excess-of-loss reinsurance design. Healthy New York is for individual workers and sole proprietors with incomes below 250 percent of the poverty level as well as for workers in small firms where at least 30 percent of the workers earn less than $32,000 per year.[14] The premiums are implicitly subsidized by reinsurance funded by the state's tobacco settlement funds. The reinsurance reimburses insurers for 90 percent of a person's annual expenses between $5,000 and $75,000; expenses above $75,000 are not covered by the reinsurance. As a result of the reinsurance, Healthy New York premiums are about half those in the standard individual (direct-pay) market in New York. Since Healthy New York began operating in 2001, more than 200,000 people have purchased coverage through it, and more than 102,000 people were actively enrolled in it as of the end of October 2005.[15]

Linking government-sponsored reinsurance to the three measures to expand use of the small-group and individual markets and of professional associations has precedents. Even more important, the combination of measures provides an opportunity to help and ease the anxieties of a growing number of uninsured workers (and their families) as we make the transition to a very changed economy and workplace.

THE URGENT NEED TO RESTRUCTURE OUR HEALTH INSURANCE SYSTEM

We are on the brink of enormous change in employer roles in sponsoring and paying for fringe benefits. The fifty-year old implicit compact between workers and big business that precluded any need for a national health insurance system is breaking. The recent changes in the economy and in employer-employee relationships are not going to be reversed. Even when the economy finally recovers from the mild recession we have been in since 2001, we are not returning to the world of large manufacturing companies and relatively modest levels of international trade. Employers want to reduce their role in organizing and paying for health insurance, and that new reality is already forcing changes in our system of private and public coverage. These changes have left 45.5 million people outside of the U.S. system of health insurance.

The Risks Involved in Doing Nothing

The lack of attention to people who have lost access to employer-sponsored coverage over the last decade suggests that many policymakers believe the uninsured, especially the middle-class uninsured, can obtain coverage as individuals or as members of small groups in the private markets. But as we saw in earlier chapters, this view is incorrect. With their concerns about adverse selection, insurers avoid applicants they expect to have high expenses. Further, because the risks of covering extremely high-cost people are greater in the individual and small-group markets, the premiums per person are substantially higher than for large groups. The high premiums discourage small employers that want to sponsor health insurance for their employees, and the recent annual increases of 30 percent and more for small-group premiums simply scare small businesses. Many have stopped covering their employees or have altered their relationships with people who work with them. Middle-class people who are not turned down by insurers nevertheless often cannot afford to buy coverage with premiums as high as they are in the individual market, and low-income people do not even bother to apply.

As more workers lose access to employer-sponsored coverage, adverse selection in the individual and small-group markets is likely to grow. Healthier people with middle-class incomes will opt to be uninsured rather than pay 15 percent or more of their incomes for coverage. We are already seeing this with people like Sam and Paul. It is unrealistic to expect that most people who lose access to employer-sponsored coverage will be able to buy their own insurance in the private markets. It is even more unrealistic to expect low-income people to be able to buy private policies. They simply do not have the means to pay deductibles of $2,000 to $5,000, plus monthly premiums of $200 and more for single coverage and $700 and up for family coverage. Seventy percent of the uninsured are in poor or low-income families; they need large subsidies to purchase private insurance, or they need reasonably priced public-private insurance programs. We can expect the number of low-income uninsured to increase as competitive pressures from foreign companies with low-wage workforces compel employers to reduce their health care coverage or outsource work to small companies that do not offer coverage.

Simply standing by and doing nothing as employers reduce their role in our health insurance system will lead to health and social calamities. A large underclass of citizens without health insurance risk not receiving appropriate medical care or running up large debts to pay for the care they do get. This has particular implications in a globalized world where old and new infectious diseases travel easily and swiftly in and out of the United States. Infectious disease experts believe it is only a matter of time before the avian flu virus mutates to affect humans and cause a flu pandemic, for example.[16] The SARS episode two years ago is another warning sign of the potential for new infectious diseases to spread quickly. Even old diseases like tuberculosis have mutated into drug-resistant strains that can be controlled only if infected people obtain prompt and consistent medical care. Uninsured people are far less likely to obtain such care, posing a threat to all of us.

Many uninsured will be bitterly disillusioned by their inability to obtain health insurance through either a job or the individual market. This outcome contains the seeds for a social disaster, especially with the increasing number of reports on links between disparities in quality of care and types of health insurance or none at all.[17] A large group of citizens without health insurance can only exacerbate class distinctions in our society, distinctions we Americans have tried hard to reduce for half a century.

A Role for Government-Sponsored Reinsurance

In designing a new structure of health insurance, the critical points to consider are whether we want to continue to have a voluntary system of health insurance and whether we want to rely on private health insurance for a majority of the population. If the answer to both is yes, then we need to address insurers' concerns about extremely high-cost people. Any new design that has almost everyone buying their own individual policies or is a combination of employer-sponsored groups and individual policies will fail unless insurers know that the very highest-cost people do not pose significant risks to their business.

The best way to address insurer concerns about adverse selection is to have the federal government assume this risk with a reinsurance program. With such a program in place, all of us would help pay for the costs of the few people who, by random bad luck, are extremely sick in a particular year. This would reduce insurers' incentives to use selection mechanisms to restrict coverage, and it would reduce premiums so that more people would buy coverage. A government-sponsored reinsurance program would force the pooling of everyone's low-probability risks from random but individually catastrophic events—which is what insurance is all about.

Appendix

Precedents for Government Assuming Responsibility for the Worst Risks

A s noted in chapter 7, there is a rich history of precedents in the United States for government, at both the federal and state level, taking responsibility for the worst risks in a variety of situations.[1] As a result of government assuming the very high risks, private insurance markets exist for lower levels of risk and other types of markets have been able to grow. For example, because the government assumes the worst mortgage risks, the secondary mortgage market is thriving, enabling a high proportion of the population to own their homes. Our economy operates far more efficiently because people and businesses can smooth out risks through insurance markets and financial markets. The same could be true with health insurance: the small-group and individual insurance markets could cover more people and operate more efficiently if the federal government were to assume the risk of extremely high-cost people by providing reinsurance to these markets.

CATASTROPHE REINSURANCE

Insurers that sell catastrophe insurance are able to buy catastrophe reinsurance because of the history of government reimbursement of large fractions of the costs of catastrophes. Indeed, the creation of the Federal Emergency Management Agency in 1978 formally acknowledged the federal government's role in disaster recovery.

The Growth of Federal Responsibility

The prevailing attitude from the late 1700s until the 1930s was that the private sector should assist victims of natural disasters. During the 1800s and through the first quarter of the twentieth century, the federal government provided disaster relief, but it was relatively rare.[2] The dominant political attitude was that governmental support was paternalistic and detrimental to the "national character" (from President Cleveland's statement vetoing a disaster relief bill in 1887).[3] David Moss marks the 1927 "great flood" of the Mississippi River as the beginning of a change in this attitude.[4] The federal government and the American National Red Cross carried out a large-scale relief effort after the 1927 flood, and even though that effort covered only about 13 percent of the total estimated damages, it received widespread publicity. Secretary of Commerce Herbert Hoover was put in charge of the relief effort, and he brought along reporters to write about the flooding and subsequent government help.[5] The use of motion pictures to provide news to the public was still a new phenomenon in 1928, and the flood provided great photo opportunities. Five motion picture companies filmed its devastating effects and the relief efforts. Their short news films, shown before feature movies in theaters across America, brought the enormity of the devastation directly to people in a way that had not been possible before.[6]

The dramatic change in attitude toward the federal government's role in the aftermath of floods is evident in the change in the amounts of money appropriated by Congress in 1927 and 1928. In 1927 Congress appropriated $10 million to help with the great flood relief effort; one year later it authorized close to $300 million for flood control projects in the floodplain of the lower Mississippi River.[7] Note that the money for flood control projects was not for disaster relief; it was for flood control to try to prevent future disasters. In subsequent years, the federal government became increasingly involved in flood control. The Flood Control Acts of 1936 and 1938 authorized federal financing of the dams and reservoirs that today are found all over the country. Prior to these acts, the federal government funded large-scale civil engineering projects only if state and local governments also contributed funds or land.

During the two decades after World War II, the federal role in disasters shifted again—relief became a central mission. In 1950 Congress passed the Disaster Relief Act, which created a permanent relief fund and gave the president the power to decide whether a disaster qualifies for federal aid. Even so, when Hurricane Carol ravaged parts of the East Coast in 1953, Red Cross spending still surpassed federal spending. By 1965, however, total federal disaster aid had been eight times that of the Red Cross for the 1964 Alaskan earthquake, flooding in Washington and Oregon, and damage along the Gulf Coast in 1965.[8] This change in the balance of federal and private relief payments reflects the expansion during the 1960s of the types of damages and economic losses that were eligible for federal flood disaster funds: damaged higher education buildings, removal of debris from private property (not just from government properties), and unemployment compensation, temporary housing, and food coupons for victims.[9]

In 1968 Congress passed the National Flood Insurance Act, which created the National Flood Insurance Program (NFIP). The NFIP marks a turning point in cooperative efforts between the government and the private sector to establish an insurance market. In the early 1950s, a number of policy analysts as well as members of Congress tried to encourage the creation of an insurance market for flood losses, since it was not available as part of homeowner and factory-owner general property and casualty policies.[10] As Edward Pasterick says, "This was primarily because of the catastrophic nature of flooding and the insurers' inability to develop an actuarial rate structure that could adequately reflect the risk to which flood-prone properties were exposed."[11] For a private market in flood insurance to succeed, these risks had to be identified for all the different geographic areas. There was general agreement that private insurers could not map the risks; insurers or even a consortium of insurers could not afford to conduct such studies.[12] The Army Corps of Engineers or another federally organized effort would be needed to conduct hydrological studies to identify the nature and extent of the risk of flooding in various areas.[13] Nonetheless, it was not until the NFIP was created in 1968 that the federal effort to identify flood risks was finally authorized.[14]

Along with the risk identification effort, the NFIP called for the development of a private insurance market for flood insurance. The original structure for this did not work well, and by 1977 the federal government had made it an all-federal program. In 1983 a restructured federal-private flood insurance program was unveiled. Private insurers were brought into the NFIP through what is called the write-your-own (WYO) program: insurers sell and service flood insurance policies under their own names but do not bear any risk—it is the federal government that underwrites and holds the risk. The participating insurers simply sell and service the policies.[15] The insurers are permitted to keep about 32 percent of the premium for administrative and production costs. In 2003, 93 companies participated in the WYO program and about 4.4 million NFIP policies were written.[16]

Federal Coordination and FEMA

The 1970 Disaster Relief Act affirmed the incremental expansions during the 1960s of what constituted disaster relief. It further expanded what could be done with federal disaster relief funds to include grants for temporary housing and legal services. It was not until 1978, however, that the Federal Emergency Management Agency was established as an independent agency to coordinate federal disaster programs. The National Flood Insurance Program was placed under FEMA in 1979. In March 2003, FEMA became part of the Department of Homeland Security.

139

As the disasters created by the terrorist attacks on September 11, 2001, the wildfires in southern California in the fall of 2003, and the hurricanes that struck the Gulf Coast and Florida in 2004 and 2005 vividly demonstrate, FEMA now plays an extraordinary and critical role in governmental response to disasters. It manages the federal and state responses and, in doing so, sets the terms by which financial aid will be provided. FEMA disbursed $4.3 billion in fiscal year 2002. A proportion of FEMA's annual disbursements come from special appropriations (presidential or congressional) after disasters. For example, as of May 2005, FEMA had paid out $5.2 billion for recovery from the four hurricanes that struck Florida in 2004. In line with relying on special appropriations after disasters, the president's fiscal year 2006 budget for FEMA included only $3.3 billion. The president had to ask Congress to appropriate more than $60 billion of special disaster funds after Hurricanes Katrina and Rita struck the Gulf Coast. To put these expenditures in perspective for helping the uninsured, note that Blumberg and Holahan estimated that a government reinsurance program for small-group health insurance would cost $5.2 billion.[17]

Government Backstopping Creates Insurance Markets

Without the current federal role in disasters, there might be no private insurers willing to sell flood insurance in many communities. The identification of flood risks in many parts of the country allowed flood insurance premiums to be established in those areas. Most important for private insurers, however, is the federal government's assumption, through the WYO program, of the very worst flood risks. Similarly, the catastrophe reinsurance market exists because the federal government provides disaster assistance. Reinsurance companies are willing to sell policies to insurers of residential and business properties for damages due to hurricanes and earthquakes only because the federal government will take responsibility for much of the very highest costs. They would not sell coverage without government backstopping of these risks.

The need for the government to take responsibility for high losses in disasters became even clearer in the summer of 2002 when insurers refused to issue liability insurance and catastrophe reinsurance for losses due to terrorist attacks. This particularly hit owners of tall buildings in New York City and other major cities. To coax insurers back into these markets, in November 2002 the federal government expanded the scope of its disaster relief by assuming responsibility for such catastrophic losses. The Terrorism Risk Insurance Act of 2002 calls for the government to pay 90 percent of the costs of any terrorist attack after losses exceed

$10 billion. As a result, the markets for liability insurance and catastrophe reinsurance are functioning again, with insurers offering terrorism coverage at reasonable rates.

The lesson from the government's role in disaster assistance is that the backstopping role of the government enables disaster-related insurance and reinsurance markets to operate and grow. Without assurance that the federal government will provide assistance, private insurers cannot determine the risks and premiums for very low-probability events that have extremely high costs.

SECONDARY MORTGAGE MARKET

The federal government's seventy-year role in the secondary mortgage market is very similar to its role in the insurance and reinsurance markets for disasters. It played a pivotal role in the development of the secondary mortgage market and the subsequent market for mortgage-backed securities. These markets depended on the federal government guaranteeing the worst risks in the home mortgage market.

Federally Insured and Guaranteed Mortgage Loans

In 1933 and 1934 the federal government took the first of several steps that enabled a secondary mortgage market to develop. These steps involved helping "deserving" people obtain home mortgages—working people who could make mortgage payments but did not have savings for a down payment and, ten years later, soldiers returning from World War II. The first step was the creation of the Home Owners Loan Corporation (HOLC) in 1933 and the Federal Housing Administration in 1934. The HOLC used government-backed bonds to purchase mortgages on which people had defaulted. The HOLC bought the mortgages from banks and other financial institutions that held the mortgages and then reinstated the mortgages—but with new terms. Until the Great Depression, mortgages for single-family homes were typically for only five to ten years, had a variable rate of interest, and did not amortize over the life of the mortgage (they did not include a payment toward the principal over the life of the mortgage). The HOLC changed these terms so that mortgages became longer-term (twenty-year), fixed-rate, fully amortizing mortgages. The intent of the new design was to reduce borrowers' desire to refinance mortgages—something which non-amortizing, short-term mortgages do because they require a large lump-sum payment at the end of the loan. The HOLC was replaced in 1938 by the Federal National Mortgage Association (known as Fannie Mae starting in the 1950s), which was supposed to help develop a secondary market for

FHA-insured mortgages. The FHA provided mortgage insurance to mortgage borrowers so mortgage investors would not fear what happened in the Great Depression: many borrowers defaulting on their mortgages. The FHA charges borrowers an insurance premium (today equal to 1.5 percent of the mortgage) when they take out the mortgage, and then an annual premium that declines over the life of the mortgage until the outstanding mortgage balance represents less than 75 percent of the property value.

Before the end of World War II, conventional mortgage lenders generally required that purchasers make down payments of at least 50 percent of the purchase price so that the mortgage insurers were not at risk for the entire value of the house if the borrower defaulted. This requirement effectively prevented people with small savings from obtaining mortgages and owning homes. They were considered high-risk by conventional mortgage insurers and lenders.

The federal role with mortgages expanded in 1944 when the Veterans Administration (VA) loan guarantee program was instituted to guarantee mortgage loans to veterans. The VA mortgage guarantee is not insurance (no premiums are paid by the mortgage borrower), but rather a guarantee by the VA (the federal government) that it will compensate lenders for losses on mortgage loans made to veterans. The amount of the guarantee varies with housing market conditions and VA authority, but it is generally about 25 percent of the price of what is considered "an adequate housing unit" in the area surrounding the house. This amount represents the equivalent of what would otherwise be a down payment in a conventional mortgage. It effectively jump-started mortgage lending to GIs, another group of risky but deserving borrowers who were returning from World War II without savings.

The FHA mortgage insurance and VA mortgage guarantee programs fundamentally altered the way risk is handled in the U.S. mortgage market. The most obvious change is that the federal government assumes the risk that high-risk mortgage borrowers might default on repaying their loans. By taking on this risk, the federal government has been widely credited with increasing the number of homeowners.[18]

The two programs also were the catalyst for an equally significant change: the creation of a national mortgage market (in addition to localized markets). The FHA and VA programs provided minimum standards for the types and quality of information that had to be obtained about the borrower and the property, including subdivision standards and credit reviews of borrowers. Standardizing the information permitted banks and other mortgage lenders to classify mortgage applications by their level of risk of default.[19] These standards provided insured or guaranteed mortgages a level of quality that allowed lending institutions that were not located near the property to judge its value without doing their own investigation (due diligence). This, in turn, made it possible for the country to develop a national mortgage market. Equally important, the standardized information made FHA- and VA-backed mortgages available for resale, creating the secondary mortgage market. The secondary mortgage market enables originating lenders to sell mortgages to other investors, which increases the amount of money available for mortgage loans. Without the secondary mortgage market, it is highly doubtful that the United States would enjoy its present homeownership rates or the increased size of many homes.

Fannie Mae and the Secondary Mortgage Market

The federal government's role in expanding the secondary mortgage market grew substantially after 1954. The Federal National Mortgage Association (Fannie Mae) was rechartered to focus on a secondary mortgage market for government-insured residential mortgages.[20] To provide FNMA with a financial base, Congress authorized it to issue stock, as well as various types of bonds (notes).[21] The U.S. Treasury was authorized to acquire as much as $2.25 billion of these notes (in 1954 dollars). The backing of the federal government was tremendously important because it enabled FNMA to borrow money at interest rates below those available in the market. The difference between what it earned on the mortgages it bought and the interest it paid investors was what permitted it to buy more government-insured mortgages in the secondary market.

The Impact of Ginnie Mae and Freddie Mac

The federal government's role in expanding the use of securities in the form of mortgage-backed stocks and bonds to increase the funds available for mortgages was significant. At the end of the 1960s, savings and loans institutions—the traditional source of conventional mortgages—were losing deposits because new ways to invest and save were being created. U.S. Treasury bills became available in smaller denominations so people with modest savings could invest in them; the establishment of mutual funds of stocks and bonds provided another investment outlet for people with small amounts of savings and people who wanted to invest in a fund with diversified risk rather than in one company. Savings and loans, meanwhile, were strictly regulated and limited in the rates of interest they could pay on savings accounts. The combined result was that less money was available from the traditional source of mortgage money.

The federal government reacted to the decline by creating two organizations that boosted the use of mortgage pools (or bundling of mortgages) in the secondary mortgage market. The Government National Mortgage Association (GNMA, or Ginnie Mae) was created by the 1968 Housing and Urban Development Act. GNMA's operations are financed through funds from the U.S. Treasury from government-issued debt. GNMA guarantees the future interest and principal payments due on pools of mortgages made up of FHA- and VA-backed mortgages. With a government-assisted guarantee of future payments, mortgages in these pools are the collateral that "securitizes" bonds or stocks that can be issued based on the pool of mortgages. Pooling these mortgages makes them attractive to a new set of investors and expands the funds available for mortgages. Investors purchase a share in a pool of mortgages (much like a fund of investments in stocks or bonds); shares in such a pool are preferable to purchasing single mortgages because a pool diversifies the risks of default or prepayment on any given mortgage. The market for FHA- and VA-backed securities was hugely popular among large investors, particularly pension funds and life insurance companies.

Congress expanded the government's support of such mortgage-backed securities by passing the Emergency Home Finance Act in 1970. The act chartered the Federal Home Loan Mortgage Corporation (FHLMC, or Freddie Mac), which was charged with expanding the secondary mortgage market for conventional mortgage originators. (At the end of the 1960s, conventional mortgages accounted for 79 percent of total residential loans.) A loan originator selling a mortgage through the FHLMC secondary mortgage market had to adhere to standardized procedures for underwriting and documentation when originating the loan. As a result, conventional mortgages rapidly became standardized, permitting individual mortgages to be pooled with similar mortgages. The pooling of mortgages by type diversifies the risks of default and prepayment by any one borrower and shifts the risks to a larger group of investors. The expansion and increase in complexity of the secondary mortgage market since 1970 has been remarkable.[22]

The secondary mortgage market and the mortgage-backed securities that are now available are a direct result of the federal government's role in guaranteeing the worst risks. Without the government's backing of risky mortgage loans and guaranteeing of pools of these loans, the nation's housing stock and rate of homeownership would be very different from what we observe today.

NEW YORK STATE'S HEALTHY NEW YORK

New York was the first state to have a state-financed reinsurance program that reimburses insurers when they have very high annual expenses for enrollees.[23] The reinsurance is restricted to insurers that participate in the Healthy New York Program, which is targeted at individual workers and sole proprietors with incomes below 250 percent of the poverty level as well as workers in small firms where at least 30 percent of the workers earn less than $32,000 per year.[24] All HMOs must participate, and the two benefits packages are standardized.[25] Healthy New York premiums are implicitly subsidized by reinsurance funded by the state's tobacco settlement funds. Originally, the reinsurance provided reimbursement of 90 percent of total annual claims between $30,000 and $100,000 for individuals with at least $30,000 of expenses in a year. In June 2003, the reinsurance-eligible "corridor" was lowered to $5,000 to $75,000—so the reinsurance now pays 90 percent of total expenses for enrollees with at least $5,000 in claims in a calendar year.[26] When Healthy New York started, the premiums were about half those quoted in the direct-pay market (the individual market for people with incomes *above* 250 percent of the poverty level).[27] Since the threshold for activating the reinsurance was lowered to $5,000, premiums have dropped even further in comparison with those available in the direct-pay market.[28]

By removing a substantial part of the losses for the high-cost enrollees from an insurer's book of business with the Healthy New York program and the direct-pay market, the state has shifted the risk of adverse selection from the insurers enrolling previously uninsured people to the broader population of the state. With relatively modest advertising, the program has attracted more than 200,000 enrollees since 2001 (102,000 of whom were active enrollees at the end of October 2005).[29] Enrollment in the program has been growing steadily since it began, and was averaging more than 7,000 new members per month throughout 2005. Total claims submitted for reinsurance reimbursement were about $35 million in 2004, which is less than what was budgeted. It is telling that a program targeted at low-income working people is growing in enrollment and has not exhausted the funds in the reinsurance pool even after the reinsurance threshold was lowered.

MEDICARE'S OUTLIER PAYMENTS AND PRESCRIPTION DRUG BENEFIT

When the prospective payment system (PPS) for paying hospitals under Medicare was implemented in 1983 and 1984, it included a provision to pay for patients with costs and/or length of stay that were far higher than expected—these patients are known as "outliers." Under the PPS, 5 to 6 percent of total hospital payments under Medicare must be made for these outliers; the current target for outlier payments is 5.2 percent.[30] Calculating whether a case at a particular hospital qualifies for an outlier payment involves several steps.[31] The threshold for outlier cases is redefined each year, and in June 2003 the method for determining outlier cases was substantially revised.[32] The bottom line is that Medicare pays a hospital for 80 percent of its costs above the threshold that defines an outlier case. Thus, Medicare is essentially providing reinsurance to hospitals with very sick Medicare patients.

The George H. W. Bush administration, in 1990, also proposed that HMOs participating in Medicare receive outlier payments for very high-cost cases.[33] The proposal was to create an outlier pool, funded from the Medicare Trust Fund, which would pay 45 percent of costs of HMO Medicare enrollees with expenditures above $50,000 (in 1990 dollars). Gail Wilensky and Louis Rossiter estimated (in 1991) that fewer than 0.5 percent of Medicare beneficiaries had costs above $50,000 per year.[34] In another study of the Bush administration's proposal, James Beebe estimated that the proposal would increase Medicare spending on managed care plans by 1.8 percent, and that if they wanted to increase spending by 5 percent, the threshold could be lowered to $32,000.[35]

The Medicare Modernization Act of 2003 is not specific about details, but it includes provisions for the federal government to assume some of the risk involved in selling prescription drug insurance to Medicare beneficiaries. The Medicare prescription drug benefit, which went into effect in January 2006, involves risk for insurers and other entities that are expected to sell the drug insurance. Regulations written since the passage of the MMA have established risk corridors such that if an insurer has an individual with expenses in excess of a complicated formula of costs, the Centers for Medicare and Medicaid Services (CMS) will provide a reinsurance payment.[36] If the insurer's costs are below the risk corridor's threshold lower level, the regulations call for CMS to reduce its total payments to the insurer. This approach guarantees that if the risk has been overestimated and costs are less than anticipated, the federal government will share in the "profits." The primary risk in the Part D benefit is due to potential adverse selection. Prescription drug use is relatively predictable—people who have chronic conditions are more likely to use prescription drugs than those who do not. Among Medicare beneficiaries in 2003, 41 percent had prescription drug expenditures below $1,000.[37] An almost equal number (40 percent) had expenditures above $2,000. Thus, without some protection from the risk that a disproportionate share of enrollees would be people with high costs, insurers were reluctant to enter the market for Medicare prescription drug coverage. The risk-sharing created by the regulations appears to have allayed their concerns—in most states, more than forty options are available to beneficiaries.

THE IMPORTANCE OF THE GOVERNMENT'S
ROLE TO PRIVATE MARKETS AND
THE ECONOMY

In sum, there is a considerable history of the federal government and some state governments taking responsibility for the worst risks in a variety of markets that are thus not only able to function efficiently but would not otherwise exist. Many people have subsequently obtained the benefits of a wide variety of services and intangibles, ranging from insurance to homeownership. The economy and society as a whole have gained in untold ways from the stability in these markets brought about by government assumption of their greatest risks. The same could be true of health insurance markets.

Notes

CHAPTER 1

1. In addition, COBRA permits people to retain access to group health insurance for up to three years if they would lose such access because of the death of or their divorce from the primary worker. If they choose to "COBRA" their group policy, they must pay 102 percent of the full premium. COBRA also allows unmarried children under the age of twenty-five who have been full-time students and covered by their parents' policy to extend their coverage for eighteen months after completing school; they must pay 102 percent of the full premium. See Patrice Flynn, "COBRA Qualifying Events and Elections, 1987–1991," *Inquiry* 31, no. 2 (1994): 215–20.

2. Determining an income threshold as the definition for being middle-class is elusive and arbitrary. I am using median household income as the threshold because I am comparing who is in the middle class and without health insurance over a twenty-five-year period. Many factors that affect incomes and who is in what type of family changed during this time—for example, the economy, the labor force participation rates of women, and the age of first marriage. Setting the threshold for middle-class at the median household income in each year is a conservative way of adjusting for the changes in such factors over the last twenty-five years. The changing factors that have had an impact on incomes and health insurance coverage are discussed in more detail in chapter 2.

3. Employees on non-agricultural payrolls have been divided, by Bureau of Labor Statistics (BLS) custom, between the goods-producing industries (natural resources and mining; construction; and manufacturing) and the service-producing industries (wholesale and retail trade; transportation and utilities; information; financial activities; professional and business services; education and health services; leisure and hospitality; other services; and federal, state, and local government). In 1959 (the year when the current industry divisions were established), 36 percent of non-agricultural employees were in goods-producing industries; by the second quarter of 2005, this figure was just 16.6 percent. People who are self-employed, proprietors, or agricultural workers are not included in these figures.

4. Author's tabulations based on Council of Economic Advisers, *2005 Economic Report of the President* (Washington: U.S. Government Printing Office, 2005),

table B-46, "Employees on Nonagriculture Payrolls, by Major Industry, 1959–2004."

5. David Autor, personal communication, June 2004. Autor also estimates that in 1949 almost 42 percent of all workers were blue-collar workers. It is difficult to estimate the change in the proportion of workers in different occupations over time. Occupations have changed, and the government's dictionary of occupations is updated every twenty-five years or so to keep up with the changes. Autor has cross-walked descriptions of occupations to be able to make this comparison over the past half-century.

6. Jon Gabel, Gary Claxton, Isadora Gil, Jeremy Pickreign, Heidi Whitmore, Erin Holve, Benjamin Finder, Samantha Hawkins, and Diane Rowland, "Health Benefits in 2004: Four Years of Double-Digit Premium Increases Take Their Toll on Coverage," *Health Affairs* 23, no. 5 (2004): 200–209. The offer rates reported by Gabel and his colleagues—using the Henry J. Kaiser Family Foundation/Health Research and Educational Trust (KFF/HRET) Surveys of Employer-Sponsored Health Benefits between 2000 and 2004 and the KPMG Survey of Employer-Sponsored Health Benefits in 1996 for firms with fewer than fifty workers—have consistently been nine percentage points higher than those found in the 1996 Medical Expenditure Panel Survey-Insurance Component (MEPS-IC) data. The surveys use different methods, and the response rate for the MEPS-IC survey is higher than the response rate for the KFF/HRET surveys. For more details, see James M. Branscome, Philip F. Cooper, John Sommers, and Jessica P. Vistnes, "Private Employer-Sponsored Health Insurance: New Estimates by State," *Health Affairs* 19, no. 1 (2000): 139–47. The bottom line, however, is that small firms are far less likely than firms with more than two hundred employees to offer health insurance benefits.

7. Marilyn E. Manser and Garnett Picot, "The Role of Self-employment in U.S. and Canadian Job Growth," *Monthly Labor Review* 122, no. 4 (1999): 10–25.

8. Cynthia Smith, Cathy Cowan, Stephen Heffler, Aaron Catlin, and the Health Accounts Team, "National Health Spending in 2004: Recent Slowdown Led by Prescription Drug Spending," *Health Affairs* 25, no. 1 (2006): 186–96.

9. Laparoscopic surgery uses a tiny tube (smaller than a thin pencil) that contains a high-intensity light and camera so that the surgeon can see the inside of the organ on a television monitor. Tiny surgical tools can also be put into the tube (or another tube), which typically is inserted into the body through a small incision close to the surgical site.

10. Author's estimates from the March 2005 Current Population Survey (CPS). Prior to rounding the estimated number, the percentage in 2004 was 63.2 percent; in 2003 it was 63.8 percent. The decline over the past two years is statistically significant.

11. The true division between employer and employee of the cost of health insurance depends on market conditions. We can see this by considering

what happens when there is an increase in health insurance premiums. When employers believe they can easily replace any employee who quits, they will likely ask the employee to pay all of the increased premium, usually in the form of forgone wage increases. Conversely, employers who believe their employees both have other opportunities and are hard to replace will absorb the increased costs. Of course, employees paid at the minimum wage cannot pay all of the increase in premium since their wages cannot go below the minimum. In this case, the employer will either pay all of the increase in premium or reduce the number of minimum-wage employees.

Since most people focus on their out-of-pocket costs when they consider the costs of health insurance benefits, I will stick with the popular view that employers pay the larger share of the premium when they sponsor health insurance.

12. Jon Gabel, Gary Claxton, Isadora Gil, Jeremy Pickreign, Heidi Whitmore, Benjamin Finder, Samantha Hawkins, and Diane Rowland, "Health Benefits in 2005: Premium Increases Slow Down, Coverage Continues to Erode," *Health Affairs* 24, no. 5 (2005): 1273–80.

13. Ibid.

14. Karen Pollitz, Richard Sorian, and Kathy Thomas, *How Accessible Is Individual Health Insurance for Consumers in Less-Than-Perfect Health?* (Menlo Park, Calif.: Henry J. Kaiser Family Foundation, 2001).

15. For a comprehensive review of the literature on the consequences of not having health insurance, see Jack Hadley, *Sicker and Poorer: The Consequences of Being Uninsured* (Washington: Kaiser Commission on Medicaid and the Uninsured, 2002).

16. Alan C. Monheit, "Persistence in Health Expenditures in the Short Run: Prevalence and Consequences," *Medical Care* 41, no. 7(supp.) (2003): III53–64.

17. See Pollitz et al., *How Accessible Is Individual Health Insurance?*

18. Institute of Medicine, *Coverage Matters: Insurance and Health Care* (Washington, D.C.: National Academy Press, 2003); Institute of Medicine. *Unequal Treatment: Confronting Racial and Ethnic Disparities in Healthcare* (Washington, D.C.: National Academy Press, 2003).

19. Leonard E. Burman and Jonathan Gruber, "Tax Credits for Health Insurance," *Tax Policy Issues and Options* No. 11 (June 2005), Washington, D.C.: Urban-Brookings Tax Policy Center; available at: www.taxpolicycenter.org/UploadedPDF/311189_IssuesOptions_11.pdf.

20. I am grateful to Patricia Swolak (personal communication, November 15, 2005), New York State Department of Insurance, Healthy New York Program, for providing these numbers.

21. See, for example, Judith Feder and Sheila Burke, eds., *Options for Expanding Health Insurance Coverage: A Report on a Policy Roundtable* (Menlo Park, Calif.: Henry J. Kaiser Family Foundation, 1999); the proposals in Jack A. Meyer and Elliot K. Wicks, eds., *Covering America: Real Remedies for the Uninsured,*

vols. 1, 2, and 3 (Washington, D.C.: Economic and Social Research Institute, 2001, 2002, 2003); the proposals in *Inquiry* 38, no. 2 (Summer 2001); and Linda J. Blumberg, John Holahan, Alan Weil, Lisa Clemans-Cope, Matthew Buettgens, Fredric Blavin, and Stephen Zuckerman, *Building the Roadmap to Coverage: Policy Choices and the Cost and Coverage Implications* (Boston: Blue Cross Blue Shield of Massachusetts Foundation, 2005), also available at: www. bcbsmafoundation. org / foundationroot / en_ US / documents / roadmapTo coverage.pdf.

CHAPTER 2

1. Stephen R. Barley and Gideon Kunda, *Gurus, Hired Guns, and Warm Bodies: Itinerant Experts in a Knowledge Economy* (Princeton, N.J.: Princeton University Press, 2004).
2. That is, using median household income as the threshold for middle-class. The 1979 median household income was $17,710 (or $42,700 in 2004 dollars, using the CPI-U-RS price index to adjust for inflation between 1979 and 2004).
3. U.S. Department of Labor, Bureau of Labor Statistics, "Job Openings and Labor Turnover: February 2005," USDL 05–622, *News*, April 12, 2005.
4. Manufacturing, construction, and mining are the principal goods-producing industries. The service-producing industries are transportation and utilities, information, financial, insurance, real estate, services (for example, business, entertainment, and health), and government.
5. Author's analyses of U.S. Department of Labor, Bureau of Labor Statistics, *Employment and Earnings* data, in Council of Economics Advisers, *2005 Economic Report of the President* (Washington: U.S. Government Printing Office, 2005), table B-46; and Lawrence Mishel, Jared Bernstein, and Sylvia Allegretto, *The State of Working America 2004–2005* (Ithaca, N.Y.: ILR Press/Cornell University Press, 2005), 173, table 2.28.
6. Establishments consist of firms that are unique and employers that are franchises or subunits of very large corporations. McDonald's, for example, is a very large corporation with thousands of locations across the United States, each one of which counts as an establishment. Some large corporations sponsor health insurance for workers at all their locations, but others treat each establishment as an independent operation or franchise.
7. Author's tabulations from U.S. Department of Labor, Bureau of Labor Statistics, Office of Employment and Unemployment Statistics, *Covered Employment and Wages* (ES-202) data. My thanks to Jim Rice of the BLS for sending me data from 1975 to 1985 that were not easily accessible in the libraries in Boston and for providing me with data from 2004 and the first quarter of 2005 that were no longer on the BLS website. It is important to note that these numbers refer to establishments rather than firms; several establish-

ments may belong to the same firm—for example, a restaurant may have several locations, each of which is its own establishment. When employment is allocated by firm, closer to half of all workers are employed by firms with more than five hundred employees (U.S. Department of Commerce, U.S. Census Bureau [various years], *Statistics of U.S. Business* and *Non-employer Statistics*).

8. Susan N Houseman, "Why Employers Use Flexible Staffing Arrangements: Evidence from an Establishment Survey," *Industrial and Labor Relations Review* 55, no. 1 (2001): 149–70; Susan N Houseman, Arne L. Kalleberg, and George A. Erickcek, "The Role of Temporary Agency Employment in Tight Labor Markets," *Industrial and Labor Relations Review* 57, no. 1 (2003): 105–27.

9. The current payroll tax rates for Social Security and Medicare are 6.2 percent and 1.45 percent, respectively. The employer and the employee each pay these taxes, for a total of 15.3 percent. The income subject to the Social Security payroll tax has a cap, which rises every year; in 2006 the maximum amount of earnings subject to the tax was $94,200. There is no limit on income subject to the Medicare payroll tax.

10. Eileen Appelbaum, Annette Bernhardt, and Richard J. Murnane, eds., *Low-Wage America: How Employers Are Reshaping Opportunity in the Workplace* (New York: Russell Sage Foundation, 2003); Paul Osterman, *Employment Futures: Reorganization, Dislocation, and Public Policy* (New York: Oxford University Press, 1988).

11. Sharon R. Cohany, "Workers in Alternative Employment Arrangements: A Second Look," *Monthly Labor Review* 121, no. 11 (1998): 3–21.

12. John F. Bregger, "Measuring Self-employment in the United States," *Monthly Labor Review* 119, nos. 1–2 (1996): 3–9.

13. Steven Hipple, "Self-employment in the United States: An Update," *Monthly Labor Review* 127, no. 7 (2004): 13–23.

14. Ibid.

15. Author's calculations based on March 2004 CPS.

16. Steven Hipple. "Contingent Work in the Late 1990s," *Monthly Labor Review* 124, no. 3 (2001): 3–27.

17. Ibid., 9. Although some of these college and university faculty may have another job, the CPS questions refer to a person's "main job—the job in which they worked the most hours." The answers to the questions about the main job determine whether it is a contingent job or not. So for the 29 percent of all college and university instructors who Hipple estimates are employed on a contingent basis, the faculty job is their primary job.

18. Ibid., 11.

19. Barley and Kunda, *Gurus, Hired Guns, and Warm Bodies*, 17.

20. Franklin Shaffer, Cross Country Healthcare, Inc., personal communication, July 29, 2004.

21. Eric Bettinger and Bridget T. Long, "Do College Instructors Matter? The

Effects of Adjuncts and Graduate Assistants on Students' Interests and Success," working paper 10370 (Cambridge, Mass.: National Bureau of Economic Research, 2004).

22. Charles J. Muhl, "What Is an Employee? The Answer Depends on the Federal Law," *Monthly Labor Review* 125, no. 1 (2002): 3–11.

23. J. J. Kuenzi and C. A. Reschovsky, "Home-Based Workers in the United States," *Current Population Reports*, series P70, no. 78 (Washington: U.S. Government Printing Office for U.S. Census Bureau, 2001).

24. Julie Hatch, "Employment in the Public Sector: Two Recessions' Impact on Jobs," *Monthly Labor Review* 127, no. 10 (2004): 38–47; U.S. Department of Commerce, U.S. Census Bureau, *Statistical Abstract of the United States: 2004–2005* (Washington: U.S. Department of Commerce, 2005), 321, table 483.

25. Data from Centers for Disease Control and Prevention, table 1–1, "Live Births, Birthrates, and Fertility Rates, by Race: United States, 1909–2000," available at: www.cdc.gov/nchs/data/statab/t001x01.pdf; and from Joyce A. Martin, Brady E. Hamilton, Paul D. Sutton, Stephanie J. Ventura, Fay Menacker, and Martha L. Munson, "Births: Final Data for 2003," *National Vital Statistics Reports* 54, no. 2 (Hyattsville, Md.: National Center for Health Statistics, 2005), table 1.

26. U.S. Department of Commerce, U.S. Census Bureau, table HH-6, "Average Population per Household and Family: 1940 to Present," June 29, 2005; available at: www.census.gov/population/socdemo/hh-fam/tabHH-6.pdf.

27. U.S. Department of Commerce, U.S. Census Bureau, table FM-1, "Families, by Presence of Own Children Under 18: 1950 to Present," June 29, 2005; available at: www.census.gov/population/socdemo/hh-fam/tabFM-1.pdf.

28. Data on birthrates by Hispanic origin were not collected by all states and the District of Columbia until 1993. In 1991 and 1992, New Hampshire did not ask for information on Hispanic origin, and in 1990 neither New Hampshire nor Oklahoma collected this information. For more details, see Brady E. Hamilton, Joyce A. Martin, and Paul D. Sutton, "Births: Preliminary Data for 2003," *National Vital Statistics Reports* 53, no. 9 (Hyattsville, Md.: National Center for Health Statistics, 2004).

29. Martin et al., "Births: Final Data for 2003," tables 4 and 9.

30. Jason Fields, "America's Families and Living Arrangements: 2003," *Current Population Reports*, series P20, no. 553 (Washington: U.S. Government Printing Office, 2004).

31. U.S. Department of Commerce, U.S. Bureau of the Census, table MS-2, "Estimated Median Age of First Marriage, by Sex: 1890 to the Present," June 29, 2005; available at: www.census.gov/population/socdemo/hh-fam/tabMS-2.pdf.

32. Fields, "America's Families and Living Arrangements."

33. U.S. Department of Commerce, U.S. Bureau of the Census, table MS-1, "Marital Status of the Population 15 Years Old and Over, by Sex and Race,

1950 to Present," June 29, 2005; available at: www.census.gov/population/socdemo/hh-fam/ms1.pdf.

34. Ibid.

35. U.S. Department of Commerce, U.S. Census Bureau, table FM-1, "Families, by Presence of Own Children Under 18: 1950 to Present," June 29, 2005; available at: www.census.gov/population/socdemo/hh-fam/tabFM-1.pdf.

36. U.S. Department of Commerce, U.S. Census Bureau, table CH-1, "Living Arrangements of Children Under 18 Years Old: 1960 to Present," June 29, 2005; available at: www.census.gov/population/socdemo/hh-fam/tabCH-1.pdf.

37. U.S. Department of Commerce, U.S. Census Bureau, *Statistical Abstract of the United States: 2004–2005* (Washington: U.S. Department of Commerce, 2005), labor force participation tables 570–579; available at www.census.gov/prod/2004pubs/04statab/pop.pdf.

38. Frank Levy, *The New Dollars and Dreams: American Incomes and Economic Change* (New York: Russell Sage Foundation, 1998).

39. Mishel et al., *State of Working America*, 158.

40. My thanks to Susan Garfield for making this point to me.

41. The SCHIPs were authorized as part of the 1997 Balanced Budget Act. Like Medicaid, the SCHIPs are funded by a combination of state and federal funds. The federal share of SCHIP funding is higher than it is for Medicaid, although the total amount of federal funding available for the SCHIPs is a block grant voted on by Congress. Thus, unlike Medicaid, the SCHIPs are not an entitlement program.

42. Kaiser Commission on Medicaid and the Uninsured, "Key Facts: Health Coverage for Low-Income Children" (Washington: Kaiser Commission on Medicaid and the Uninsured, September 2004); available at: www.kff.org/uninsured/loader.cfm?url=/commonspot/security/getfile.cfm&PageID=46994.

43. Kaiser Commission on Medicaid and the Uninsured, "In Their Own Words: The Uninsured Talk About Living Without Health Insurance" (Washington, D.C.: Kaiser Commission on Medicaid and the Uninsured, 2001); available at: www.kff.org/uninsured/2207-index.cfm.

CHAPTER 3

1. Paul Fronstin, "Sources of Health Insurance and Characteristics of the Uninsured: Analysis of the March 2004 Current Population Survey," issue brief 276 (Washington: Employee Benefit Research Institute, 2004); and author's calculations from March 2005 CPS.

2. Among the few who did foresee this transformation were Colin Clark, *The Conditions of Economic Progress* (New York: St. Martin's Press, 1957), and Victor R. Fuchs, assisted by Irving F. Leveson, *The Service Economy*, General Series vol. 87 (New York: National Bureau of Economic Research, 1968).

3. Paul Starr, *The Social Transformation of American Medicine* (New York: Basic Books, 1982), has been especially influential in promulgating this view among health policy researchers.
4. This abbreviated history of the development of employer-based health insurance owes much to Jennifer Klein, *For All Those Rights: Business, Labor, and the Shaping of America's Public-Private Welfare State* (Princeton, N.J.: Princeton University Press, 2003).
5. Ibid., 179.
6. Ibid.
7. Ibid.
8. An indemnity health insurance plan typically specifies that it will cover a stated amount for each of a variety of health services—for example, a day in the hospital or a physician's office visit. Often the stated amount has been negotiated in advance with health care providers. Indemnity plans typically require insured persons to pay several hundred (or thousand) dollars of their medical expenses before the insurance starts to pay any of those costs. This is known as a "deductible," and it restarts at the beginning of the contract year of the insurance policy. In addition, indemnity policies usually require the insured person to pay a "coinsurance rate"—a fraction of any medical expenses above the deductible. The most common coinsurance rate today is 20 percent (see Gabel et al., "Health Benefits in 2005," 1273–80). Many but not all indemnity policies also have what is known as a "stop loss": a maximum amount of out-of-pocket expenditures that an insured person has to pay during a year. Until health maintenance organizations (HMOs) and other forms of managed care plans became widespread in the 1980s, a large majority of Americans had indemnity health insurance.
9. Len Burman, *The Tax Treatment of Employment-Based Health Insurance* (Washington: Congressional Budget Office, 1994), 5. The 1943 IRS ruling was that employers' contributions to group health insurance policies were exempt from taxation. But in 1953 the IRS ruled that employers' contributions to individual health insurance policies were taxable.
10. Klein, *For All Those Rights*, 225.
11. Other taxes also may be used to finance health insurance, but taxes on income are the primary source of revenue for the insurance systems.
12. Thomas Piketty and Emmanuel Saez, "Income Inequality in the United States, 1913–1998," *Quarterly Journal of Economics* 118, no. 1 (2003): 1–39. The 2000 estimate comes from the updated table Piketty and Saez reprinted in the National Bureau of Economic Research working paper version (8467) of this article.
13. Economic Policy Institute, "CEO Pay," *Facts and Figures: State of Working America* (March 2005); available at: www.epinet.org.
14. Health care spending data from Katharine Levit, Cynthia Smith, Cathy Cowan, Art Sensenig, Aaron Catlin, and the Health Accounts Team,

"Health Spending Rebound Continues in 2002," *Health Affairs* 23, no. 1 (2004): 147–59. The CPI was used to account for general price inflation between 1960 and 2004.

15. Per capita expenditures come from Smith et al., "National Health Spending in 2004." The CPI was used to account for general price inflation between 1980 and 2004.

16. Mishel et al., *The State of Working America 2004–2005*, 154. The CPI was used to account for general price inflation between 1979 and 2004.

17. Philip F. Cooper and Barbara S. Schone, "More Offers, Fewer Takers for Job-Based Health Insurance," *Health Affairs* 16, no. 6 (1997): 142–49.

18. Ibid.

19. People who belong to groups formed for reasons other than insurance often also buy insurance as a group activity if the members do not have access to employer-sponsored coverage. For example, farmers or ranchers who belong to cooperatives to sell their product often obtain group insurance through the cooperative.

20. The purpose of some of these models, known as risk adjustment models, is to provide insurers (or medical care providers) with an adjustment to an average premium where the adjustment provides additional (or less) compensation for covering an individual who has predictably higher (or lower) medical expenses based on his or her known characteristics. See Arlene Ash, Frank Porell, Leonard Gruenberg, Eric Sawitz, and Alexa Beiser, "Adjusting Medicare Capitation Payments Using Prior-Hospitalization Data," *Health Care Financing Review* 10, no. 4 (1989): 17–30; Randall P. Ellis and Arlene S. Ash, "Refinements to the Diagnostic Cost Group Model," *Inquiry* 32, no. 4 (1995): 418–29; Wynand P. M. M. van de Ven and Randall P. Ellis, "Risk Adjustment in Competitive Health Plan Markets," in *Handbook of Health Economics*, vol. 1A, edited by Anthony J. Culyer and Joseph P. Newhouse (Amsterdam: Elsevier Science, 2000).

21. See van de Ven and Ellis, "Risk Adjustment in Competitive Health Plan Markets"; Joseph P. Newhouse, "Patients at Risk: Reform and Risk Adjustment," *Health Affairs* 13, no. 1 (1994): 132–46; Joseph P. Newhouse, "Reimbursing Health Plans and Health Providers: Efficiency in Production Versus Selection," *Journal of Economic Literature* 34, no. 3 (1996): 1236–63; Joseph P. Newhouse, Melinda B. Buntin, and John D. Chapman, "Risk Adjustment and Medicare: Taking a Closer Look," *Health Affairs* 16, no. 5 (1997): 26–43.

22. Of course, an employer could decide, after the differential selection is observed, to subsidize the employees who chose the policy that has a disproportionate share of high-risk employees. But the difference in total premiums for each of the plans would reflect the difference in average risk levels of the pools of people in each plan.

23. Nelda McCall and H. S. Wai, "An Analysis of the Use of Medicare Services by the Continuously Enrolled Aged," *Medical Care* 21, no. 6 (1983): 567–85;

W. P. Welch, "Medicare Capitation Payments to HMOs in Light of Regression Toward the Mean in Health Care Costs," in *Advances in Health Economics and Health Services Research: Biased Selection in Health Care Markets*, edited by Richard M. Scheffler and Louis F. Rossiter (Greenwich, Conn.: JAI Press, 1985); Michael J. Goodman, Douglas W. Roblin, Mark C. Hornbrook, and John P. Mullooly, "Persistence of Health Care Expense in an Insured Working Population," in *Advances in Health Economics and Health Services Research: Risk-Based Contributions to Private Health Insurance*, edited by Richard M. Scheffler and Louis F. Rossiter (Greenwich, Conn.: JAI Press, 1991); Marian Gornick, Alma McMillan, and James Lubitz, "A Longitudinal Perspective on Patterns of Medicare Payments," *Health Affairs* 12, no. 2 (1993): 140–50; Monheit, "Persistence in Health Expenditures in the Short Run: Prevalence and Consequences."

24. In December 1990, the Financial Accounting Standards Board (FASB), a private-sector organization that establishes financial accounting and reporting standards, issued FASB statement 106, which requires companies that offer retiree health benefits to show that they are accumulating sufficient funds for those benefits. With this change, the business sector became acutely aware of the costs of health benefits.

25. Author's calculations based on BLS, *Employment and Earnings* data, in Council of Economic Advisers, *2005 Economic Report of the President*, table B-46.

CHAPTER 4

1. Marc L. Berk and Alan C. Monheit, "The Concentration of Health Care Expenditures, Revisited," *Health Affairs* 20, no. 2 (2001): (9–18); Monheit, "Persistence in Health Expenditures."

2. Berk and Monheit, "The Concentration of Health Care Expenditures, Revisited."

3. Monheit, "Persistence in Health Expenditures," III56, table 1.

4. Smith et al., "National Health Spending in 2004."

5. Monheit, "Persistence in Health Expenditures."

6. Although it is people in the top 1 percent of the spending distribution who cause insurers the most anxiety, they are almost equally apprehensive about people in the top 2 to 5 percent. People in the top 2 percent have expenses above $30,000, and people in the top 5 percent have expenses above $15,000. These thresholds are likely to have been higher in 2005 simply because the types of medical care (including pharmaceuticals) available have expanded since 1996 and I have not accounted for that here.

7. A fourth distinct market for private health insurance is the market for Medi-Gap insurance for senior citizens who are eligible for Medicare and want to purchase supplementary insurance to cover costs not covered by Medicare.

However, the market for MediGap insurance shares many characteristics with the individual market, so I am not including it in this discussion.

8. Klein, *For All Those Rights*, 219–24.

9. My thanks to Profs. Michelle Mello of Harvard School of Public Health, John Manning of Harvard Law School, and Victor P. Goldberg of Columbia Law School for their discussions with me on this point.

10. U.S. Code, title 15, ch. 20, sect. 1012 (from the McCarran-Ferguson Act).

11. Gail A. Jensen and Michael A. Morrisey, "Employer-Sponsored Health Insurance and Mandated Benefit Laws," *Milbank Quarterly* 77, 4 (1999): 425–59.

12. Deborah Chollet, Adele Kirk, and Marc Chow, *Mapping State Health Insurance Markets: Structure and Change in the States' Group and Individual Health Insurance Markets, 1995–1997* (Washington, D.C.: Academy for Health Services Research and Health Policy [now AcademyHealth], 2000).

13. Ibid.

14. In the thirty years since ERISA was passed, the federal government has exercised its powers to preempt states' regulatory authority over health insurance only once—in 1978 the Pregnancy Discrimination Act (which was an amendment to Title VII of the Civil Rights Act) required that all group health insurance policies cover the costs of maternity care in the same manner as any other medical care.

15. My thanks to Joe Newhouse, who reminded me of this important point.

16. Jensen and Morrisey, "Employer-Sponsored Health Insurance and Mandated Benefit Laws."

17. In many states there is a clear distinction between agents and brokers: agents generally sell products from only one insurance company, whereas brokers sell policies for a set of competing companies. However, the distinction between agents and brokers is increasingly blurred as states permit people to obtain licenses to be both. Brokers can also act as "wholesale brokers," serving as intermediaries between insurers and agents. For more details, see Deborah W. Garnick, Katherine Swartz, and Kathleen C. Skwara, "Insurance Agents: Ignored Players in Health Insurance Reform," *Health Affairs* 17, no. 2 (1998): 137–43.

18. It is not even necessary that everyone in a group that is offered the bundle purchase the entire bundle. When a bundle is offered, people often enroll in all the parts because then they do not have to search for information about alternatives. Thus, the insurance company gains enrollees in each of the parts who do not have high expectations of needing the insurance—that is, they are low risks for the different types of insurance in the bundle.

19. One might expect risks in life insurance to be highly correlated with risks in health insurance, but in fact they are not. My thanks to Zvi Bodie for pointing this out to me years ago.

20. Several of the uninsured people I spoke with were somewhat embarrassed

to admit that they had started to find out more information about insurance options but had not pursued it. It seemed as if they just did not know how to judge whether the prices and coverage they were quoted seemed reasonable. Those who were Web-savvy also were skeptical of some of the offers available online.

21. Garnick, Swartz, and Skwara, "Insurance Agents."

22. Very few people who are offered employer-sponsored insurance (ESI) turn it down and remain uninsured. Papers by Philip Cooper and Barbara S. Schone and by Peter Cunningham show that between 15 and 20 percent of those offered employer-sponsored coverage turn it down, but among those people, three-quarters are covered by a policy from another family member, usually a spouse. See Cooper and Schone, "More Offers, Fewer Takers for Employment-Based Health Insurance"; Peter Cunningham, "Choosing to Be Uninsured: Determinants and Consequences of the Decision to Decline Employer-Sponsored Health Insurance," working paper (Washington, D.C.: Center for Studying Health Insurance Change, 1999).

23. To be sure, insurers also work to reduce their administrative costs, but they are primarily focused on reducing adverse selection and lowering the risk of covering people with very high costs.

24. Medical underwriting—sometimes called experience rating—usually entails asking questions about the applicant's history of health care use, determining whether the applicant or a family member has any of a list of specific medical conditions, and sometimes giving a medical exam. The underwriting process essentially determines whether a person will pay the base premium for the policy plus an additional amount. Thus, if a person's health status is poor, actuarial underwriting practices would yield a higher premium than that for an otherwise similar person in excellent health. Similarly, when insurers set premiums for policy renewals, medical underwriting can yield high premiums for people who have had expensive medical care in the previous six to twelve months, or it may lead to outright denial of renewal of coverage. Depending on state regulations, medical underwriting may be used by insurers writing policies for individuals, small groups, and particular individuals within small groups. At the other extreme of the premium-setting options is community rating. With community rating, everyone—regardless of age, sex, occupation, or other characteristics—is charged the same premium for the same policy. Some states permit what is termed modified community rating: setting different rates by factors such as geographic area of residence, age, and sex. Community rating is always applied to a particular type of plan—single, husband-wife, adult plus child(ren), or family. See Mark Merlis, "Fundamentals of Underwriting in the Nongroup Health Insurance Market: Access to Coverage and Options for Reform," Background paper (Washington, D.C.: National Health Policy Forum, George Washington University, April 13, 2005).

25. Joseph P. Newhouse, "Is Competition the Answer?" *Journal of Health Economics* 1 (1982): 110–16; Joseph P. Newhouse, "Cream Skimming, Asymmetric Information, and a Competitive Insurance Market," *Journal of Health Economics* 3 (1984): 97–100; Newhouse, "Reimbursing Health Plans and Health Providers"; Deborah Chollet and Adele Kirk, *Understanding Individual Health Insurance Markets* (Menlo Park, Calif.: Henry J. Kaiser Family Foundation, 1998); Katherine Swartz and Deborah W. Garnick, "Can Adverse Selection Be Avoided in a Market for Individual Health Insurance?" *Medical Care Research and Review* 56, no. 3 (1999): 373–88; Katherine Swartz and Deborah W. Garnick, "Lessons from New Jersey's Creation of a Market for Individual Health Insurance," *Journal of Health Politics, Policy, and Law* 25, no. 1 (2000): 45–70.

26. Deborah Stone, "The Struggle for the Soul of Health Insurance," *Journal of Health Politics, Policy, and Law* 18, no. 2 (1993): 287–317; Richard G. Frank, Thomas G. McGuire, Jay P. Bae, and Agnes Rupp, "Solutions for Adverse Selection in Behavioral Health Care," *Health Care Financing Review* 18, no. 3 (1997): 109–22.

27. Newhouse, "Patients at Risk."

28. Pollitz, Sorian, and Thomas, *How Accessible Is Individual Health Insurance?*, ii.

29. Ibid.

30. Swartz and Garnick, "Lessons from New Jersey's Creation of a Market."

31. Pollitz et al., *How Accessible Is Individual Health Insurance?*, 31–32; General Accounting Office, *Private Health Insurance: Millions Relying on Individual Market Face Cost and Coverage Trade-offs*, GAO/HEHS-97-8 (Washington: U.S. Government Printing Office, 1996).

32. My thanks to Karen Pollitz (personal communication, April 4, 2005) for providing me with details on the exceptions.

33. Chollet and Kirk, *Understanding Individual Health Insurance Markets*, iii.

34. Pollitz et al., *How Accessible Is Individual Health Insurance?*, 7–23.

35. Newhouse, "Reimbursing Health Plans and Health Providers."

36. Insurers would argue that consumers are not all alike, and therefore they are offering different benefit designs in response to consumers' demands for a variety of policies. Moreover, the insurers would say, if they did not respond to the desires of low-risk consumers, their competitors would, and they would end up with high-risk, higher-cost enrollees. This may all be true, but the different benefit designs also work to insurers' advantage as a selection mechanism.

37. Len M. Nichols and Linda J. Blumberg, "A Different Kind of 'New Federalism'? The Health Insurance Portability and Accountability Act of 1996," *Health Affairs* 17, no. 3 (1998): 25–42.

38. In a GAO survey of seven states' individual health insurance markets, the vast majority of the companies did not actually sell individual insurance to any applicant. Instead, these companies had a "book of business" (see chap-

ter 6) of individual policies that were conversions from group policies or were restricted to people who were self-employed and belonged to associations of similarly self-employed people. See GAO, *Private Health Insurance*, and Chollet, Kirk, and Chow, *Mapping State Health Insurance Markets*.

39. Michael A. Morrisey and Gail A. Jensen, "State Small Group Insurance Reform," in *Health Policy, Federalism, and the American States*, edited by Robert F. Rich and William D. White (Washington, D.C.: Urban Institute Press, 1996).

40. As of mid-2005, thirty-three states had high-risk pools (West Virginia's provision for a high-risk pool took effect in July 2005). In addition, Idaho and Tennessee have different arrangements for high-risk people that are similar to but not formal high-risk pools. See Communicating for Agriculture and the Self-Employed, Inc., *Comprehensive Health Insurance for High-Risk Individuals, 2004–2005*, 18th ed. (Bloomington, Minn.: Communicating for Agriculture and the Self-Employed/National Association of State Comprehensive Health Insurance Plans, 2004).

41. Alain Enthoven, "The History and Principles of Managed Competition," *Health Affairs* 12 (supp.) (1993): 24–48.

42. The states included New York, New Jersey, and Massachusetts; also, the National Association of Insurance Commissioners (NAIC) included standardized benefits packages in its model legislation for individual insurance.

43. In New York the premiums vary by county. In Suffolk County on eastern Long Island, the least expensive family policy in the individual market was an HMO plan for $1,663.

44. Alan C. Monheit, Joel C. Cantor, Margaret Koller, and Kimberley S. Fox, "Community Rating and Sustainable Individual Health Insurance Markets: Trends in the New Jersey Individual Health Coverage Program," *Health Affairs* 23, no. 4 (2004): 167–75; Mark C. Hall. "An Evaluation of New York's Reform Law," *Journal of Health Policy, Politics, and Law* 24, no. 1 (2000): 71–100.

PART II

1. The most recently established state pool is West Virginia's, which became operational in July 2005. Idaho has an arrangement for high-risk individuals that is quite similar but is not a formal high-risk pool.

2. Reinsurance for health insurance was first proposed on January 18, 1954, when President Eisenhower suggested a $25 million federal reinsurance fund to enable and encourage private insurers to broaden the types of people to whom they offered coverage. The reinsurance would have covered 75 percent of any "abnormal" losses. The proposal also called for insurers to voluntarily purchase and finance the reinsurance. It was defeated in part because insurers did not want to finance it. Twenty-five years later, a similar voluntary reinsurance fund was part of the Carter health plan; it would

have allowed HMOs and self-insured companies to buy reinsurance for costs for an individual above $25,000 (in 1979 dollars). The reinsurance fund was not even discussed in congressional hearings on the bill. Stuart Altman has said that reinsurance also was discussed during the Nixon administration when national health insurance proposals were on the table. However, I have not seen a reference to it in any legislation that was considered by the Congress. Federal reinsurance for health insurance was mentioned in the Congressional Research Service's 1988 report, "Insuring the Uninsured: Options and Analysis," prepared for the House of Representatives' Subcommittee on Labor-Management Relations and the Subcommittee on Labor Standards of the Committee on Education and Labor, and the Subcommittee on Health and the Environment of the Committee on Energy and Commerce, and the Senate Special Committee on Aging; see Library of Congress, Congressional Research Service. *Insuring the Uninsured: Options and Analysis* (Washington: U.S. Government Printing Office, 1988). Also, in 1991 the Health Insurance Association of America (HIAA) proposed that a private, not-for-profit reinsurance mechanism be established to pay for high-risk individuals and high-risk employer groups covered by private health insurance; see Carl J. Schramm, "Health Care Financing for All Americans," *Journal of the American Medical Association* 265, no. 24 (1991): 3296–99. This proposal was different in two ways from what I am proposing here: it called for a private reinsurer rather than the federal government acting as the reinsurer, and it called for targeting the employer groups and individuals known to be at high risk, rather than people whose actual medical expenses were high. The proposal was never published with details.

CHAPTER 5

1. Between 1987 and the end of 1993, Tennessee had a high-risk pool known as the Tennessee Comprehensive Health Insurance Pool (TCHIP). Almost 3,500 people were participating in the pool until they were moved into the state's TennCare program starting in 1994. TennCare began operations in 1994 with a federal Medicaid waiver to cover people previously covered by Medicaid as well as uninsured people with incomes above the poverty level and "uninsurable" people who previously would have been eligible for TCHIP. In November 2004, however, TennCare was dramatically scaled back because of state financial problems; it now no longer covers people who are uninsurable with incomes above the poverty level. Legislation to set up a new high-risk pool was introduced in the state legislature in 2004, but it did not pass. As a result, as of April 2005, Tennessee does not have a mechanism to guarantee portability of insurance coverage to the individual market for people leaving the group markets.

2. See, for example, Lori Achman and Deborah Chollet, *Insuring the Uninsur-*

able: *An Overview of State High-Risk Health Insurance Pools* (New York: Commonwealth Fund Task Force on the Future of Health Insurance, 2001); James Studnicki, "State High-Risk Insurance Pools: Their Operating Experience and Policy Implications," *Employee Benefits Journal* 16, no. 2 (1991): 32–36; George E. Rejda, Michael J. McNamara, and Gerald P. Hanner, "State High-Risk Pools for the Uninsurable: A Critical Analysis," *Journal of the American Society of CLU and ChFC* 47, no. 5 (1993): 61–73.

3. Tennessee is counted in this group of nine states that had implemented high-risk pools by 1989. However, Tennessee ended its pool in 1995 after transitioning all the risk-pool enrollees into TennCare.

4. As noted earlier, West Virginia's high-risk pool became operational in July 2005.

5. Jim Mayhew, Centers for Medicare and Medicaid Services, personal communication, April 22 and 25, 2005.

6. Legislation has been proposed in the Congress to provide $75 million to offset losses in fiscal year 2006, but as of November 2005, the legislation had not been acted upon. Given the costs of responding to Hurricanes Katrina, Rita, and Wilma, it seemed unlikely that Congress would pass the legislation in the current term.

7. The benefits packages are relatively generous and are usually in line with the benefits packages of policies sold in the states' individual markets.

8. "One percent" was the response given in a congressional hearing to a question about how many people are uninsured because they are uninsurable, but it has always been unclear whether the 1 percent was of the uninsured population or the total population. At various times I have heard the answer ascribed to Karen Davis, now president of the Commonwealth Fund, and to Gail Wilensky, former administrator of the Health Care Financing Administration (now the Center for Medicare and Medicaid Services [CMS]), adviser to former President George H. W. Bush, and currently a senior fellow at Project Hope. Bovjberg and Koller state that "most experts guess that it [the uninsurable population] totals about one percent of the general population," but they do not provide a source; see Randall R. Bovjberg and Christopher F. Koller, "State Health Insurance Pools: Current Performance, Future Prospects," *Inquiry* 23, no. 2 (1986): 111–21, 111.

Another estimate of the number of uninsurables comes from Frakt, Pizer, and Wrobel, who define the uninsurable population as "individuals who were uninsured and who either could not work, were limited in the type of work they could do, or received any disability or worker's compensation income." As they note, their "approach suggests that roughly one percent of the total population and six percent of the uninsured population is uninsurable"; see Austin B. Frakt, Steven D. Pizer, and Marian V. Wrobel,

"High-Risk Pools for Uninsurable Individuals: Recent Growth, Future Prospects," *Health Care Financing Review* 26, no. 2 (2004–2005): 73–87.

9. Communicating for Agriculture and the Self-Employed, *Comprehensive Health Insurance for High-Risk Individuals, 2004–2005*, 25; Bruce Abbe, vice president of public affairs, Communicating for Agriculture and the Self-Employed, personal communication, April 6, 2005.

10. Achman and Chollet, *Insuring the Uninsurable*; Deborah Chollet, "Expanding Individual Health Insurance Coverage: Are High-Risk Pools the Answer?" *Health Affairs* (Web exclusive) (October 23, 2002): 349–52. To place another perspective on this number, 230,000 people lost their jobs in Ohio between January 2001 and the summer of 2004.

11. California Managed Risk Medical Insurance Board, "MRMIP Subscriber and Health Plan Data: December 2005 Summary," available at: www.mrmib. ca.gov/MRMIB/MRMIPRptSum.pdf.

12. Achman and Chollet, *Insuring the Uninsurable*, 2. Communicating for Agriculture and the Self-Employed, which does an annual review of the high-risk pools, does not collect this type of information and could not verify the estimate.

13. To be HIPAA-eligible, a person must have had health insurance coverage for eighteen months with no gaps in coverage of more than sixty-three days within or after the eighteen-month period, and he or she must have exhausted any coverage available under COBRA or any other state or federal program. Data on the states that use their risk pools to cover people eligible under HIPAA come from Communicating for Agriculture and the Self-Employed, *Comprehensive Health Insurance for High-Risk Individuals, 2004–2005*, 288, and Bruce Abbe, personal communications, January 2004 and April 2005.

14. Only four states officially have waiting lists or caps on part of their programs so as to control pool expenses. Illinois and Louisiana have capped enrollment and established waiting lists for previously uninsured people who are eligible; people who are HIPAA-eligible can enroll without a waiting period or cap on enrollment. California had a waiting list between 1999 and late 2003, and then in September 2003 it restructured its pool. California's goal is to have a steady state of about 10,225 people enrolled each year in its high-risk pool. After "incubating" in the pool for three years, people would switch to the individual market, where they would have guaranteed-issue coverage at a premium equal to 110 percent of the high-risk pool premium. Florida has closed its high-risk pool since 1991 because of inadequate funding; it is entertaining the idea of creating a new pool for high-risk people not currently enrolled in the first pool.

15. My thanks to Bruce Abbe (personal communication, April 6, 2005) for making this point.

16. Bruce Abbe, personal communication, January 2004.
17. Deborah Chollet, "Expanding Individual Health Insurance Coverage: Are High-Risk Pools the Answer?" *Health Affairs* (Web exclusive) (October 23, 2002): 349–52.
18. Communicating for Agriculture and the Self-Employed, *Comprehensive Health Insurance for High-Risk Individuals, 2004–2005*.
19. Given the costs relative to incomes, it should not be a surprise that Stearns and her colleagues found, in a study of eight states' high-risk pools established before 1988, that the lowest-risk enrollees were more likely to disenroll in any given month than were the higher-risk enrollees; see Sally C. Stearns and Thomas A. Mroz, "Premium Increases and Disenrollment from State Risk Pools," *Inquiry* 32, no. 4 (1995–96): 392–406; Sally C. Stearns, Rebecca T. Slifkin, Kenneth Thorpe, and Thomas A. Mroz, "The Structure and Experience of State Risk Pools: 1988–1994," *Medical Care Research and Review* 54, no. 2 (1997): 224–38.
20. Communicating for Agriculture and the Self-Employed, *Comprehensive Health Insurance for High-Risk Individuals, 2004–2005*, 13.
21. Bruce Abbe, personal communication, January 2004.
22. My calculations are based on data in Communicating for Agriculture and the Self-Employed, *Comprehensive Health Insurance for High-Risk Individuals, 2004–2005*, 25–26. I do not include West Virginia, which just started its risk pool in 2005; Idaho, which does not have a true risk pool; or New Hampshire, which did not implement its risk pool until 2002.

    Just as a small proportion of the general population accounts for a large proportion of total medical expenses, it is also true that a few people in each state's high-risk pool are responsible for a large share of the high-risk pool's expenses. The Minnesota Comprehensive Health Association (MCHA), Minnesota's high-risk pool, discovered that 272 enrollees in 1999 (less than 1 percent of its total enrollment) incurred 30 percent of the pool's total expenses; see Minnesota Comprehensive Health Association *MCHA Annual Report: 1999/2000* (Minneapolis, Minn., 2000). Data from the high-risk pools in California and Illinois in 1999 show a similar pattern of concentrated expenses; see California Major Risk Medical Insurance Program (MRMIP), *1999 Fact Book for the Major Risk Medical Insurance Program* (Sacramento, Calif., 1999), available at: www.mrmib.ca.gov; Illinois Comprehensive Health Insurance Plan, *1999 Annual Report and Financial Summaries* (Springfield, Ill.: Department of Insurance, 2000), available at: www.chip.state.il.us/downloads/1999annl.pdf.
23. Based on comparisons of my calculations from Communicating for Agriculture and the Self-Employed, *Comprehensive Health Insurance for High-Risk Individuals, 2004–2005*, 25–26; and Communicating for Agriculture and the Self-Employed, Inc., *Comprehensive Health Insurance for High-Risk Individuals, 2003–2004*, 17th ed. (Bloomington, Minn.: Communicating for Agriculture

and the Self-Employed/National Association of State Comprehensive Health Insurance Plans, 2003), 23–24.

24. This is one reason why Congress authorized up to $100 million for state high-risk pools in the Trade Adjustment Assistance Reform Act of 2002. Eighty percent of these funds were to be used to help states cope with the losses in their pools.

25. Both Illinois and Louisiana rely on assessments on insurers to finance the difference between premium revenues and costs for the small number of enrollees who are using the high-risk pool for HIPAA-guaranteed portability of group to individual market coverage.

26. Wisconsin uses general revenues to fund its subsidy program for low-income people who are eligible for the high-risk pool. Wisconsin also pays providers at the Medicaid-provider reimbursement rate, thereby partially "taxing" providers to help finance the program (Bruce Abbe, personal communication, April 12, 2005).

27. Communicating for Agriculture and the Self-Employed, *Comprehensive Health Insurance for High-Risk Individuals, 2004–2005,* 26. Firms that self-insure their employees' health costs are exempt from state taxes on health insurance policies sold in the state because of ERISA (Employee Retirement Income Security Act of 1974). As a result, if a large number of workers in a state work for self-insured firms, a large share of health care coverage dollars are exempt from high-risk pool assessments that are based on insurance premiums. Further, the insurer assessments based on share of total premium revenues in the state fall disproportionately on insurers that sell policies in the individual and small-group markets. In states with a large share of the labor force employed in self-insured firms, the disproportionate burden of the assessment mechanism based on total premiums has been recognized. Some states have responded by also assessing stop-loss insurers and reinsurers—that is, insurers that sell policies to self-insured firms that want insurance protection against a high total of individual claims. (Stop-loss coverage, a variation of reinsurance, does not have layers of coverage above an initial threshold; instead, it is simply coverage for claims above a threshold level so that the self-insured firm does not face all of the losses above the stop-loss level.) This has been done through assessments based both on covered lives and on earned premiums where the revenue base includes the premiums of stop-loss insurers and reinsurers. For more on this last point, see Pat Butler, "ERISA Complicates State Efforts to Improve Access to Individual Insurance for the Medically High Risk," *State Coverage Initiatives Issue Brief* 1, no. 3 (Washington, D.C.: Academy for Health Services Research and Health Policy [now AcademyHealth], 2000).

28. The low enrollments may, however, be masking high turnover among enrollees. It has been estimated that Minnesota, with 32,641 people enrolled as of the end of June 2003, has had more than a quarter-million people

enrolled in its high-risk pool since it started in 1977; see B. Bruce Zellner, David K. Haugen, and Bryan Dowd, "A Study of Minnesota's High-Risk Health Insurance Pool," *Inquiry* 30, no. 2 (1993): 170–79.

29. All the enrollment numbers are current as of a mix of December 31, 2003, and June 2004, and come from Communicating for Agriculture and the Self-Employed, *Comprehensive Health Insurance for High-Risk Individuals, 2004–2005.*

30. Ibid. The enrollment numbers for Minnesota, Oregon, and Nebraska are as of December 31, 2003.

31. See note 14.

32. John Bertko and Sandra Hunt, "Case Study: The Health Insurance Plan of California," *Inquiry* 35, no. 2 (1998): 148–53; Laura Tollen and Michael Rothman, "Case Study: Colorado Medicaid HMO Risk Adjustment," *Inquiry* 35, no. 2 (1998): 154–70; David Knutson, "Case Study: The Minneapolis Buyers Health Care Action Group," *Inquiry* 35, no. 2 (1998): 171–77; Vicki M. Wilson, Cynthia A. Smith, Jenny M. Hamilton, Carolyn W. Madden, Susan M. Skillman, Bret Mackay, James S. Matthisen, and David A. Frazzini, "Case Study: The Washington State Health Care Authority," *Inquiry* 35, no. 2 (1998): 178–92.

33. "Earned premium" is an accounting term for the portion of the premium for which the time period covered by the policy has passed. Thus, for example, the earned premium for the previous year is the amount of premium revenue that was paid for coverage for that time period.

34. The premiums for the reinsurance policies are typically determined by calculating how much would be required in premium revenues over five years to cover the reinsurer's exposure to losses in one year. Thus, the premium reflects what would be needed to break even within five years if the reinsurer or seller of the stop-loss policy had to pay the full amount of its exposure to losses once in five years. (Note that the reinsurance is for a stated or "capped" exposure to losses.) These premiums can be expensive. Without data on premiums paid for reinsurance and health insurance policies, we do not know how the burden of assessments based on premiums would be shared among self-insured firms and firms and people that purchase health insurance policies.

35. Man-made disasters have also caused insurers to stop providing insurance. During the mid to late 1960s, there was a shortage of fire insurance available to firms and people located in urban areas thought to be at risk for fires related to civil rights riots. Washington, D.C., Detroit, Newark, Chicago, and Los Angeles were the best-known sites of such rioting, but the fire insurance shortages arose in many urban areas across the country. As a result, Congress passed the 1968 Urban Property Protection and Reinsurance Act, which established fair access to insurance requirements (FAIR).

These led to what are known as FAIR plans, which all property-casualty insurers are required to participate in. The insurers were protected against catastrophic losses through reinsurance made available by and purchased from the federal government. Interestingly, no claims were ever made against the federal reinsurance, and it went out of existence when the 1968 act sunsetted in 1983. See Howard Kunreuther, "Insurability Conditions and the Supply of Coverage," in *Paying the Price: The Status and Role of Insurance Against Natural Disaster in the United States*, edited by Howard Kunreuther and Richard J. Roth Sr. (Washington, D.C.: Joseph Henry Press/ National Academy Press, 1998), 48.

36. Chad Terhune and Theo Francis, "Hurricanes Squeeze Insurers of Last Resort," *Wall Street Journal*, October 24, 2005.

37. Kunreuther, "Insurability Conditions and the Supply of Coverage."

38. See Swartz and Garnick, "Lessons from New Jersey's Creation of a Market for Individual Health Insurance."

39. Ibid.

40. This incentive has what economists call a moral hazard aspect to it since it encourages behavior that is not the intent of the incentive. In this case, the incentive to get large companies to share the burden of high-cost people was taken advantage of by companies with small market shares. They realized that the loss assessment mechanism permitted them to shift most of the losses they might incur to the large insurers, thus limiting the risk they faced.

41. The moral hazard incentive to small insurers to not worry about losses was noticed by some designers of the IHCP. They did not expect small insurers to take on the risks of selling policies in the individual market, however, and consequently forgot about the moral hazard embedded in the regulations. The significant losses were obvious by late 1996 and early 1997, and so, by June 1997, the legislature had altered the loss assessment mechanism, effective January 1, 1998. The losses incurred by the small insurers led to chaotic pricing in the IHCP, many insurers' premiums rose rapidly, and the number of enrollees declined markedly in response to the smaller insurers raising their premiums. See Swartz and Garnick, "Lessons from New Jersey's Creation of a Market for Individual Health Insurance."

42. As Newhouse notes, however, even with the relatively low level of predictive power of the current risk adjustment models, so long as an insurer is just a little better than its competitors at making such predictions, it will make a great deal more profit. This is why insurers spend so much effort trying to develop risk selection mechanisms that are better than the mechanisms of their competitors at estimating a person's predictable medical expenses. See Newhouse, "Patients at Risk."

43. Ministry of Health, Welfare and Sport of the Netherlands, "Health Insur-

ance in the Netherlands: The New Health Insurance System from 2006" (The Hague, September 2005): 5; available at www.minvws.nl/images/ health-insurance-in-nl_tcm11-74566.pdf.

44. What follows is based on descriptions and analyses by the following: Erik M. van Barneveld, René C. J. A. van Vliet, and Wynand P. M. M. van de Ven, "Mandatory High-Risk Pooling: An Approach to Reducing Incentives for Cream Skimming," *Inquiry* 33, no. 2 (1996): 133–43; Erik M. van Barneveld, Leida M. Lamers, René C. J. A. van Vliet, and Wynand P. M. M. van de Ven, "Mandatory Pooling as a Supplement to Risk-Adjusted Capitation Payments in a Competitive Health Insurance Market," *Social Science and Medicine* 47, no. 2 (1998): 223–32; Erik M. van Barneveld, René C. J. A. van Vliet, and Wynand P. M. M. van de Ven, "Risk Sharing Between Competing Health Plans and Sponsors," *Health Affairs* 20, no. 5 (2001): 253–62; Wynand van de Ven and Randall P. Ellis, "Risk Selection, Risk Adjustment, and Risk Sharing: Lessons from Europe and the Americas," working paper (Boston: Boston University, Department of Economics, 2003); Wynand P. M. M. van de Ven, René C. J. A. van Vliet, and Leida M. Lamers, "Health-Adjusted Premium Subsidies in the Netherlands," *Health Affairs* 23, no. 3 (2004): 45–55.

45. Van de Ven, van Vliet, and Lamers, "Health-Adjusted Premium Subsidies in the Netherlands."

46. Wynand P. M. M. van de Ven, Konstantin Beck, Florian Buchner, Dov Chernichovsky, Lucien Gardiol, Alberto Holly, Leida M. Lamers, Erik Schokkaert, Amir Shmueli, Stephan Spycher, Carine Van de Voorde, René C. J. A. van Vliet, Jürgen Wasem, and Irith Zmora, "Risk Adjustments and Risk Selection on the Sickness Fund Insurance Market in Five European Countries," *Health Policy* 65, no. 1 (2003): 75–98.

47. Van de Ven, van Vliet, and Lamers, "Health-Adjusted Premium Subsidies in the Netherlands," 54.

48. Van de Ven and Ellis, "Risk Selection, Risk Adjustment, and Risk Sharing."

49. Van Barneveld, van Vliet, and van de Ven, "Risk Sharing Between Competing Health Plans and Sponsors."

CHAPTER 6

1. The reinsurer also protects itself from the moral hazard incentive that all insurance contains. The moral hazard incentive is to do riskier activities simply because the person or company has insurance. In this case, the moral hazard incentive is for the originating insurer to cover risks that it would not without the reinsurance. Thus, by requiring the originating insurer to retain a portion of the risk, the reinsurer is hoping to offset the moral hazard incentive of the reinsurance.

2. The increased ease of worldwide communication since the mid-1980s has

made the growth of reinsurance possible. Since reinsurance covers losses that are so large they threaten the financial reserves of the insured company, the companies that sell reinsurance must themselves have diversified portfolios so that they can bear the risk of such large losses. Financial syndicates of people and companies around the world have made it possible for larger losses to be covered by reinsurance and for more types of companies to purchase reinsurance.

3. Some researchers have argued that information asymmetry is a problem with reinsurance markets because the firms that want to buy reinsurance may know far more about the particular risks they are bearing than any outsider; see David M. Cutler and Richard J. Zeckhauser, "Reinsurance for Catastrophes and Cataclysms," in *The Financing of Catastrophe Risk*, edited by Kenneth A. Froot (Chicago: University of Chicago Press, 1999). However, most reinsurers limit their risk exposure by providing reinsurance only in situations where information assures them that the risk is random. For example, the probability of an earthquake or hurricane in a particular place in a particular year is essentially random. No one has developed models that accurately predict them. Under these circumstances, asymmetric information does not exist in the market. See also John H. Cochrane, "Comment on Cutler and Zeckhauser, 'Reinsurance for Catastrophes and Cataclysms,'" in Froot, *The Financing of Catastrophe Risk*.

4. There are two ways this can be done. One is for the original insurer to retain most of the premium revenues, which of course permits the original insurer to have a more rapid growth in assets. This permits the insurer to sell more business than it otherwise would be capable of if it had to retain assets in reserve funds for all of the risk covered by its policies. The reinsurer sets a yearly premium for the amount of the face policy that is being reinsured. The second type of quota share arrangement is often called a "coinsurance plan." Under this arrangement, the original insurer cedes a share of the premiums to the reinsurer in exchange for the reinsurer bearing a pro rata share of the risk. In this case, the reinsurer gains from the growth in assets. In addition, because the original insurer has expenses in selling the original policy and then administering the policy, the reinsurer pays a "ceding commission" to the original insurer.

5. A company purchasing reinsurance may also buy different layers from different reinsurers. It may buy one or two layers from one company and then other layers from another company—perhaps because one reinsurer is unwilling to sell coverage beyond some level. Similarly, a reinsurance company might be willing to sell layers for all of an insurer's different policies—or the reinsurance company could choose to sell reinsurance only for particular types of policies based on the characteristics of the people purchasing them or the cost-sharing and benefits covered by the policies. A reinsurer might set such restrictions if it feels that the original insurer's

policies have highly correlated risk—that is, if one person has high expenses, many other people might also have high expenses.

6. By efficient use, I mean that the benefits of the medical care used are worth the costs and that there is not a less costly treatment that would have the same benefit. Unfortunately, because insurance pays most of the costs of medical care, it creates an incentive for people to seek (and physicians to provide) medical care that is sometimes of dubious benefit but is costly. Insurance policies can be designed to encourage the use of cost-effective health care, such as screening and diagnostic tests for cancer and heart disease so that health problems can be caught early. More efficient use of care also can be achieved by policies that encourage the use of networks of medical providers; such networks can take advantage of shared medical information about patients, reducing the need for repeating diagnostic tests and allowing greater consultation between providers.

7. M. Susan Marquis and Stephen H. Long, "Trends in Managed Care and Managed Competition, 1993–1997," *Health Affairs* 18, no. 6 (1999): 75–88; Barbara Steinberg Schone and Philip F. Cooper, "Assessing the Impact of Health Plan Choice," *Health Affairs* 20, no. 1 (2001): 267–75; Sally Trude, "Who Has a Choice of Health Plans?," issue brief 27 (Washington, D.C.: Center for Studying Health System Change, 2000).

8. Kaiser Family Foundation and Mathematica Policy Research, "Medicare Advantage and Medicare Beneficiaries," *Medicare Advantage Monthly Tracking Report* (October 2004); available at: www.kff.org/medicare/upload/Medicare-Advantage-Monthly-Tracking-Report-September-2004.pdf.

9. David M. Cutler and Sarah Reber, "Paying for Health Insurance: The Trade-off Between Competition and Adverse Selection," *Quarterly Journal of Economics* 113, no. 2 (1998): 433–66; Thomas C. Buchmueller and Paul J. Feldstein, "The Effect of Price on Switching Among Health Plans," *Journal of Health Economics* 16, no. 2 (1997): 231–47.

10. Nichols and Blumberg, "A Different Kind of 'New Federalism'?"

11. My thanks to Joe Newhouse for raising this issue.

12. Many states have already sold their tobacco settlement funds, so this is not an option for them.

13. The Eisenhower administration's proposal for reinsurance for health care (described in the appendix) failed in part because it relied on the insurers voluntarily paying premiums into the proposed reinsurance fund. Insurers vigorously opposed this, and there is no reason to believe they would behave any differently today.

14. Linda J. Blumberg and John Holahan, "Government as Reinsurer: Potential Impacts on Public and Private Spending," *Inquiry* 41, no. 2 (2004): 130–43.

15. The Urban Institute researchers' proposal was developed for the Blue Cross Blue Shield of Massachusetts Foundation under its "Roadmap to Coverage" initiative. See especially Blumberg et al., *Building the Roadmap to Coverage*.

16. Lewin Group. *Bush and Kerry Health Care Proposals: Cost and Coverage Compared* (Falls Church, Va.: Lewin Group, 2004); also available at www.lewin .com.

17. Kerry's plan also called for tax credits for small employers that offered coverage to employees through what was called the Congressional Health Plan; this was estimated to cost $384.9 billion over the ten years. The Lewin Group estimated that the reinsurance program, by lowering premiums by an estimated $774 billion over the ten years, and the small-employer tax credits would increase production and employment in the United States and the incomes of workers, leading to an increase in tax revenues of $414.7 billion over the ten years. How much of the increase in tax revenues would be due to the reinsurance rather than the tax credit parts of the plan was not clear. The net federal cost of the Kerry reinsurance and small-employer tax credit proposal therefore would be almost $700 billion over ten years.

18. This back-of-the-envelope calculation involves four steps. We need to estimate:

1. The percentage of costs that the people in the ninety-ninth percentile of the expenditure distribution are responsible for.

2. The number of people with individual and small-group coverage.

3. The costs of people with individual and small-group coverage.

4. The costs that would be covered by the originating insurers.

For the first, Monheit has estimated that in 1996 the people in the ninety-ninth percentile of the health care expenditure distribution accounted for 28 percent of all expenses (see Monheit, "Persistence in Health Expenditures in the Short Run"). People of all ages are included in Monheit's estimate, so it includes expenditures for elderly people, who may have higher-than-average expenditures. (Indeed, 17.2 percent of the expenditures of people in the ninety-ninth percentile are for people who died in 1996, although of course not all of those who died were sixty-five years of age or older.) Although we are interested in the expenses of the non-elderly who are in the top 1 percent of the health expenditure distribution, let's accept the 28 percent estimate provided by Monheit's calculations and assume that this percentage holds for people in the individual and small-group markets.

For the number of people covered by individual and small-group insurance, we begin with the fact that there were almost 177 million people younger than sixty-five with private health insurance in 2004 and that, of these, 9.6 percent had individual coverage (see Carmen DeNavas-Walt, Bernadette D. Proctor, and Cheryl H. Lee, "Income, Poverty, and Health Insurance Coverage in the United States: 2004," *Current Population Reports*, series P60, no. 229 (Washington: U.S. Government Printing Office, 2005). We do not know how many of the people with employment-based insurance have small-group coverage. But approximately one-quarter of the labor force in the private sector works for an employer (as opposed to an "establishment") with fewer than fifty employees, and less than half of all such workers have coverage from their employer (see Robert J. Mills and Shailesh Bhandari, "Health Insurance Coverage in the United States: 2002," *Current Population Reports*, series P60, no. 223 (Washington: U.S. Government Printing Office, 2003). We can estimate then that perhaps 12 percent of the people with private insurance have small-group coverage. Together with the 9.6 percent who have individual coverage—rounded up to 10 percent—perhaps 22 percent of the population with private coverage have individual or small-group insurance. This is approximately 40 million people.

To obtain an estimate of the health care costs of people with individual and small-group coverage, we start with the fact that in 2004 private health insurance paid for $658.5 billion of health services and supplies (see Smith et al., "National Health Spending in 2004," exhibit 2). We can round this to $660 billion for our back-of-the-envelope calculation. Then, using our estimate that 22 percent of the non-elderly population with private coverage have individual or small-group insurance, we can estimate that they account for 22 percent of the $660 billion of expenditures paid by private health insurance—or roughly $145 billion in 2003.

The costs that would be covered by the originating insurers rather than the reinsurance fund include all of the costs of a person below the reinsurance threshold level and then the cost-sharing required for the various layers of reinsurance. We estimated above that 40 million people have individual or small-group coverage, so approximately 400,000 of these people will have medical expenses in the ninety-ninth percentile of the expenditure distribution. If we assume that the threshold level for reinsurance is $50,000, then $20 billion (400,000 times $50,000) would be assumed by the originating insurers before the reinsurance started.

Finally, we put all these numbers together for our back-of-the-envelope calculation. We apply the 28 percent estimate to the $145 billion and arrive at $41 billion as the costs of people in the ninety-ninth percentile of the expenditure distribution among those with individual and small-group coverage. We subtract the $20 billion for the costs below the threshold level and arrive at $21 billion as the cost that will be shared with the reinsurance program. The reinsurance program would require that the original insurers share in these costs, with different levels of cost-sharing for different layers of costs above the threshold at which reinsurance commences. People who have medical costs in the ninety-ninth percentile will have widely varying costs—some will have costs just above the threshold, and others will have costs running well above $1 million. We do not know this distribution of costs. However, we can estimate that the reinsurance program will pay 85 to 90 percent of these costs—or $17.9 billion to $18.9 billion in 2004. Adjusting for inflation since 2004, these estimates are $18.5 billion to $19.5 billion in 2005 dollars.

This is a lower-bound estimate of how much it might cost to have a federal reinsurance program for the individual and small-group markets because it does not account for the expected growth in the number of people who would find it easier and cheaper to obtain coverage in these markets.

19. Center on Budget and Policy Priorities, "The Estate Tax: Myths and Realities," February 9, 2005; available at: www.cbpp.org/pubs/estatetax.htm.

20. See "Florida Hurricane Recovery Passes $5.2 Billion," May 27, 2005; available at: www.fema.gov/news/newsrelease.fema?id=17555.

21. As explained in the appendix, Healthy New York in New York State saw premiums for individuals decline by about half from those in the standard individual (direct-pay) market, a far greater decline than the 15 to 20 percent that many were expecting.

22. David M. Lawrence, "My Mother and the Medical Care Ad-hoc-racy," *Health Affairs* 22, no. 2 (2003): 238–42.

23. See chapter 4 for discussion of how I estimated these thresholds.

24. Burman and Gruber, "Tax Credits for Health Insurance."

CHAPTER 7

1. Gabel et al., "Health Benefits in 2005."

2. Ibid.

3. Ibid. The average disguises substantial variation in the rate at which premiums increased during this time. For example, between 2003 and 2004, premiums on average increased 11.2 percent, but more than one-quarter of all workers, especially those in smaller firms, faced annual increases above 15 percent. See Gabel et al., "Health Benefits in 2004"; Jon Gabel, Gary Claxton, Erin Holve, Jeremy Pickreign, Heidi Whitmore, Kelley Dhont, Samantha Hawkins, and Diane Rowland, "Health Benefits in 2003: Premiums Reach Thirteen-Year High as Employers Adopt New Forms of Cost-Sharing," *Health Affairs* 22, no. 5 (2003): 117–26.

4. Author's calculations based on BLS data on the consumer price index and Council of Economic Advisers, *2005 Economic Report of the President*, table B-49, "Productivity in the Business Sector."

5. Employee Benefit Research Institute, "EBRI Research Highlights: Health Benefits," EBRI Special Report SR-41 (Washington, D.C.: EBRI, 2003).

6. Gabel et al., "Health Benefits in 2004."

7. Katharine Levit, Cynthia Smith, Cathy Cowan, Art Sensenig, Aaron Catlin, and the Health Accounts Team, "Health Spending Rebound Continues in

2002," *Health Affairs* 23, no. 1 (2004): 147–59; Ernst R. Berndt, "The U.S. Pharmaceutical Industry: Why Major Growth in Times of Cost Containment?" *Health Affairs* 20, no. 2 (2001): 100–14.

8. Smith et al., "National Health Spending in 2004."
9. See, for example, Karla J. Hanson, "Is Insurance for Children Enough? The Link Between Parents' and Children's Health Care Use Revisited," *Inquiry* 35, no. 3 (1998): 294–302; Amy Davidoff, Lisa Dubay, Genevieve Kenney, and Alshadye Yemane, "The Effect of Parents' Insurance Coverage on Access to Care for Low-Income Children," *Inquiry* 40, no. 3 (2003): 254–68.
10. David A. Moss, *When All Else Fails: Government as the Ultimate Risk Manager* (Cambridge, Mass.: Harvard University Press, 2002).
11. Edward T. Pasterick, "The National Flood Insurance Program," in *Paying the Price: The Status and Role of Insurance Against Natural Disaster in the United States*, edited by Howard Kunreuther and Richard J. Roth Sr. (Washington, D.C.: Joseph Henry Press/National Academy Press, 1998).
12. See ch. 5, n. 2.
13. See *Federal Register* 69, no. 148 (August 3, 2004): 346826–29.
14. Katherine Swartz, *Healthy New York: Making Insurance More Affordable for Low-Income Workers* (New York: Commonwealth Fund, 2001).
15. My thanks to Patricia Swolak (personal communication, November 15, 2005), New York State Department of Insurance, Healthy New York Program, for providing these numbers.
16. See *Nature* 435 (May 26, 2005), which is devoted to avian flu.
17. Institute of Medicine, *Unequal Treatment*.

APPENDIX

1. Mark R. Greene, "The Government as an Insurer," *Journal of Risk and Insurance* 43, no. 3 (1976): 393–410; Mark R. Greene, "A Review and Evaluation of Selected Government Programs to Handle Risk," *Annals of the American Academy* 443 (1979): 129–44; Moss, *When All Else Fails.*
2. David A. Moss, "Courting Disaster? The Transformation of Federal Disaster Policy Since 1803," in *The Financing of Catastrophe Risk*, edited by Kenneth A. Froot (Chicago: University of Chicago Press, 1999).
3. Cleveland quoted in ibid., 313.
4. Ibid., 308–14.
5. John M. Barry, *Rising Tide: The Great Mississippi Flood of 1927 and How It Changed America* (New York: Simon & Schuster, 1997).
6. Douglas Gomery, Professor of Journalism, University of Maryland, personal communication, November 2, 2003.
7. Barry, *Rising Tide*, 406; Moss, "Courting Disaster?" 313.
8. Moss, "Courting Disaster?" 315. The Good Friday Alaskan earthquake of March 1964 was the most powerful earthquake to strike North America in

the twentieth century. It devastated the downtown of Anchorage, in part because of huge landslides. The tsunamis caused by the earthquake wreaked significant damage on towns and villages along the coast of the Gulf of Alaska, particularly in Prince William Sound. The earthquake and tsunamis caused 125 deaths (115 from the tsunamis) and an estimated $311 million (equal to $1.96 billion in 2005 dollars) in property damage. Because so much damage was caused by the tsunamis, the federal relief efforts were funded under the flood relief disaster funds. For more details, see George Pararas-Carayannis, "The March 27, 1964, Great Alaska Earthquake," available at: www.drgeorgepc.com/Earthquake1964Alaska.html.

9. Moss, "Courting Disaster?" 317.
10. Pasterick, "The National Flood Insurance Program."
11. Ibid., 127.
12. It is striking that Title II of the Eisenhower administration's proposed health reinsurance legislation (83 HR 8356) called for the secretary of Health, Education, and Welfare to conduct studies and "collect much needed data on the incidence of sickness and its effects on the use of medical care facilities and services. . . . The FHA has restrictions on maximum insurable loan amounts, which vary with the geographic region in which the loan is made"; HEW Secretary Oveta Culp Hobby, statement before Committee on Interstate and Foreign Commerce, hearings on health reinsurance legislation (83 HR 8356), March 24, 1954, 26. Clearly, there were members of the administration and Congress who believed that federal efforts were needed to quantify risks so that the insurance industry might then offer insurance policies.
13. Pasterick, "The National Flood Insurance Program," 126, 128.
14. The flood hazard identification process was very slow in part because community participation in the identification process is voluntary. In 1973 the Flood Disaster Protection Act gave communities an incentive to participate by denying nonparticipating communities certain types of federal assistance in their floodplains. By 1998, 18,760 communities had joined the NFIP flood risk identification effort; of these, about one-third are considered low-risk (ibid., 129).
15. Ibid., 135.
16. Edward Pasterick, personal communications, November 18, 2003, and March 22, 2006. The percentage that insurers are permitted to keep for administrative and production costs was 32.6 percent for many years, but was 31.9 percent in 2003, and is 30.8 percent in 2006.
17. Blumberg and Holahan, 2004. "Government as Reinsurer."
18. It is noteworthy that reference was made to the FHA in a March 1954 congressional hearing on the Eisenhower administration's proposal for reinsurance for health insurers. Rep. John Bennett pointed out that prior to 1938 no mortgage lender would lend beyond fifteen years for mortgages, but the FHA stimulated lenders to lend for twenty years and then twenty-five. Rep.

Bennett said he expected that a reinsurance pool for insurers would similarly stimulate insurers to offer health insurance policies to people who were not then viewed as good risks. Rep. John Bennett, statement before House Committee on Interstate and Foreign Commerce, hearings on health reinsurance legislation (83 HR 8356), March 25, 1954, 54.

19. The quality of the house construction, the neighborhood, whether the house was a single family dwelling or a multiple dwelling unit, and the income of the mortgagee relative to the size of the mortgage were factored into a risk rating.

20. FNMA was originally chartered by the federal government in 1938 as part of the Reconstruction Finance Corporation. The 1954 congressional rechartering carried the directive that it be transformed into a privately owned and managed corporation.

21. Sellers of mortgages to FNMA had to buy the stock, which provided FNMA with capital and resulted in widespread private-sector ownership of FNMA.

22. At least four different types of securities are now available in conjunction with this market: mortgage-backed bonds, mortgage pass-through securities, mortgage pass-through bonds, and collateralized mortgage obligations. The securities known as collateralized mortgage obligations (CMOs) are securities issued in different maturity (time to payoff) classes, known as tranches, against a common pool of mortgages. The expected maturity classes might be for three, five, and seven years, for example. The tranches in the secondary mortgage market are quite similar to the layers of reinsurance discussed earlier. Investors in CMOs can manage their exposure to risk and level of investment return by choosing the tranches of the mortgages in which they want to invest.

23. New York recognized the potential role of government as a reinsurer as early as 1989, when the Department of Health developed a proposal for universal health insurance known as the Universal New York Health Care (UNY-Care). Included in this proposal was the provision that there be a stop-loss limit of approximately $25,000 per patient per year for inpatient hospital services and $25,000 per patient per year for out-of-hospital services. The UNY-Care proposal did not advance for a number of reasons, the primary one being that it was quite ambitious: it called for a single-payer authority that would have required new administrative capacities that made insurers and health care providers uneasy. In addition, by 1990 the state's economy was slumping, making people nervous about paying the estimated $1.2 billion to $1.9 billion to finance the state's share of the costs for universal health insurance in the state. The chances that the UNY-Care proposal or any of its administrative components would be enacted were further hurt by the untimely death in 1990 of the commissioner of health for New York, Dr. David Axelrod, one of its primary proponents.

For more details, see Dan E. Beauchamp and Ronald L. Rouse, "Universal New York Health Care—A Single-Payer Strategy Linking Cost Control and Universal Access," *New England Journal of Medicine* 323, no. 10 (1990): 640–44.

24. Swartz, *Healthy New York*.

25. One package provides prescription drug coverage while the other does not. This change went into effect in June 2003.

26. Originally, an enrollee's claims were eligible for reinsurance if the total was more than $30,000. The reinsurance pool paid 90 percent of the claims between $30,000 and $100,000. But because very few claims had been submitted for reimbursement by April 2003, the Department of Insurance reduced the threshold and the corridor for reimbursement, effective June 2003. The Health Care Reform Act of 2000 (HCRA) also established a reinsurance pool for the direct-pay market. This pool provides reinsurance of 90 percent of all claims that fall between $20,000 and $100,000 for enrollees who have at least $20,000 of claims in a calendar year.

27. Swartz, *Healthy New York*.

28. Lewin Group, in partnership with Empire Health Advisers, *Report on Healthy New York Program* (2003); available at: www.ins.state.ny.us/website2/hny/reports/hnylewin.pdf.

29. My thanks to Patricia Swolak (personal communication, November 15, 2005), New York State Department of Insurance, Healthy New York Program, for providing these numbers.

30. My thanks to Julian Pettingil (personal communication, April 22, 2005) of the Medicare Payment Advisory Commission for walking me through the revisions to the rules for outlier payments to hospitals; he is not responsible for any misunderstandings I still may have.

31. See the Medicare Payment Advisory Commission brief "Medicare Hospital Outlier Payment Policy" (December 2002) for a succinct explanation. Centers for Medicare and Medicaid Services, *Medicare News*, June 5, 2003 (available at: www.cms.hhs.gov/media/press/release.asp?Counter=749) has an update on 2003 revisions to how the outlier payments are determined. The *Federal Register* (69, no. 154 [August 11, 2004]: 49,275–78) also contains an explanation of the revisions to the FY 2005 outlier threshold.

32. For a case to qualify as an outlier in fiscal year 2005, the costs had to exceed the prospective payment rate for the diagnosis related group (DRG), plus any medical education and disproportionate share hospital (DSH) payments, plus any add-ons for new technology, plus $25,800 (see *Federal Register* 69, no. 154 [August 11, 2004]: 49,278). Thus, the threshold varies by DRG.

33. Gail R. Wilensky and Louis F. Rossiter, "Coordinated Care and Public Programs," *Health Affairs* 10, no. 4 (1991): 62–77.

34. Ibid., 75.
35. James C. Beebe, "An Outlier Pool for Medicare HMO Payments," *Health Care Financing Review* 14, no. 1 (1992): 59–63.
36. See *Federal Register* 69, no. 148 (August 3, 2004): 46, 826–29.
37. Kaiser Family Foundation, "Fact Sheet: Medicare and Prescription Drugs" (Menlo Park, Calif.: Henry J. Kaiser Family Foundation, 2003); available at: www.kff.org / medicare / loader.cfm?url= / commonspot / security / getfile .cfm&PageID=14186.

References

Achman, Lori, and Deborah Chollet. 2001. *Insuring the Uninsurable: An Overview of State High-Risk Health Insurance Pools.* New York: Commonwealth Fund Task Force on the Future of Health Insurance.

Agency for Healthcare Research and Quality, Center for Financing, Access, and Cost Trends. 2003. 2003 Medical Expenditure Panel Survey-Insurance Component, table 1.A.2. Available at: www.meps.ahrq.gov/MEPSDATA/ic/2003/Tables_I/TIA2.pdf.

Appelbaum, Eileen, Annette Bernhardt, and Richard J. Murnane, eds. 2003. *Low-Wage America: How Employers Are Reshaping Opportunity in the Workplace.* New York: Russell Sage Foundation.

Ash, Arlene, Frank Porell, Leonard Gruenberg, Eric Sawitz, and Alexa Beiser. 1989. "Adjusting Medicare Capitation Payments Using Prior-Hospitalization Data." *Health Care Financing Review* 10(4): 17–30.

Barley, Steven R., and Gideon Kunda. 2004. *Gurus, Hired Guns, and Warm Bodies: Itinerant Experts in a Knowledge Economy.* Princeton, N.J.: Princeton University Press.

Barry, John M. 1997. *Rising Tide: The Great Mississippi Flood of 1927 and How It Changed America.* New York: Simon & Schuster.

Beauchamp, Dan E., and Ronald L. Rouse. 1990. "Universal New York Health Care—A Single-Payer Strategy Linking Cost Control and Universal Access." *New England Journal of Medicine* 323(10): 640–44.

Beebe, James C. 1992. "An Outlier Pool for Medicare HMO Payments." *Health Care Financing Review* 14(1): 59–63.

Berk, Marc L., and Alan C. Monheit. 2001. "The Concentration of Health Care Expenditures, Revisited." *Health Affairs* 20(2): 9–18.

Berndt, Ernst R. 2001. "The U.S. Pharmaceutical Industry: Why Major Growth in Times of Cost Containment?" *Health Affairs* 20(2): 100–14.

Bertko, John, and Sandra Hunt. 1998. "Case Study: The Health Insurance Plan of California." *Inquiry* 35(2): 148–53.

Bettinger, Eric, and Bridget T. Long. 2004. "Do College Instructors Matter? The Effects of Adjuncts and Graduate Assistants on Students' Interests and Success." Working paper 10370. Cambridge, Mass.: National Bureau of Economic Research.

Blumberg, Linda J., and John Holahan. 2004. "Government as Reinsurer: Potential Impacts on Private and Public Spending." *Inquiry* 41(2): 130–43.

Blumberg, Linda J., John Holahan, Alan Weil, Lisa Clemans-Cope, Matthew Buettgens, Fredric Blavin, and Stephen Zuckerman. 2005. *Building the Roadmap to Coverage: Policy Choices and the Cost and Coverage Implications.* Boston: Blue Cross Blue Shield of Massachusetts Foundation. Available at: www.bcbsma foundation.org/foundationroot/en_US/documents/roadmapTocoverage.pdf.

Bovjberg, Randall R., and Christopher F. Koller. 1986. "State Health Insurance Pools: Current Performance, Future Prospects." *Inquiry* 23(2): 111–21.

Branscome, James M., Philip F. Cooper, John Sommers, and Jessica P. Vistnes. 2000. "Private Employer-Sponsored Health Insurance: New Estimates by State." *Health Affairs* 19(1): 139–47.

Bregger, John F. 1996. "Measuring Self-employment in the United States." *Monthly Labor Review* 119(1–2): 3–9.

Buchmueller, Thomas C., and Paul J. Feldstein. 1997. "The Effect of Price on Switching Among Health Plans." *Journal of Health Economics* 16(2): 231–47.

Burman, Len. 1994. *The Tax Treatment of Employment-Based Health Insurance.* Washington: Congressional Budget Office.

Burman, Leonard E., and Jonathan Gruber. 2005. "Tax Credits for Health Insurance." *Tax Policy Issues and Options* 11. Washington, D.C.: Urban-Brookings Tax Policy Center. Available at: www.taxpolicycenter.org/UploadedPDF/311189_IssuesOptions_11.pdf.

Butler, Pat. 2000. "ERISA Complicates State Efforts to Improve Access to Individual Insurance for the Medically High-Risk." State Coverage Initiatives issue brief vol. 1, no. 3. Washington, D.C.: Academy for Health Services Research and Health Policy (now AcademyHealth).

California Major Risk Medical Insurance Program (MRMIP). 1999. *1999 Fact Book for the Major Risk Medical Insurance Program.* Sacramento, Calif.: MRMIP. Available at: www.mrmib.ca.gov.

California Managed Risk Medical Insurance Board. 2006. "MRMIP Subscriber and Health Plan Data: December 2005 Summary." Available at: www.mrmib.ca.gov/MRMIB/MRMIPRptSum.pdf.

Centers for Disease Control and Prevention. 2005. Table 1–1, "Live Births, Birth-rates, and Fertility Rates, by Race: United States, 1909–2000." Available at: www.cdc.gov/nchs/data/statab/t001x01.pdf.

Centers for Medicare and Medicaid Services. *Medicare News,* June 5, 2003.

Chollet, Deborah. 2004. "The Role of Reinsurance in State Efforts to Expand Coverage." State Coverage Initiatives issue brief 5, no. 4. Washington, D.C.: Academy Health.

Chollet, Deborah J., and Adele M. Kirk. 1998. *Understanding Individual Health Insurance Markets.* Menlo Park, Calif.: Henry J. Kaiser Family Foundation.

Chollet, Deborah, Adele Kirk, and Marc Chow. 2000. *Mapping State Health Insurance Markets: Structure and Change in the States' Group and Individual Health Insurance Markets, 1995–1997.* Washington, D.C.: Academy for Health Services Research and Health Policy (now AcademyHealth).

182

Clark, Colin. 1957. *The Conditions of Economic Progress*. 3rd ed. New York: St. Martin's Press.

Cochrane, John H. 1999. "Comment on Cutler and Zeckhauser: Reinsurance for Catastrophes and Cataclysms." In *The Financing of Catastrophe Risk*, edited by Kenneth A. Froot. Chicago: University of Chicago Press.

Cohany, Sharon R. 1998. "Workers in Alternative Employment Arrangements: A Second Look." *Monthly Labor Review* 121(11): 3–21.

Communicating for Agriculture and the Self-Employed, Inc. 2003. *Comprehensive Health Insurance for High-Risk Individuals, 2003–2004*. 17th ed. Bloomington, Minn.: Communicating for Agriculture and the Self-Employed/National Association of State Comprehensive Health Insurance Plans.

———. 2004. *Comprehensive Health Insurance for High-Risk Individuals, 2004–2005*. 18th ed. Bloomington, Minn.: Communicating for Agriculture and the Self-Employed/National Association of State Comprehensive Health Insurance Plans.

Cooper, Philip, and Barbara S. Schone. 1997. "More Offers, Fewer Takers for Employment-Based Health Insurance." *Health Affairs* 16(6): 142–49.

Council of Economic Advisers. 2005. *2005 Economic Report of the President*. Washington: U.S. Government Printing Office for the White House.

Cunningham, Peter J. 1999. "Choosing to Be Uninsured: Determinants and Consequences of the Decision to Decline Employer-Sponsored Health Insurance." Working paper. Washington, D.C.: Center for Studying Health Insurance Change.

Cutler, David M., and Sarah Reber. 1998. "Paying for Health Insurance: The Trade-off Between Competition and Adverse Selection." *Quarterly Journal of Economics* 113(2): 433–66.

Cutler, David M., and Richard J. Zeckhauser. 1999. "Reinsurance for Catastrophes and Cataclysms." In *The Financing of Catastrophe Risk*, edited by Kenneth A. Froot. Chicago: University of Chicago Press.

Davidoff, Amy, Lisa Dubay, Genevieve Kenney, and Alshadye Yemane. 2003. "The Effect of Parents' Insurance Coverage on Access to Care for Low-Income Children." *Inquiry* 40(3): 254–68.

DeNavas-Walt, Carmen, Bernadette D. Proctor, and Cheryl H. Lee. 2005. "Income, Poverty, and Health Insurance Coverage in the United States: 2004." *Current Population Reports*, series P60, no. 229. Washington: U.S. Government Printing Office for U.S. Census Bureau.

Economic Policy Institute. 2005. "Facts and Figures: CEO Pay." In *State of Working America 2004–2005*. Washington, D.C.: EPI (March). Available at: www.epinet.org/books/swa2004/news/swafacts_ceopay.pdf.

Ellis, Randall P., and Arlene S. Ash. 1995. "Refinements to the Diagnostic Cost Group Model." *Inquiry* 32(4): 418–29.

Employee Benefit Research Institute. 2003. "EBRI Research Highlights: Health Benefits." Special report SR-41. Washington, D.C.: EBRI.

Enthoven, Alain. 1993. "The History and Principles of Managed Competition." *Health Affairs* 12 (supp.): 24–48.

Feder, Judith, and Sheila Burke, eds. 1999. *Options for Expanding Health Insurance Coverage: A Report on a Policy Roundtable.* Menlo Park, Calif.: Henry J. Kaiser Family Foundation.

Fields, Jason. 2004. "America's Families and Living Arrangements: 2003." *Current Population Reports*, series P20, no. 553. Washington: U.S. Government Printing Office for U.S. Census Bureau.

Flynn, Patrice. 1994. "COBRA Qualifying Events and Elections, 1987–1991." *Inquiry* 31(2): 215–20.

Frakt, Austin B., Steven D. Pizer, and Marian V. Wrobel. 2004–2005. "High-Risk Pools for Uninsurable Individuals: Recent Growth, Future Prospects." *Health Care Financing Review* 26(2): 73–87.

Frank, Richard G., Thomas G. McGuire, Jay P. Bae, and Agnes Rupp. 1997. "Solutions for Adverse Selection in Behavioral Health Care." *Health Care Financing Review* 18(3): 109–22.

Fronstin, Paul. 2004. "Sources of Health Insurance and Characteristics of the Uninsured: Analysis of the March 2004 Current Population Survey." Issue brief 276. Washington, D.C.: Employee Benefit Research Institute.

Froot, Kenneth A. 1999. "Introduction." In *The Financing of Catastrophe Risk*, edited by Kenneth A. Froot. Chicago: University of Chicago Press.

———, ed. 1999. *The Financing of Catastrophe Risk.* Chicago: University of Chicago Press.

Fuchs, Victor R., assisted by Irving F. Leveson. 1968. *The Service Economy.* General Series vol. 87. New York: National Bureau of Economic Research.

Gabel, Jon, Gary Claxton, Isadora Gil, Jeremy Pickreign, Heidi Whitmore, Erin Holve, Benjamin Finder, Samantha Hawkins, and Diane Rowland. 2004. "Health Benefits in 2004: Four Years of Double-Digit Premium Increases Take Their Toll on Coverage." *Health Affairs* 23(5): 200–9.

Gabel, Jon, Gary Claxton, Isadora Gil, Jeremy Pickreign, Heidi Whitmore, Benjamin Finder, Samantha Hawkins, and Diane Rowland. 2005. "Health Benefits in 2005: Premium Increases Slow Down, Coverage Continues to Erode." *Health Affairs* 24(5): 1273–80.

Gabel, Jon, Gary Claxton, Erin Holve, Jeremy Pickreign, Heidi Whitmore, Kelley Dhont, Samantha Hawkins, and Diane Rowland. 2003. "Health Benefits in 2003: Premiums Reach Thirteen-Year High as Employers Adopt New Forms of Cost Sharing." *Health Affairs* 22(5): 117–26.

Garnick, Deborah W., Katherine Swartz, and Kathleen C. Skwara. 1998. "Insurance Agents: Ignored Players in Health Insurance Reform." *Health Affairs* 17(2): 137–43.

General Accounting Office (GAO). 1996. *Private Health Insurance: Millions Relying on Individual Market Face Cost and Coverage Trade-offs.* GAO/HEHS-97–8.

Washington: U.S. Government Printing Office for General Accounting Office.

Goodman, Michael J., Douglas W. Roblin, Mark C. Hornbrook, and John P. Mullooly. 1991. "Persistence of Health Care Expense in an Insured Working Population." In *Advances in Health Economics and Health Services Research: Risk-Based Contributions to Private Health Insurance*, edited by Richard M. Scheffler and Louis F. Rossiter. Greenwich, Conn.: JAI Press.

Goodwin, Barry K., and Vincent H. Smith. 1995. *The Economics of Crop Insurance and Disaster Aid*. Washington, D.C.: AEI Press.

Gornick, Marian, Alma McMillan, and James Lubitz. 1993. "A Longitudinal Perspective on Patterns of Medicare Payments." *Health Affairs* 12(2): 140–50.

Greene, Mark R. 1976. "The Government as an Insurer." *Journal of Risk and Insurance* 43(3): 393–410.

———. 1979. "A Review and Evaluation of Selected Government Programs to Handle Risk." *Annals of the American Academy* 443: 129–44.

Hadley, Jack. 2002. *Sicker and Poorer: The Consequences of Being Uninsured*. Washington, D.C.: Kaiser Commission on Medicaid and the Uninsured.

Hall, Mark C. 2000. "An Evaluation of New York's Reform Law." *Journal of Health Policy, Politics, and Law* 24(1): 71–100.

Hamilton, Brady E., Joyce A. Martin, and Paul D. Sutton. 2004. "Births: Preliminary Data for 2003." *National Vital Statistics Reports* 53, no. 9. Hyattsville, Md.: National Center for Health Statistics.

Hanson, Karla J. 1998. "Is Insurance for Children Enough? The Link Between Parents' and Children's Health Care Use Revisited." *Inquiry* 35(3): 294–302.

Hatch, Julie. 2004. "Employment in the Public Sector: Two Recessions' Impact on Jobs." *Monthly Labor Review* 127(10): 38–47.

Hipple, Steven. 2001. "Contingent Work in the Late 1990s." *Monthly Labor Review* 124(3): 3–27.

———. 2004. "Self-employment in the United States: An Update." *Monthly Labor Review* 127(7): 13–23.

House Committee on Interstate and Foreign Commerce. 1954. Hearings on health reinsurance legislation, 83 HR 8356. (March 24–26, 30, 31; April 1, 2, 5, 8; May 5–7).

Houseman, Susan N. 2001. "Why Employers Use Flexible Staffing Arrangements: Evidence from an Establishment Survey." *Industrial and Labor Relations Review* 55(1): 149–70.

Houseman, Susan N., Arne L. Kalleberg, and George A. Erickcek. 2003. "The Role of Temporary Agency Employment in Tight Labor Markets." *Industrial and Labor Relations Review* 57(1): 105–27.

Hyde, Alan. 2003. *Working in Silicon Valley: Economic and Legal Analysis of a High-Velocity Labor Market*. Armonk, N.Y.: M. E. Sharpe.

Illinois Comprehensive Health Insurance Plan. 2000. *1999 Annual Report and Fi-*

nancial Summaries. Springfield, Ill.: Department of Insurance. Available at: www .chip.state.il.us/downloads/1999annl.pdf.

Institute of Medicine. 2003. *Coverage Matters: Insurance and Health Care*. Washington, D.C.: National Academy Press.

———. 2003. *Unequal Treatment: Confronting Racial and Ethnic Disparities in Healthcare*. Washington, D.C.: National Academy Press.

Jensen, Gail A., and Michael A. Morrisey. 1999. "Employer-Sponsored Health Insurance and Mandated Benefit Laws." *Milbank Quarterly* 77(4): 425–59.

Kaiser Commission on Medicaid and the Uninsured. 2001. "In Their Own Words: The Uninsured Talk About Living Without Health Insurance." Washington, D.C.: Kaiser Commission on Medicaid and the Uninsured. Available at: www.kff.org/uninsured/2207-index.cfm.

———. 2004. "Key Facts: Health Coverage for Low-Income Children." Washington, D.C.: Kaiser Commission on Medicaid and the Uninsured. Available at: www.kff.org/uninsured/loader.cfm?url=/commonspot/security/getfile .cfm&PageID=46994.

Kaiser Family Foundation. 2003. "Fact Sheet: Medicare and Prescription Drugs." Menlo Park, Calif.: Henry J. Kaiser Family Foundation. Available at: www.kff .org/medicare/loader.cfm?url=/commonspot/security/getfile.cfm&PageID= 14186.

———, with Mathematica Policy Research. 2004. "Medicare Advantage and Medicare Beneficiaries." Medicare Advantage Monthly Tracking Report (September). Available at: www.kff.org/medicare/upload/Medicare-Advantage-Monthly-Tracking-Report-September-2004.pdf.

Klein, Jennifer. 2003. *For All Those Rights: Business, Labor, and the Shaping of America's Public-Private Welfare State*. Princeton, N.J.: Princeton University Press.

Knutson, David. 1998. "Case Study: The Minneapolis Buyers Health Care Action Group." *Inquiry* 35(2): 171–77.

Kuenzi, J. J., and C. A. Reschovsky. 2001. "Home-Based Workers in the United States." *Current Population Reports*, series P70, no. 78. Washington: U.S. Government Printing Office for U.S. Census Bureau.

Kunreuther, Howard. 1998. "Insurability Conditions and the Supply of Coverage." In *Paying the Price: The Status and Role of Insurance Against Natural Disaster in the United States*, edited by Howard Kunreuther and Richard J. Roth Sr. Washington, D.C.: Joseph Henry Press/National Academy Press.

Lawrence, David M. 2003. "My Mother and the Medical Care Ad-hoc-racy." *Health Affairs* 22(2): 238–42.

Levit, Katharine, Cynthia Smith, Cathy Cowan, Art Sensenig, Aaron Catlin, and the Health Accounts Team. 2004. "Health Spending Rebound Continues in 2002." *Health Affairs* 23(1): 147–59.

Levy, Frank. 1998. *The New Dollars and Dreams: American Incomes and Economic Change*. New York: Russell Sage Foundation.

Lewin Group. 2004. *Bush and Kerry Health Care Proposals: Cost and Coverage Compared*. Falls Church, Va.

Lewin Group, in partnership with Empire Health Advisers. 2003. *Report on Healthy New York Program 2003*. Available at: www.ins.state.ny.us/website2/hny/reports/hnylewin.pdf.

Lewis, Christopher M., and Kevin C. Murdock. 1999. "Alternative Means of Redistributing Catastrophic Risk in a National Risk-Management System." In *The Financing of Catastrophe Risk*, edited by Kenneth A. Froot. Chicago: University of Chicago Press.

Library of Congress. Congressional Research Service. 1988. *Insuring the Uninsured: Options and Analysis*. Washington: U.S. Government Printing Office.

Manser, Marilyn E., and Garnett Picot. 1999. "The Role of Self-employment in U.S. and Canadian Job Growth." *Monthly Labor Review* 122(4): 10–25.

Marquis, M. Susan, and Stephen H. Long. 1999. "Trends in Managed Care and Managed Competition, 1993–1997." *Health Affairs* 18(6): 75–88.

Martin, Joyce A., Brady E. Hamilton, Paul D. Sutton, Stephanie J. Ventura, Fay Menacker, and Martha L. Munson. 2005. "Births: Final Data for 2003." *National Vital Statistics Reports* 54, no. 2. Hyattsville, Md.: National Center for Health Statistics.

McCall, Nelda, and H. S. Wai. 1983. "An Analysis of the Use of Medicare Services by the Continuously Enrolled Aged." *Medical Care* 21(6): 567–85.

McGill, Dan M. 1994. "Reinsurance," revised by Jeremy S. Holmes and James F. Winberg. In *McGill's Life Insurance*, edited by Edward E. Graves. Bryn Mawr, Penn.: American College.

Medicare Payment Advisory Commission. 2002. *Report to the Congress: Medicare Payment Policy*. Washington: Medicare Payment Advisory Commission.

———. 2002. "Medicare Hospital Outlier Payment Policy." Washington: Medicare Payment Advisory Commission (December).

———. 2003. *Report to the Congress: Medicare Payment Policy*. Washington: Medicare Payment Advisory Commission.

Merlis, Mark. 2005. "Fundamentals of Underwriting in the Nongroup Health Insurance Market: Access to Coverage and Options for Reform." Background paper. Washington, D.C.: National Health Policy Forum, George Washington University (April 13).

Meyer, Jack A., and Elliot K. Wicks, eds. 2001. *Covering America: Real Remedies for the Uninsured*, vol. 1. Washington, D.C.: Economic and Social Research Institute.

———. 2002. *Covering America: Real Remedies for the Uninsured*, vol. 2. Washington. D.C.: Economic and Social Research Institute.

———. 2003. *Covering America: Real Remedies for the Uninsured*, vol. 3. Washington, D.C.: Economic and Social Research Institute.

Mills, Robert J., and Shailesh Bhandari. 2003. "Health Insurance Coverage in the

United States: 2002." *Current Population Reports*, series P60, no. 223. Washington: U.S. Government Printing Office for U.S. Census Bureau.

Ministry of Health, Welfare and Sport of the Netherlands. 2005. "Health Insurance in the Netherlands: The New Health Insurance System from 2006." The Hague: Ministry of Health, Welfare and Sport of the Netherlands (September). Available at: www.minvws.nl/images/health-insurance-in-nl_tcm11-74566.pdf.

Minnesota Comprehensive Health Association. 2000. *MCHA Annual Report: 1999/2000*. Minneapolis, Minn.

Mishel, Lawrence, Jared Bernstein, and Sylvia Allegretto. 2005. *The State of Working America 2004–2005*. Ithaca, N.Y.: ILR Press/Cornell University Press.

Monheit, Alan C. 2003. "Persistence in Health Expenditures in the Short Run: Prevalence and Consequences." *Medical Care* 41(7-supp.): III53–64.

Monheit, Alan C., and Joel C. Cantor, eds. 2004. *State Health Insurance Market Reform: Towards Inclusive and Sustainable Insurance Markets*. New York: Routledge.

Monheit, Alan C., Joel C. Cantor, Margaret Koller, and Kimberley S. Fox. 2004. "Community Rating and Sustainable Individual Health Insurance Markets: Trends in the New Jersey Individual Health Coverage Program." *Health Affairs* 23(4): 167–75.

Morrisey, Michael A., and Gail A. Jensen. 1996. "State Small Group Insurance Reform." In *Health Policy, Federalism, and the American States*, edited by Robert F. Rich and William D. White. Washington, D.C.: Urban Institute Press.

Moss, David A. 1999. "Courting Disaster? The Transformation of Federal Disaster Policy Since 1803." In *The Financing of Catastrophe Risk*, edited by Kenneth A. Froot. Chicago: University of Chicago Press.

———. 2002. *When All Else Fails: Government as the Ultimate Risk Manager*. Cambridge, Mass.: Harvard University Press.

Muhl, Charles J. 2002. "What Is an Employee? The Answer Depends on the Federal Law." *Monthly Labor Review* 125(1): 3–11.

Newhouse, Joseph P. 1982. "Is Competition the Answer?" *Journal of Health Economics* 1: 110–16.

———. 1984. "Cream Skimming, Asymmetric Information, and a Competitive Insurance Market." *Journal of Health Economics* 3: 97–100.

———. 1994. "Patients at Risk: Reform and Risk Adjustment." *Health Affairs* 13(1): 132–46.

———. 1996. "Reimbursing Health Plans and Health Providers: Efficiency in Production Versus Selection." *Journal of Economic Literature* 34(3): 1236–63.

Newhouse, Joseph P., Melinda B. Buntin, and John D. Chapman. 1997. "Risk Adjustment and Medicare: Taking a Closer Look." *Health Affairs* 16(5): 26–43.

Nichols, Len M., and Linda J. Blumberg. 1998. "A Different Kind of 'New Federalism'? The Health Insurance Portability and Accountability Act of 1996." *Health Affairs* 17(3): 25–42.

Osterman, Paul. 1988. *Employment Futures: Reorganization, Dislocation, and Public Policy.* New York: Oxford University Press.

Pararas-Carayannis, George. N.d. "The March 27, 1964, Great Alaska Earthquake." Available at: www.drgeorgepc.com/Earthquake1964Alaska.html.

Pasterick, Edward T. 1998. "The National Flood Insurance Program." In *Paying the Price: The Status and Role of Insurance Against Natural Disaster in the United States,* edited by Howard Kunreuther and Richard J. Roth Sr. Washington, D.C.: Joseph Henry Press/National Academy Press.

Piketty, Thomas, and Emmanuel Saez. 2003. "Income Inequality in the United States, 1913–1998." *Quarterly Journal of Economics* 118(1): 1–39.

Pollitz, Karen, Richard Sorian, and Kathy Thomas. 2001. *How Accessible Is Individual Health Insurance for Consumers in Less-Than-Perfect Health?* Menlo Park, Calif.: Henry J. Kaiser Family Foundation.

Rejda, George E., Michael J. McNamara, and Gerald P. Hanner. 1993. "State High-Risk Pools for the Uninsurable—A Critical Analysis." *Journal of the American Society of CLU and ChFC* 47(5): 61–73.

Schone, Barbara S., and Philip F. Cooper. 2001. "Assessing the Impact of Health Plan Choice." *Health Affairs* 20(1): 267–75.

Schramm, Carl J. 1991. "Health Care Financing for All Americans." *Journal of the American Medical Association* 265(24): 3296–99.

Smith, Cynthia, Cathy Cowan, Stephen Heffler, Aaron Catlin, and the Health Accounts Team. 2006. "National Health Spending in 2004: Recent Slowdown Led by Prescription Drug Spending." *Health Affairs* 25(1): 186–96.

Starr, Paul. 1982. *The Social Transformation of American Medicine.* New York: Basic Books.

Stearns, Sally C., and Thomas A. Mroz. 1995–96. "Premium Increases and Disenrollment from State Risk Pools." *Inquiry* 32(4): 392–406.

Stearns, Sally C., Rebecca T. Slifkin, Kenneth Thorpe, and Thomas A. Mroz. 1997. "The Structure and Experience of State Risk Pools: 1988–1994." *Medical Care Research and Review* 54(2): 224–38.

Stone, Deborah A. 1993. "The Struggle for the Soul of Health Insurance." *Journal of Health Politics, Policy, and Law* 18(2): 287–317.

Studnicki, James. 1991. "State High Risk Insurance Pools: Their Operating Experience and Policy Implications." *Employee Benefits Journal* 16(2): 32–36.

Swartz, Katherine. 2001. *Healthy New York: Making Insurance More Affordable for Low-Income Workers.* New York: Commonwealth Fund.

———. 2001. "Justifying Government as the Backstop in Health Insurance Markets." *Yale Journal of Health Policy, Law, and Ethics* 2(1): 89–108.

Swartz, Katherine, and Deborah W. Garnick. 1999. "Can Adverse Selection Be Avoided in a Market for Individual Health Insurance?" *Medical Care Research and Review* 56(3): 373–88.

———. 2000. "Lessons from New Jersey's Creation of a Market for Individual Health Insurance." *Journal of Health Politics, Policy, and Law* 25(1): 45–70.

Terhune, Chad, and Theo Francis. 2005. "Hurricanes Squeeze State Insurers of Last Resort." *Wall Street Journal*, October 24.

Tollen, Laura, and Michael Rothman. 1998. "Case Study: Colorado Medicaid HMO Risk Adjustment." *Inquiry* 35(2): 154–70.

Trude, Sally. 2000. "Who Has a Choice of Health Plans?" Issue brief 27. Washington, D.C.: Center for Studying Health System Change.

U.S. Department of Commerce. U.S. Bureau of the Census. 2005. *Statistical Abstract of the United States: 2004–2005*. Washington, D.C.: U.S. Department of Commerce. Available at: www.census.gov/prod/2004pubs/04statab/pop.pdf.

———. Various years. *Statistics of U.S. Business*. Available at: www.census.gov/csd/susb/susb.htm.

———. Various years. *EPCD, Non-employer Statistics*. Available at: www.census.gov/epcd/nonemployer/.

U.S. Department of Labor. U.S. Bureau of Labor Statistics. 2001. "Contingent and Alternative Employment Arrangements, February 2001" (news release, May 24). Washington: U.S. Bureau of Labor Statistics. Available at: www.bls.gov/news.release/conemp.nr0.htm.

———. 2005. "Job Openings and Labor Turnover: February 2005." *News*, USDL 05–622. Washington: U.S. Bureau of Labor Statistics (April 12).

U.S. Department of Labor. Office of Employment and Unemployment Statistics. *Covered Employment and Wages* (Quarterly Census of Employment and Wages: "Private Industry by Supersector and Age of Establishment: Establishments and Employment, First Quarter 1975 to 2005).

van Barneveld, Erik M., Leida M. Lamers, René C. J. A. van Vliet, and Wynand P. M. M. van de Ven. 1998. "Mandatory Pooling as a Supplement to Risk-Adjusted Capitation Payments in a Competitive Health Insurance Market." *Social Science and Medicine* 47(2): 223–32.

van Barneveld, Erik M., René C. J. A. van Vliet, and Wynand P. M. M. van de Ven. 1996. "Mandatory High-Risk Pooling: An Approach to Reducing Incentives for Cream Skimming." *Inquiry* 33(2): 133–43.

———. 2001. "Risk Sharing Between Competing Health Plans and Sponsors." *Health Affairs* 20(5): 253–62.

van de Ven, Wynand P. M. M., Konstantin Beck, Florian Buchner, Dov Chernichovsky, Lucien Gardiol, Alberto Holly, Leida M. Lamers, Erik Schokkaert, Amir Shmueli, Stephan Spycher, Carine van de Voorde, René C. J. A. van Vliet, Jürgen Wasem, and Irith Zmora. 2003. "Risk Adjustments and Risk Selection on the Sickness Fund Insurance Market in Five European Countries." *Health Policy* 65(1): 75–98.

van de Ven, Wynand P. M. M., and Randall P. Ellis. 2000. "Risk Adjustment in Competitive Health Plan Markets." In *Handbook of Health Economics*, vol. 1A, edited by Anthony J. Culyer and Joseph P. Newhouse. Amsterdam, the Netherlands: Elsevier Science B.V.

———. 2003. "Risk Selection, Risk Adjustment, and Risk Sharing: Lessons from

Europe and the Americas." Working paper. Boston: Boston University, Department of Economics.

van de Ven, Wynand P. M. M., René C. J. A. van Vliet, and Leida M. Lamers. 2004. "Health-Adjusted Premium Subsidies in the Netherlands." *Health Affairs* 23(3): 45–55.

Welch, W. P. 1985. "Medicare Capitation Payments to HMOs in Light of Regression Towards the Mean in Health Care Costs." In *Advances in Health Economics and Health Services Research: Biased Selection in Health Care Markets*, edited by Richard M. Scheffler and Louis F. Rossiter. Greenwich, Conn.: JAI Press.

Wiatrowski, William J. 2004. "Documenting Benefits Coverage for All Workers." Washington: U.S. Department of Labor, Bureau of Labor Statistics (May 26). Available at: www.bls.gov/opub/cwc/print/cm20040518ar01p1.htm.

Wilensky, Gail R., and Louis F. Rossiter. 1991. "Coordinated Care and Public Programs." *Health Affairs* 10(4): 62–77.

Wilson, Vicki M., Cynthia A. Smith, Jenny M. Hamilton, Carolyn W. Madden, Susan M. Skillman, Bret Mackay, James S. Matthisen, and David A. Frazzini. 1998. "Case Study: The Washington State Health Care Authority." *Inquiry* 35(2): 178–92.

Zellner, B. Bruce, David K. Haugen, and Bryan Dowd. 1993. "A Study of Minnesota's High-Risk Health Insurance Pool." *Inquiry* 30(2): 170–79.

Index

Boldface numbers refer to figures and tables.

demographic trends, 28–34

Department of Commerce, **30, 31, 32**

Department of Health and Human Services, 115

Department of Homeland Security, 139

Department of Treasury, 143, 144

diabetes, 64

Disaster Relief Act: (1950), 138; (1970), 139

discrimination, 57

distribution of income, 49

divorce rates, 31

Dowd, B., 168n28

earned premium, 168

EBRI (Employee Benefit Research Institute), 175n5

Economic Policy Institute, 156n13

economic trends, 18–23, 126–27

educational attainment, and health insurance, 36

education and health services industry, 3, **22**

Eisenhower administration, 132, 162–63n2, 172n13, 177n12, 18

Emergency Home Finance Act (1970), 144

Employee Benefit Research Institute (EBRI), 175n5

Employee Retirement Income Security Act (ERISA) (1974), 68, 94, 167n27

employer benefits, 47. *See also* employer-sponsored health insurance

employers: health care expenditures, prediction of, 57–58; health insurance reform position, 125–28

employer-sponsored health insurance: average total premium per month, 7–8; benefits of, 7; decline in, 59; employees enrolled in, 53–54; employees turning down coverage, 160n22; firms offering by size, **52;**

history of, 45–47, 126; number or percentage of Americans holding, 7, 44; pooling in, 56–57; premiums, 51–58; self-insurance, 68; tax incentives for, 47; trade-off with wages, 48–51; transparency of employer contributions to, 48

employment: industry shifts, 3–4; job opportunities, 18–19; nonpermanent employees, 23–28

Enthoven, A., 79–80, 162n41

entrepreneurs, 26–28, 51

Erickcek, G., 153n8

ERISA (Employee Retirement Income Security Act) (1974), 68, 94, 167n27

estate tax, 119

excess-of-loss reinsurance, 105, 106, 108–9, 132–33

experience rating, 160n24

fair access to insurance requirements (FAIR), 168–69n35

family structure, 32–33

Fannie Mae (Federal National Mortgage Association) (FNMA), 131–32, 141, 143, 178n20

FASB (Financial Accounting Standards Board), 158n24

Federal Emergency Management Agency (FEMA), 84, 101, 119, 137, 139–40

Federal Employees Health Benefits Program (FEHBP), 119

federal funding: reinsurance program, 116–17; of state high-risk pools, 86

Federal Home Loan Mortgage Corporation (FHLMC) (Freddie Mac), 144

Federal Housing Administration (FHA), 131, 141, 142, 144, 177n12, 18

Federal National Mortgage Association (FNMA) (Fannie Mae), 131–32, 141, 143, 178n20